A Widow's Tale

Linda Swan Burhenne

ISBN 978-1-63814-753-4 (Paperback)
ISBN 978-1-63814-754-1 (Digital)

Covenant Books
11661 Hwy 707
Murrells Inlet, SC 29576
www.covenantbooks.com

For Jack, of course.

Introduction

On May 18, 2020, my husband, Jack, died. He had endured the effects of an enlarged prostate for over five years, and when his kidneys began their unexplained shutdown, he made the decision to refuse a "medicalized" life and to let his time here on earth come to an end.

Part of grieving the loss of not just my companion but our forty-seven-year journey together has been a complete review of my life. I decided I wanted to share what memories I have that may be of interest, not just for my children but for anyone else as well. I grew up in the very heart of the baby boom, and if you didn't, it would be hard for you to understand just how thoroughly and completely things have changed in the last sixty years.

I have spent my whole adult life swimming against the current of the culture. I am a Christian wife who believes in and tried hard to walk out godly submission in a day when such a lifestyle, at the very least, exposes one to wondering mockery. I am a practicing charismatic, yes, really. I was a public official for twenty-four years trying to bring the ideals of my faith to bear in a way that might make a difference. I was a Christian homeschooler privileged to serve on a public school board *while homeschooling*. My husband and I raised six children together, another choice that some people seem to find inexplicable.

This series of essays is my attempt to share what and why and when and how. I have tried to be honest and truthful but also reasonably kind. I am not asking for approval. I am not apologizing. I am not bragging. No one knows better than me how often and how badly I failed to live up to the ideals that have informed my life. I am telling my story in my words and may God let the chips fall where they may.

On Grief and Becoming Myself Alone

Since my husband's death, I have had occasion to be in touch with a number of people around my age who have also lost a spouse. The difference between their experiences and mine is that in almost every other case, the spouse passed without warning. At first, I felt so badly for them. Jack and I had time to prepare, and that is a gift. However, I have realized that my experience was pretty harrowing too. I had to be with him day after day for months, knowing he was going to die and watching his decline, dealing with its consequences, never really knowing how to interpret what was happening, never knowing where we were on the trajectory, and almost alone in the middle of the covid pandemic. It was tough.

When I knew that Jack's life was going to end and mine was going to continue, I started wondering what that would be like. I anticipated some relief at being freed from a fairly heavy-handed headship. At the same time, I wondered where my spiritual covering would come from—we even talked about it once. I thought I might be afraid for my safety, alone out in the country. I expected to enjoy being able to do some of the things around our home that Jack had resisted. I would have money, and I would spend some. I could not even imagine what having no companion would be like after so many years together.

Things have turned out a little differently than I expected. I *have* enjoyed doing the projects I felt were needed to be a good steward of the land Jack brought us to. I had the dead trees cut down. I had aeration installed in the pond. I demolished the back garage and replaced its function with a much smaller shed in a much better location. I bought a riding lawn mower, which, honestly, probably saved my life. I replaced all the old electronics with newer versions. Put the house deed in my name with a transfer on death to the kids attached. Put the investments in my name and updated the beneficiaries.

Those things were pretty straightforward and easy decisions. And the nuts and bolts of them kept me mentally busy for a while, which seems to be one of the things widowed people do as they cope with loss. It may be part of the general review that leads to saying goodbye to a big part of one's life. It turns out I am not as afraid of being alone as I expected to be. I am trying to cultivate a prayer life that includes asking God for protection, but in the meantime, it is not fear that keeps me awake at night.

What keeps me awake is my journey through assimilating, not just Jack's death but also our life together. I have listened to the music mixes he made in anticipation of his death and meditated on the significance of each song choice. As so many widowed people do, I sorted and albumed the mass of family photos that used to live in a giant heap in the hutch. Doing that brought me up close and personal to Jack's earlier days, which I call "Jack in the time of youth and beauty." In some ways, I fell in love all over again.

I have also spent hours combing through the many folders on his computer into which he sorted the massive correspondence that consumed so much of his time and mental energy throughout his life. There are written exchanges with columnists and elected officials going back decades. There are whole email exchanges with friends and relatives and total strangers in which he opened the storehouse of his memories and thoughts to try to connect. Some of them I have printed in order to create what I call "The Book of Jack." If any of his children or grandchildren decide at some point they would like to know him better, they can read the things he wrote over a lifetime that might help with that. It is a treasure trove—years of trying and trying, not just to connect but to influence and to understand.

As I read these writings, I recognized the depth and breadth of a whole other life he led as his own self, apart from me. Although my own thought life has bubbled along through the years, so much of what I actually did was ultimately an effort to gain his approval, much like a child with their father. And approval was what he always withheld. No one of his family, myself included, ever thought deeply enough, wrote clearly enough, battled hard enough, brought change enough, *cared* enough. It was a losing cause.

Of course, his approval was separate and apart from his love. But his love was hard to experience separate from approval. I have laid awake for hours parsing through what I said, what he said, what we did, what it all really means, why it happened as it did, how it all fits into the framework of the larger picture of our relationship. And what it means to love and be loved.

I have had people say to me, "I'm so sorry you have lost the love of your life." Was he? Maybe God is the love of my life and Jack's life, and he and I tried as best we could to facilitate that in and for each other. "I know that you and Jack were soul mates more than my wife and I ever were." Were we? I'm not sure I know what a soul mate is or if I even believe there is such a thing. Ultimately, a great deal of my interior life was entwined around what Jack felt was important.

What I have come to believe through hours and hours of reading, looking at pictures, listening to the music mixes he made, and contemplating alone through the quiet of the night is that Jack truly loved me, and I truly loved him. Yet we did not bring that to fruition for each other as successfully as we might have. And I have suffered a great deal of sadness, much more than I anticipated, as I have assimilated this belief.

Based upon every conversation I have had with or about widows, it seems that the first emotion a person feels after the death of a spouse is guilt. I should have done this, I should have said that, why was I not kinder in those final days, hours, moments. But this is the shallow guilt, the easy guilt. You vanquish it by remembering that you were doing the best you could out of the flawed person you are in sometimes very difficult circumstances. You hope he knew that, and you think he did.

But the later guilt…the guilt that winds its way through all the thoughts since then as reality reveals itself is harder to conquer. Why did I not receive his love with the joy it deserved? Why was he sometimes so hard on me? Why did I always react with defenses and stubbornness? Why was I so proud?

Part of the lingering effects of this later guilt is that there is no way to make reparation. I do not have Jack here to apologize to or to declare love for or to hug. I find myself wishing I could tell him what I think I have learned. I have to believe that many widows long, like me, to have just one more conversation to clear up those last few misunderstandings, missed opportunities, to actively exchange love just once more. That you can't ever is so sad.

Over the first six months, I had several dreams about Jack and all were either overtly or covertly negative. He is a vampire, he is leaving me for someone else, he is too busy to talk to me or to hear the things I want to share with him. I felt awful about these dreams and finally had the sense to ask God about them. What h e showed me is that I had deeply hidden anger at my husband. And that the source of the anger was the many hurts he had inflicted over the years, as happens in all relationships and which I had hoarded up in my heart. When I would think about Jack, up would pop this thing he did, that thing he said, and it was all I could think about. So I asked God what to do about it.

I believe in the reality and working of spiritual beings, both for good and for ill. I have a book that helps me when I want to deal with the devil and his works and ways. Using the book, I began to dig really deeply into my heart and into my past. I was able to realize that the negativity I was feeling about Jack and whether or not he even loved me was being facilitated by a spirit of rejection and that the power of this being entered my life long before I met Jack.

By faith and prayer, I have rooted out the spirit of rejection and use awareness, scripture, prayer, and worship to keep it from coming back as it tries to do fairly often. When it was gone, I was able to perceive the sludge left inside and to ask Jesus to cleanse me, repair the scars, to give me back the whole, clean heart that he wants me to enjoy. I am daily experiencing his power to do this. The spirit of rejection had been tormenting me for years, and it is unbelievably freeing to escape it. Having rid myself of its power freed me to ask God what I still need to apologize to Jack for, and he has been gracious to show me things where I hurt Jack in my own unkindness and ignorance.

Then I engaged in a process of inner healing where I imagined myself in a very safe place. I had Jesus with me, and Jack came in. With Jesus to mediate, I was able to tell Jack what I had been feeling. I was able to confess my wrongs against him as God brought them to mind. To confess, to repent, to ask for and receive forgiveness. Jack was able to do the same, Jesus with a hand on each of our shoulders. Inner healing is releasing me to see and appreciate the full spectrum of Jack's tender heart and to begin to truly believe in the love he kept telling me was there. It is releasing me to feel joy once more.

In some ways, I can hardly wait to move on to my home in heaven at least in part because of my hope that it will be Jack who comes for me when my time here is done. I am much less apprehensive about my death, having accompanied Jack to his. I never feared *being* dead but had some qualms about *getting* dead. Not so much now. When I think of maybe perfecting the love we had without it being spoiled by the sin that pervades life in human flesh, I know our first hug will be so sweet. I really look forward to being able to sing with him in heaven as I never really could here on earth.

Once this process was complete, I began to reflect on the fact that for so much of my grief journey I have been like someone on a crowded sidewalk with a zillion busy people rushing forward while I faced backward. I was spending so much time looking back that at some point, wallowing in the pain of that had become, for me at least, self-indulgent. I figuratively have faced front now. I am actually avoiding the activities I had spent so much time on like reading his letters, looking at his pictures, and listening to his music mixes because it hurts and makes me cry. I literally prayed one day, "God, I am so tired of being sad. Could you please heal me?" I think he is.

It was around this time that I had a different sort of dream about my husband. I dreamed I had taken my tear-stained self to church looking for Jack. I finally found him in the parking lot after the service. He had a little leather satchel and he was circulating, talking to people about contracts and gathering little snippets of paper. As I tried to talk to him, it became clear to me that he was busy. And after

I awoke, I realized he is busy doing the work God has for him now. I have found this thought a comfort ever since.

Now that I have one year behind me, I realize that the old normal is gone for me. I thought at some point I would get back to "normal," but now I think whatever normal will be is not yet in view. I found a quote by L. M. Montgomery that expresses how I feel: "It seems as if gladness were killed in me. Perhaps someday, a new kind of gladness will be born in my soul, but the old kind will never live again."

This is not meant to discourage anyone—it is just my reality. I have also concluded that no one can really understand or, honestly, try to offer comfort to a widow unless that person has suffered the loss of a spouse. Sorry, people, you don't get it until you have lived it. Period.

Now that I am alone, I am beginning to realize that the next step for me is to figure out who God wants me to be as my own separate self. This is taking some time because extricating myself from Jack's and my life together is a process. It's not just the physical and emotional life, it is the oneness of spirit. As I detangle, there is an open wound in that spot that over time is healing. Longtime widows have told me it takes a long time or even that it *never* gets better. Well...

I know Jack might have wanted me to be like him, a warrior on Facebook. I am not doing that. I do not want to pound my head against a wall I can never breach. At least not for now. I read the news every day and am horrified by what is happening at all levels of life. Unfortunately, I am starting to wonder if God is letting this country reap the bitter fruit of our rejection of him and his ways, that he is finally pressing the smite button. I may buy a gun.

I have finally moved forward in managing the investments. I have formed some very basic principles and, based on them, am finding trustworthy people to help me.

I am not committing to any more animals at this time.

I am praying a lot, and because I am alone, I am praying out loud. Not sure what the dog thinks about that, but it just seems right to pray out loud. I have had some wonderful and, I feel, effective worship times here at home. I am sometimes engaged in spiritual warfare as the Lord leads. I have found a church in Tennessee that I like, and it is feeding me for now.

How and when and what I eat has changed pretty significantly. I am still avoiding restaurants and grocery stores. I have begun to cook again a little.

I keep reaching out to people in an effort to not be too lonely with varying degrees of success. This is extra challenging during the ebb and flow of an international pandemic. I sometimes fear maybe I just do not do friendship very well. Maybe I'm bad at reading people. Maybe I'm just too self-centered. The spirit of rejection can cause a person to avoid the risk of rejection by avoiding the people, which is not conducive to authentic friendship. Maybe I will do better in this respect now that that spirit is gone.

I'm pretty sure remarriage is not in my future. I cannot imagine being that vulnerable again much less being willing to undertake another such catastrophic loss. I mean, it took me eight years to get over the loss of our dog! Also, Scripture tells widows to stay widows if they can. I am comfortable with that at this time.

What I do know is that I will find ways to be useful. I have always been animated by the desire to help. Helping is what I do. As long as I am physically able, I will contribute somehow.

Because God is working pretty hard with me regarding the sort of person he expects me to be going forward, I'm excited to see where he decides to plug me in.

On When I Was
a Little Girl

I was born on May 15, 1953, at nine forty-nine in the morning in a private hospital in Bay Village, Ohio, belonging to the Sheppard family. Yes, that Sheppard family. I'm not sure who delivered me as the practice was shared among Dr. Sam Sheppard and his father and brother. I don't know how my mother got hooked up with them for her care, but my folks drove all the way to Bay Village from Mentor for my birth. It was the following year when the murder of Dr. Sheppard's wife took place. I wonder if that was weird for my mom.

The very first memory I have is of sitting on a picnic blanket surrounded by food and being afraid of the yellow jackets that were hovering. I don't know where or when that was.

I am the second oldest of six children, four boys and two girls. By the time my sister Susan was born, I was nine years old and the only girl with three brothers. When my father came in the front door on the morning of her birth and announced I had a sister, I jumped for joy and cracked my elbow on a chair back on the way down. Funny bone. Oww!

My parents were always real estate gadflies. By the time I was born, less than three years after they married, they were already living in their third house. They had bought a dream house on Lakeshore Boulevard in Mentor at about the same time my dad tried to be a car salesman. It is my understanding they almost went bankrupt, sold the dream house, and moved to a house on Hendricks Road, whose water came through a sand filter that apparently let earthworms come out the faucets on occasion.

My first real memories are from when we lived on Bellflower Road in Mentor. They must have moved there when I was two or three years old. I remember that our house was new, but that there was some kind of problem with there being "water in the heat pipes", which ran through the slab foundation. I do remember my parents had bought a pink rug for my bedroom that had black water stains from whatever the issue was.

I can remember looking out my bedroom window and seeing the train tracks to the south so that would have been before the Route 2 freeway was built. It was in fact built while we lived there. I remember sledding down the hill formed by the overpass before the roadway opened.

The times were so different then. Mothers stayed at home and so did kids. We made our own fun and did not require adult input to find things to do. There was a fluid bunch of kids that gathered for group games like kick the can and beckon (an iteration of hide-and-seek). Our yard was often the site for these games since we were sort of central in the grouping of homes on the corner of Bellflower and Center Street. I remember my brother Bruce and his friends got their picture in the paper for "fishing in the ditch." I also remember when Mama Kitty had a litter of kittens in the corner of our dining room. When the kittens went to live in the garage, they were killed by the neighborhood tomcat. That was a little traumatic. I mean, there were pieces...

One time, we were playing doctor—no, not that kind of doctor. There were little round red and blue and black bumps on the maple leaves, much like sprinkles on Christmas cookies, and we pretended they were pills, and we ate them. They tasted bitter. I learned later they were bug eggs.

Another time, in the spring, we noticed the iris buds looked like pencils, so naturally, we picked them and wrote all over the patio with them. We got in a good bit of trouble for that one. I told you we made our own fun.

Generally speaking, I think I was probably a fairly hard kid to raise. The fact that I could never seem to overcome my aversion to being teased probably made me a pain in the neck. I actually remember throwing a temper tantrum in the living room of our neighbor across the street. You know, on the floor, thrashing. I always wondered if I might not have gotten the lap time that would have maybe made me different. Hard to say.

The dynamics of our family included dealing with my dad's temper. He would let you get away with a thing nine times and the tenth, and you never knew which was going to be the tenth, he would explode. He threw me down the stairs once. We had knuckle marks in the walls. After my grandfather's death, his mother was visiting, and we were looking at wedding pictures. I asked why his parents were by my mom and hers by him, and he totally blew up at me. I have literally no idea why. I was nine.

I will say I always thought my mother could have done a better job of protecting us, but she was pretty diffident with my dad. Later, when she was demented and thought she was eighteen and juggling several suitors, there was one she liked but was worried that he had a bad temper. I always thought that might have been my dad in her mind. After his death, I don't really think she went through anything like the grief that I am experiencing. When asked if she would ever consider remarriage, she declared stoutly, "I'm not putting myself under some man's thumb again!"

This aspect of my upbringing led to a determination that I was not going to let the father of my kids overdo his treatment of them. This was seldom an issue except a couple times when the younger boys in their teen years pushed the old man too far. I know I got between Mike and Jack once and had a bruise to show for it.

One of the things I remember was my parents having to deal with my brother Scott's psoriasis. He was probably only two or three years old when it showed up. It is apparently unusual for such a young child to have it. I can still recall the smell of the pine tar soap they used to bathe him.

I also had a constant battle with my older brother Bruce teasing me. Continually. He would push my face into mud puddles. He would mock me beyond bearing, and then I would get into trouble for the resulting explosion. I have never been able to learn not to rise to that kind of bait, even now. Why is that? It was so bad that as an adult, he once apologized. "I don't know why they let me do that."

We lived on Bellflower for seven years, so my early childhood was there. I attended Center Street School for first and second grades. It was an old building, and I can remember receiving polio vaccine in the hallways. The same hallways we used for civil defense drills. You know, in case someone sent an atom bomb to Lake County. I also remember the election of 1960 and how partisan the kids were. Though my family was Republican, it was pretty cool to stand at the window of our second-grade classroom and watch John Kennedy and his wife ride by in a red convertible.

When I was in the first grade, there was a bully, a sixth grader, who terrorized the playground at recess. One day, I got so mad I went after him 'cause a six-year-old girl can take on an eleven-year-old boy. Mostly, I remember trying to kick him, and he grabbed my foot. That made me even madder because even at that age, I could feel the mockery in it. I have always to this day hated a bully.

One day at recess, I found a flower bulb lying on the ground. I picked it up and brought it home. We planted it out by our back patio, and it turned out to be a deep-purple iris. How did I, at six, know that lumpen thing was something to save and plant?

Back then, my closest friend in the neighborhood was Lynn who lived across the street. Her dad was a serious gardener, so the yard was landscaped with lots of shrubs. We used to gather up the grass clippings from his mowing to lay out on the ground like walls and furniture to make houses. We also spent a lot of time catching bees in jars. I never got stung, but she did once. Her mother ran the hose on the ground in the front garden to make a paste of mud to put on the sting. It was from Lynn that I caught chicken pox.

I was in the second grade, and by that time, my mother had me drying dishes after dinner. I clearly recall asking her to scratch my back while I was helping her, and that was when she discovered the pox. I had a fairly normal case, but poor Scott's case was quite dreadful.

By that time, my dad was a customer engineer for IBM, and one of the companies he serviced was Wayside Gardens. In those days, due to the soil composition of Mentor and the climate that came from proximity to Lake Erie, Mentor was world famous for the roses that were raised there. My dad was garden-hearted and had a wonderful rose garden along our front walk. It seemed to me that those blossoms were as big as dinner plates. He fed them with a smelly powdered concoction in a burlap bag he had got from Wayside Gardens.

He also purchased and planted a Crimson King maple tree behind our house. I remember him being disappointed that it never did very well. That tree is still there, on Bellflower Road, though all the brick ranches are gone, and that corner has become commercial. And that tree is still kind of spindly and poor-looking. He was right; it never prospered.

Somewhere during those years, a family named Bartholomew moved in for a while. Lisa Bartholomew was really into things like ghosts and witches. She talked about them a lot. She told me once that when she got up that morning, there was orange blood on the floor of her bedroom. I am pretty sure it was from her that I developed fear of the dark that stayed with me until I became a mother and had to get over it in order to do infant care at night.

Another family came whose dad was in the military. At that time, there was a missile installation called a Nike site in Lake County. I think the daughter's name was Kim. I can remember playing dress up in her garage using old curtains my mom had given us. I also remember their dog following her brother around, eating the contents of his droopy diaper. Eww… It was their dog that bit me and almost took out my eye. Good times.

Halloween was a pretty big deal back then in kid world though emphatically not in grown-up world, unlike today. I had a princess costume that I wore for at least a couple of years. There was a full-face plastic mask that stayed on with an elastic band. I still remember how damp and breath-smelling it got over the course of the night. We each had a pillowcase we used to collect our candy. You would come home and dump out the take on the floor and sort the good stuff from the not so good stuff. Apples? Pennies? Raisins?

One of my mother's parenting practices was to require a daily nap. I had to nap every afternoon until I was five at which time I was allowed to "rest" instead. (There was no kindergarten in Mentor back then.) I did not enjoy napping. In fact, I did not nap. I suffered from boredom while being required to lay around for an hour or two while my mom went next door for coffee. I figured out how to make a little ghost out of a tissue. I drew pictures on the wall in my bedroom. I got up and tried out my mother's bright-red lipstick. I got Scott to help me build a train from our kid-sized chairs out in the living room.

It was during one of these excursions that my dad unexpectedly came home in the middle of the day. When he checked on me and saw the lipstick on my face, he started to ask me about what I had been doing, and of course, I said "nothing." I may have suggested that three-year-old Scott got out of bed, climbed up into the closet, obtained a red crayon, and wrote on my face while I slept.

Dad tried and tried to get me to confess. He promised if I would tell the truth, he would not spank me. So I told the truth, and he spanked me. Obviously the injustice of this lingers. It helped me form my own parenting style. I think my kids would tell you I might have been firm (I mean, they called me Sarge), but I never went back on a promise like that.

One of the big fun parts of this time in my life was our relationship with my widowed grandmother. She was my mother's mother, and my mother was an only child. My grandmother worked as the manager of the Hough Bakery at Harvard and Lee in Cleveland. She had a nice two-bedroom apartment in walking distance to her job. I remember visiting there and the smell of the gas stove that I had not encountered before.

She would have things for us to do when we visited. I know she always saved her McCall's magazines for me so I could cut out the Betsy McCall paper dolls they printed every month. Even then, I remember being frustrated that the dolls were in a different pose every month, so you could only use the clothes from that month on that doll. It seemed so wasteful. Why couldn't the doll be in the same pose so the clothes could accumulate? She also had a car for the boys to play with that was made to fall apart. That is, you would put it all together and roll it as fast as you could toward the wall, and when it hit, it would fall apart. Actually, it would kind of explode. Seriously.

My grandma would let us come and stay with her at her apartment in Cleveland one at a time. I remember going on a bus with her and visiting a department store that had a snack bar. I remember hearing about the rapid transit though I'm not sure she took me on that. I remember sleeping with her and opening the dresser drawer and smelling my grandfather's Old Spice cologne she had kept all those years. (I gave Jack's Old Spice to our grandson Noah for Christmas this year. I wanted him to know it's nice for a man to take the trouble to smell good.) My grandpa had died of cancer long before I was born.

After the car sales fiasco, my dad's job with IBM was to go around to all their clients in a given area and maintain and repair their equipment. This really fit into his skill set and also let him buy a new car regularly, which he liked. My parents began a friendship with a couple whose husband was my dad's coworker. The McKinneys were their lifelong friends, and I still occasionally hear from Kay McKinney.

My folks would go over to the McKinneys' house every Friday night to play cards, and my grandmother would stay with us. This required my dad to drive into Cleveland every Friday to pick her up and bring her to our house because neither she nor my mother ever learned to drive. And when she got there, she always had a bag of Hough Bakery goodies in tow. Can you imagine?

Little pecan pies and corn toastems, good bread and birthday cakes, kuchen and ribbon candy. What could be better than a grandma who managed a bakery? She was quite round, and we were pretty much all the family she had. She would let us get up after my parents left, and we would sit with her on the couch, for some reason always in the dark, and she would tell us stories about our mother's childhood. The time she turned over a board in the park and disturbed a bees' nest. The time she rode home in the wagon busily unreeling the toilet paper the whole way. We loved it.

In 1962, my parents decided to move again, this time into a five-bedroom house on Robinwood Drive in the Mentor Headlands area. My mother was expecting a fifth child, and my grandmother was going to retire and live with us. Once again, the house was new. In fact, the neighborhood was new, and at the time we moved, it was only half built. I was halfway through third grade. Because of a redistricting in the school district after second grade that had moved me to a different elementary school, this move brought me to the third elementary school I had attended.

By the time we moved to the Headlands, we were pretty well established in our attendance at Zion Lutheran Church in Painesville. I was baptized and married there, sang in the choir and taught Sunday school there, was active in the youth group and formed my familiarity with the Bible there. As a kid, you have your life at home and your neighborhood, your life at school and, for me, my life at church.

The story of my life in the Headlands is told pretty thoroughly elsewhere (see chapter *On Pam*). But I do want to say here that having my grandmother move in with us kind of destroyed the grandma mystique. It must have been pretty crappy for her too. She was diagnosed with diabetes shortly after we moved, and for some reason, my parents were always critical of her relationship with her doctor and doubtful about the diagnosis. It made for unnecessary tension. When my mom had her sixth and last baby, I remember my grandmother being kind of weirdly overprotective of him. I have to imagine that it was tough for two women who couldn't drive to be cooped up together in that little house on that little street. I am convinced that the experience of living with her mother lay at the core of my mom's adamant desire *not* to live with any of us even in her ultimately demented state (see chapter *On Letting Go.*)

There are a few things that happened while we lived in the Headlands that were very formative to my later years. One was being tapped to go into Mentor's gifted program at school. At that time, Mentor would gather the twenty-five or thirty brightest fourth graders from around the school district and comb them into a single class at Rice Elementary, the fourth elementary school I would attend. My brother Bruce was picked for the program, and then I was and so was Scott. It was called the AT class for "academically talented."

Before that time, I never thought of myself as any different from my classmates. That is, I thought everyone was just like me. After being picked for the class, I thought of myself as a cut above. Right or wrong. Mostly wrong. A kid that age needs a proper humility. In other words, it was probably good for me educationally but not so good for my character.

It was around this time that Pam and I briefly experimented with smoking. Everyone smoked then, and it was not hard to get hold of cigarettes. I remember being frustrated that I couldn't get the smoke to come out my nose. Because I did not know that smoking involved actually inhaling the smoke, which I truly never did. Duh. Fortunately, my brother tattled on me, and my folks put a stop to the smoking experiment. Thanks, Bruce. For real.

I was probably nine when I had to get stitches. I had been drying dishes while my mom talked on the phone. She had the phone cord stretched across the kitchen, and I had to bend down to get to the table where I was piling the dishes as I dried them. I miscalculated and caught my eyebrow on the corner of the counter and split the skin. My mom turned around and said, ever so calmly, "Jane, I need to go. Linda just gashed her head." A couple weeks later, I was back at the doctor for a tetanus shot because I had stepped on a nail sticking out of a board behind one of the unfinished houses up the street. Good times.

Then there was the fire. I had begun to build a babysitting business and was doing pretty well. One evening, I was babysitting at a home across the street from my house. While I cleaned up from their snack, one of the boys took his parents' lighter, crawled under the bed, and tried to light a Christmas candle but instead lit the mattress. In the moment when I opened that bedroom door and saw nothing but flames, I had a choice of what to do. I slammed the door and immediately thought of running to the front door and yelling, "Fire!" But instead, drawing on school fire drills, I called the fire department, shut all the doors, turned off all the lights and got the kids out. I was eleven years old. What I learned from this was that in the moment of severe challenge I would be able to come through and do the necessary thing. That I would not panic. That's a really good thing to know about oneself.

At around that same time, I learned I could sing. Now I had always sung. But it was kid singing. In the youth choir at church, my friend and I decided to goof around by singing as loudly as we could. And suddenly, I had an adult-sounding, pretty good singing voice. At eleven, I was given solos. I had to stand up in front of all these people I knew who knew me and open my mouth and sing. I had to remember the words and not let my pounding heart distract me from the task at hand. I had to accept the resulting compliments with grace. And I learned I could do it. As a result, I have never been afraid of public speaking because I know what it is to face and conquer that type of fear. Once again, something good to know about oneself.

When I was ten or eleven, as Christmas was approaching, I noticed the bags and boxes in my parents' closet, and as so many of us do, I decided to snoop. Among the contents of the bags was a cranberry-colored wool skirt, obviously for me. When Christmas came, as I opened each present, I kept waiting to find the skirt I knew was coming. At the end of the day, I realized that knowing what I was going to receive had completely ruined Christmas for me. It was the anticipation and the mystery that made for the best Christmas, and I had destroyed that. I decided I would never do that again.

Peeking at the gifts was like cheating at solitaire. It's a game you play alone. No one knows if you cheat or not. But if you cheat, do you ever really win? Nowadays, especially with the advent of the Internet, there is all kinds of cheating going on. Old-fashioned virtues like honesty and kindness and purity and humility are ignored as so many people pursue their most wicked and base impulses. But here's the problem, all the people who think no one knows what they do have forgotten the One who knows it all. Listen people, God sees. No one will escape having to face the things they have done in secret. Never cheat at solitaire because you only cheat yourself.

Not long after that, prepubescence struck. For me, that meant that my nose suddenly became quite large. My life on the bus was hell for two years as I endured merciless teasing. My mother used to try to get me to ignore it, but *I could not ignore* it. I actually remember the moment one day when I looked in my bedroom mirror and said to myself, "This is the face God gave me." When I accepted this immutable fact, I kind of relaxed. The teasing became mostly meaningless because, dude, that nose *was* big, especially on a kid-sized face. When I stopped caring, the teasing did stop. (Sorry, Mom.) I have to say that the few times my nose came up in later years, I was always a little surprised that anyone cared. Because I don't.

In the late spring of the year shortly before I turned thirteen, I was asked on a date by a fifteen-year-old boy from my church. At the age of twelve, I was allowed by my parents to accept and go on this date. We were supposed to go to a movie, but that didn't work out, so instead we spent some time at his house while his parents were entertaining friends. I did not enjoy this experience. I was horribly self-conscious and uncomfortable the whole time because I was *too young*! From this experience, I formed the conviction that I did not want my children to date until they were at least sixteen and mostly held to it.

When I got into early adolescence, my friendship with Pam diminished. In those last couple of years in the Headlands, I was friends with Caroline and Marcia. Marcia was unusual for the times in that her parents both worked, leaving her at home alone during school vacations. In those times, we did our best to get into mischief while the parents were gone. I had my first kiss as a thirteen-year-old in her living room from a boy I had met when we were allowed to hang around Painesville on Saturdays. We had invited him and his friends to hang out with us unsupervised. It was an incredibly dangerous situation that could have gone really wrong.

Shortly after this, my parents decided to move again. It needs to be understood that throughout those years, my parents were always looking at houses. They would go for rides to look at houses. They would come up with schemes to buy houses that either worked out or didn't. My dad was constantly drawing house plans for what he would build if he could. I am not sure what this did to the sense of stability in our home, but I will say I was aware even as a child that this behavior was indicative that my parents were putting their interests above the interests of their kids. Right or wrong, this knowledge led to my own determination as a parent to prioritize my kids above myself. To this day, I wonder what drove them in this area.

I was at the end of eighth grade when we moved again, this time to Jackson Street in Painesville. It was late spring. What a crappy kid time of year to move. There was not enough time to build any friendships before the end of school, and the following year would take me into high school. It was tough.

Although high school is not exactly a time of being a "little girl", the immaturity that marks those years (believe me, I have the diaries to prove it) makes me include them in this section. In the main, I enjoyed high school. I participated in many extracurricular activities. Many of them were calculated to bring me into the orbits of the popular kids. Like so many high school students, I longed for the acceptance and respect given to that golden group. I never really made it in. Fortunately, I eventually stopped caring.

When I was fifteen, I went into town one Saturday with my dad to help him with some errands. He went to the bank and sent me to the post office. As I walked that way, a young man approached me and asked for some road directions. I gave them and went and bought stamps.

When I came out, he was hanging around in front of the building and started to walk beside me as I headed toward the bank. I was puzzled but polite as he made a little chitchat, and then he said, "Do you put out for fifty bucks?"

"What?"

The second time he asked his question, I suddenly understood what he was asking, and I abruptly stopped walking. He kept going and disappeared around the corner.

I was obviously shocked, and you know what I thought right away? What was it about me in my ponytail with the blue bow that made him think he could ask me such a thing? It got worse when I told my dad what happened, and he laughed. I had thought he would and should be mad. That he would want to find and thrash this kid. But he laughed. It was like having cold water flicked in my face. From that, I learned that in some fundamental ways, I was really on my own.

I was a cheerleader for a couple of years. I really loved being a cheerleader. It was just as fun as it looked like it would be and really helped me to feel I had made a place for myself at school. At the end of my sophomore year, when the girls of my class should have been moved up into the varsity rank, for some reason, the people who decided, decided to skip most of the girls from my class and bring up a bunch of freshmen into the varsity group, leaving us behind as JV. This was a crushing disappointment for me. It was also possibly one of the best things that ever happened to me. Because when the opportunity to get a job came about in the late summer before my junior year, being JV made it easy for me to drop out of cheering in order to start to work.

Now I had always tried to develop moneymaking opportunities for myself. I started babysitting at eleven, and in that summer between sophomore and junior years, I had a paper route. I was part of a large family where money was adequate, but there would be nothing for college. While I was a good and successful student (class rank number 5 of 244), there were not the opportunities for help then that there are now.

The job I got was to work as a waitress at a small restaurant in Painesville every weekday from four to seven o'clock. This ruled out participating in a lot of the things teenage girls do. It also put me squarely into regular contact with the adult world. When this happens to a reasonably perceptive kid, it changes the priorities. Suddenly, all those school concerns fell into a proper perspective in relation to the larger world. For me, I think this was a good thing. It certainly helped me relax about whether or not the clique was going to let me in. I earned $1 an hour, plus tips of which a quarter was a good one. On such pay, I was able to save enough to mostly pay for one year of college.

I was in high school in the late sixties, a time of social unrest in some ways as revolutionary as what we are experiencing now. My generation rebelled against authority in ways big and small. Why can't we wear jeans to school? Why can't we grow our hair long?

Drugs became available, and some kids used them indiscriminately. I knew kids who had bad trips *at school*. As sheltered as I was, I had opportunities to partake of marijuana more than once. The standard protocol was that someone would produce or roll a joint, and it was passed around the circle. When it came to me, I just passed it on. When questioned, I simply said, "I don't smoke cigarettes. Why would I smoke a joint?"

During high school, my folks kept a pretty tight rein on me. I was not allowed to go to parties and the like. But one of the quirks of my upbringing was that my parents, in particular my dad, had the conviction that once a kid was eighteen, his job as a father was done. Though I still lived in their house during the summer after high school, there were no more curfews or other controls. It was weird. Even though I had resented the restrictions, having none felt a little like being abandoned. That being said, I was functionally out at barely eighteen. I was financially independent at nineteen.

Though lack of money and wanting to be with Martin, the guy who passed for a boyfriend in my life, were reasons I dropped out of college, truthfully, the main reason I dropped out was lack of a specific ambition. I could not justify further debt in the absence of a burning career goal. Had I had such a goal, I am confident I would have found a way. So I stayed home, got an adult job, and began trying to live an adult life.

One of the bright spots of this period was that I got to experience effectively owning a horse. Because Martin was working in an adult job and still living at home, he had a lot of disposable income that he spent pretty freely. One thing he did was buy a horse, a ten-year-old palomino mare, for a girl with whom he had been friends (and occasionally more than friends) in high school. And weirdly, she never really did much with the horse besides pay the rent for her stall. But because he had bought the horse, Martin was comfortable telling me I could use Sunny as much as I wanted, and I did. He even bought me a decent saddle. I really love that I got to do that once in my life.

When I had paid off my college loan, I started to look for an apartment. I found a two-bedroom apartment at the corner of Jackson and Watson Streets in Painesville. Casting around for a roommate, I ended up calling Rita who was someone I had often walked to school with back in the day. I knew she was still in town and was working at the local newspaper office. She was all-in.

Rita was a great roommate. She paid her share of the bills, didn't mind washing dishes as I didn't mind cleaning, she made no judgments of my activities, and I left her alone as well. We lived together for nine months until I climbed into a big blue van in the predawn darkness of September 5, 1973, with my beautiful new husband and drove away.

On Pam

When I was a young girl, my best friend for several years was Pam C. After my family moved away, years after, Pam and I reconnected. By then, she was about to be married and enter a life of Christian camp ministry. We exchanged letters, and she sometimes visited for the rest of her life, which ended in the crash of a small plane in the mountains of Montana on a beautiful Sunday afternoon in May of 1992. It was a joyride. She was thirty-nine years old.

When I turned fifty in 2003, I decided to write down everything I could remember about our early friendship and share it with her daughters. What follows is what I sent.

* * * * *

I got to thinking the other day and realized there is a whole, pretty significant part of your mother's life that no one remembers in this life but me. I never forget her, and I decided I wanted to write down what I could recall of our friendship so that someone else can remember when we are both gone.

Pam and I were best friends from before we were nine until we were almost thirteen. The times were very different then from what they're like now. We were born in the very heart of the baby boom. Moms mostly stayed home. Most families had lots of kids. I only had one friend whose parents were divorced. The neighborhood where we lived in the Headlands was all new houses, part of the building boom that took place to meet the needs of the times. In fact, when we both moved onto Robinwood, the street was only half finished being built.

Our house was what my parents called a "bedroom" house. That is, fairly small living spaces but lots of bedrooms. Ours had five bedrooms to accommodate my parents, four children, and my grandmother, who was just then coming to live with us. My mother was eight months pregnant.

We moved early in 1962, and my sister was born March 6. Right around that time, Pam's family moved in kitty corner across the street. There were also four children in her family, and her mom was pregnant. Your aunt Georgia was born that spring.

Everyone knows that little girls are big on "best" friends. And that the girl who fits that description changes a lot. It wasn't like that for Pam and me. We were *always* each other's best friend. As I look back, I think it was that we had so much in common. It was interesting to me, later in life, to see how much our adult lives ended up similar.

Pam was three days older than me. I will admit it always bugged me that she was older than me. I have a strong personality and thought of myself as the leader in our relationship, and in many ways, I was. Yet when I got reacquainted with Pam as an adult, I saw how incomplete my perception had been. Pam became just as strong a leader as I had ever been.

There were several things that bound us together beyond being in the exact same place in life.

One was a deep and abiding love for horses. We both loved horses like mad and would have done anything to have contact with one. I hope you can imagine my envy when as an adult, Pam got to have steady contact with horses. Oh, was I jealous!

When we played horses, there was any number of approaches we took. At that time, there was a stretch of woods between our street and the next one over. It was obvious someone planned to develop it into another street someday because a bulldozer had gone down the middle of the woods and removed trees. But then it was left to sit, and nothing happened to it during the five years I lived there. We used to go to the north end of the woods where the houses on a short beginning of the street ended. These were the days of TV Westerns, and we were lady sheriffs, so our feet danced around the way as horses do, and we held the reins in front of us. Then we would get on that path and "gallop" all the way to the other end, managing our restive mounts with the "reins" we held.

We used to like to draw pictures of horses too. One summer day on Pam's back patio, we drew one picture after another. Blacks with white manes and tails. Pintos and bays, rearing and running and grazing. Brown and white and palomino, we wanted one of each.

Another thing we used to pretend was that we were in a horse show. We set up a course of jumps starting at Pam's patio. We'd jump over a couple of picnic benches, over the hedge into the next yard, then "canter" around a big curve and to the big jump. There was a tree right on the property line whose two trunks came up in the shape of a big V. It was pretty tough to jump through there, but of course, we did. We both often had scratches on both arms from brushing against the tree bark.

One summer, we somehow decided it would be cool to be horses on our hands and knees. Oh my, our knees were just black with grass stains for weeks as we "cantered" around on all fours, shaking our "manes" and neighing. (I seem to remember that being a time when we also got into screaming. TV had taught us the importance of being able to scream convincingly. My recollection is that your mom was a much better screamer than me.)

In the Headlands, there is a Fourth of July celebration with a parade and carnival every summer. It was so fun to sit on the side of the road and catch free candy. Then we'd go down by the community center and throw darts at balloons or toss bean bags for little prizes. One year, they had pony rides, and the owner let Pam and me actually lead the ponies around all day for free.

The only instruction was that we weren't supposed to let the ponies snatch at the grass, the way they always do. Wouldn't you know that a newspaper photographer came to snap our picture just as my wayward pony had grabbed at some grass, and I was trying to pull the grass out of its mouth. So there I was in the paper, holding a real pony's reins, "feeding" it a "snack"! That was my only hands-on experience with horseflesh as a child. We must have been about ten.

One of the best things about those years was having the run of the woods. Pam and I spent so much time wandering the woods and the edges of the swamp down at the end of the street. Though they had been bulldozed once, our woods were actually pretty pristine. In the spring, they were just full of a progression of wildflowers and birds. My dad had got into bird-watching when we moved there, and he used to watch the woods with an old pair of opera glasses. One spring, he was beside himself because he saw an ivory-billed woodpecker, a huge, pterodactyl-looking thing that was supposed to be extinct. Of course, it was really a pileated woodpecker, but it was still cool.

One summer day, we decided to follow a trail we'd often seen but never taken. It led away from our street, along the swamp past the ends of several other streets into a different patch of woods. We walked and walked. Finally, we came to a tree-covered hillside that faced out over a different section of the swamp. Here, someone had made a small, dugout cabin. It was half into the ground and roofed with slanting logs. Pam and I appropriated it and visited often. We dug little shelves into the dirt walls. We used to carry these cheesy little pocketknives, and we used them to cut holes into the sides of the huge acorns under the trees in that part of the woods. Then we stuck in sticks to make "pipes." Why? How should I know? We were kids.

I have always been an early-rising morning person. Your mom definitely wasn't. The year after we moved into our houses, the builder came back and put in curbs and sidewalks down our street. I can't tell you how many summer mornings I sat on the curb in front of my house, waiting for your mom to appear so the fun could begin. Our street ran north and south, the north end toward the lake and the south end toward the swamp.

That first summer, Pam and I befriended a plumber who was working on the new houses that were slowly going up down our street. We used to hang around sometimes and watch him work. We were especially fascinated by the lead he used to sweat the pipes together. He had a torch and a little metal pot that he would melt the lead in. One day, he took a tool and stuck it into the sand floor where he was working and poured a little of the liquid lead into the holes. Then he pulled out the pieces of lead and gave them to us. We thought that was so cool! I remember being fascinated by the disproportionate weight of the lead compared to its size.

One of the more dangerous things we did that summer was play on the roofs of the new houses. The workmen would leave their ladders after work, and up we'd go. I can still close my eyes and remember what Robinwood looked like from the top of one of those houses. We also played inside the unfinished homes. What a shock to discover that that nice, soft-looking pink insulation would leave a person feeling prickly all over! That was also the summer I stepped on a nail. I used to wear rubber flip-flops. That was a pretty nasty feeling, stepping on an upturned nail sticking up from a board and then looking into the hole in the bottom of my foot.

When you went to the south end of our street, you found yourself standing at the top of a steep incline maybe ten or twelve feet above the level of the swamp. You were looking across a panorama of silvered dead trees and acres and acres of cattails and swamp grasses. We were always afraid of the swamp, as indeed we needed to be, because there was quicksand. We only played on the very edges. At the foot of the little cliff at the end of our street, a huge tree had been tipped over in a storm and lay on its side in the swamp water with half of the roots jutting up to the sky. Oh, the fun we had with that tree. Once, we pretended it was an airplane, and the trunk was the walkway between the seats. Mostly though, it was a house, and the usable branches were different rooms.

One summer day, we were playing on one of the huge branches that lay like a walkway across a pond of swamp water. The dark water was warm and still and full of green duckweed and little brown snails. You could smell this rank, swampy stink. We would reach in and pull up wads of the weed and lay out beds for our little snail children. Somehow, in the course of moving around on that mossy branch, I lost my footing and fell into the water. That was not good. Going home covered head to toe in black swamp muck was not going to be well received. I can still remember the combination of the ickiness of being covered in muck, walking down the street in squishing wet sneakers, and the fear of what my mom would say about the condition of my clothes. As it turned out, I was able the sneak in and avoid a confrontation, but I still remember the stink.

At the foot of that same little cliff was the base of a very tall tree. I think it might have been a sycamore. The huge trunk went straight up, beyond the clifftop, even well above the tops of the houses on our street before there was a single branch. When it did branch, the limbs were enormous. Up the side of that tree, someone had nailed a bunch of pieces of two by four into a kind of ladder. One day, your mother decided it would be cool for the two of us to climb that ladder.

Oh! That climb still remains in my memory as one of the most terrifying events of my life! Pam was always more daring than I was, and I don't remember her being especially scared. (There was another time when she decided to *walk* up the incline formed by a tree that had tipped over and stuck among the branches of another tree. I went up on my bottom.) I can tell you the day we climbed that ladder I was beyond frightened. It's not that we didn't climb trees, we did, all the time. But this one was so high and the limbs, when you finally got to the top of the ladder, were so big there was nothing you felt safe holding onto. I don't know if Pam ever climbed it again, but I can tell you, once was enough for me!

Also at the base of that cliff was a tumble of tree stumps. Apparently, when they cleared the land for our street, they just bulldozed the stumps down to the end, and there they stayed in a wilderness jumble. You could crawl in among them because they were full of little "caves." We would play there every now and then, and I can still remember the damp earth smell in those caves. When we got thirsty, we would just take a handful of the water that trickled from the cement stormwater pipe that drained into the swamp right there.

Many of the families growing up on Robinwood at that time had different signals by which the children were called home at the end of the day. Your grandfather had a bright, piercing whistle he could produce at will to call Pam and her brothers and sisters. My father had mounted a bell outside our sliding doors. How many times did we come out of the woods at the foot of the street, and walking fast, knowing it was late, we'd ask the kids we passed, "Did the bell ring?" "Did my dad whistle?"

So far, I've made it sound like the only time we played was in summer. We also spent a lot of time in the woods during the winter. There was a hillside among the trees at the swamp end of the street where we went to sled. It was called "double hill" because it went down a ways, flattened, and then down again. I had a white vinyl winter coat one year with red fur trim. I used to go down that hill on my back with my knees hugged to my chest. Vinyl is really slick on snow! We had a neighbor boy one year who missed his aim and hit a tree, breaking his leg. That was a pretty big deal, seeing the ambulance go down our street to get him.

The other time the fire station up by the community center sent a truck to Robinwood was when the little boys I was babysitting set the house on fire, but of course, that's another story.

One other thing we did in the winter was to slide on the ice. The best way to slide on the ice was in our school shoes because the soles were hard enough that you could really go a long way. So we'd put on our fleece-lined red rubber boots over our shoes and dutifully buckle up. Then as soon as we were out of sight of home, we'd take them off, slide around all we wanted, put them back on, and go home, which was fine until you hit a patch of ice thin enough to let your foot go through. Then you went home with a "soaker" and tried not to get caught. The ice we slid on was over big puddles that formed in the woods during the winter. We *never* went into the swamp or walked on ice there. There were no ponds or lakes or anything like that where we lived, so the only danger to us was in getting a wet foot.

Another thing Pam and I liked to do was sing. We sang a lot. One day, we had gone up to the store at the north end of our street. This was a little strip shopping center with a grocery store, bakery, drugstore, library branch, with a freestanding ice cream store out in the north part of the parking lot. For some reason that escapes me to this day, we decided one time to spend about two hours marching up and down in front of the grocery store, singing the Oscar Mayer wiener song at the top of our lungs. Ask your Dad, I bet he can still sing it. "Oh, I'd love to be an Oscar Mayer wiener. That is what I'd truly like to be…"

You know, at that ice cream store, you could get a really nice cone for ten cents. Sometimes when we needed money, we would go door to door through the neighborhood asking for pop bottles. We often got a whole wagon load. Back then, you bought pop in returnable bottles. When you took them back to the store to be reused, you got your deposit back. It was two cents on the Pepsi bottles and a whopping ten cents on the quart ginger ale bottles. One bottle was good for a nice big ice cream cone. It was worth a little begging!

Money could be an issue for us because it could be hard to come by. I had always lived in a suburb with a mom who didn't drive, so I'd never had regular contact with the temptations of a candy counter. That first summer, Pam and I decided a good way to get candy was to just take it. Yes, we stole candy from the drugstore. And then, one day, we got caught. Oh, that still ranks as one of the great humiliations of my life. It was a good lesson though, and I was lucky it came to me early in life. I don't really know how Pam felt about it because I don't remember a time we talked about it. I can tell you we never stole again though.

There was a lady who lived one door away from my house. Her name was Trudy, and she was an unusual person. She was very fun-loving and outgoing. She was the kind of person who really went all out for Halloween, dressing up as a witch and handing out candy in her yard. I know lots of people do that sort of thing now, but believe me, back then, that was unusual. For some reason, she kind of took to Pam and me. She taught us to knit, which I still do on occasion. The other really significant thing she did was give us her old prom dresses.

Pam's was a pink sheath with spaghetti straps. It was covered from top to bottom with tiny horizontal pink lace ruffles. Mine was blue, strapless, with a full, chiffon bouffant skirt. Oh my goodness, we sashayed around in those dresses endlessly. We used to play on the patio behind your mom's house because we used the sliding glass doors like a huge mirror. About that time, we started to experiment with things like Kleenex and socks as shirt stuffers to give ourselves nice bosoms. I think the summer we were eleven was when we started to actively pursue that first kiss.

That summer was also the one I have always thought of as the "Barbie" summer. Living next door to your mom was an unusual little family. Both parents worked, and they had only one child, a daughter a year older than Pam and me. Her name was Linda Mooney. Her parents were much older than most in our street and rented their house while most people we knew were buying.

Linda's mother worked at a department store, and about once a week, she brought something new for Linda's Barbie collection.

Linda's house had five bedrooms, and the entire upstairs was full of her stuff. One bedroom was a big electric train setup. The other was the Barbie room. Her lifestyle was a new thing to Pam and me because she had so much stuff at a time when neither of us had much. (I remember being amazed at noticing a cake on top of the fridge that took *days* to disappear. At our house, you got your piece *today*, or you missed out!) Linda had the Barbie bedroom and living room sets and a huge box of clothes. She had the car and the Ken and Midge and a Barbie with wigs. Pam and I each had a shoebox for a bed and one doll with a handful of outfits. The summer we were eleven, we spent all day everyday up in the Barbie room, weaving fantasies and practicing to be grown-up.

And here's the odd thing. I haven't really seen or spoken to Linda Mooney in nearly forty years, but two weeks ago, she was on the front page of the local paper. She had stepped in front of a tractor trailer in Willoughby and had been killed. So now there's only me to remember the kitchen we made for the Barbie house that filled an outspread blanket on the floor of the Barbie room in Linda Mooney's house in the summer of '64.

Today is your mother's fiftieth birthday. How I wish she were here to talk to about how it feels to be fifty. Take it as a gift from both of us to know a little about your mom that maybe you didn't know before. I will never forget her. God bless, Linda Burhenne.

On Faith

I do not remember a time in my life when I did not believe in God. As a very young child, I remember saying and believing, "Jesus died on the cross to take away my sins." It was as simple as that for me. In some ways, it still is.

I was raised in the Lutheran Church/Missouri Synod. Even today, LCMS teaches *sola scriptura*, only Scripture. I have always believed it. David and Goliath, Daniel and the Lions, Noah and the Ark, Adam and Eve, I believe in them all. God said it; I believe it.

When I got to high school, I remember being in a biology class, and someone asked me incredulously, "You believe in Adam and Eve?" Well...yeah. In an English class, the teacher asked us if we believed that mankind was basically good or basically bad. I was the only one who said bad. "If mankind is basically good, why is the world so messed up?" No one had an answer for that.

Around the end of my junior year, I started running into a different breed of young Christian. These kids just seemed to be relating to God on a different level than me despite my churchgoing upbringing. As I considered the way they were and that it was different from me, I began to experience the Holy Spirit manifesting himself in my thought life.

Now here's the most important thing for anyone to understand about my faith journey. The big stuff was always supernatural. By supernatural, I mean beyond the norm, not in a weird way. I began to hear thoughts in my mind that I know were not my own. I know that actually does sound weird, but I can only say, this is what I experienced.

For example, I would think about wanting to do a certain thing or go a certain place, and occasionally, I would hear in my mind the

thought, *Only if God wants it.* I know these thoughts did not origi-
nate with me. This went on for some period of time.

Then one day in July of 1970, I was at home, lying on my bed,
not feeling well. As will happen sometimes in the adolescent girl's
brain, I toyed in my thoughts with how people would react if something bad happened to me. Immediately, that thought of, *Only if God
wants it*, popped up. Then I thought, *My life is surrendered to God.*
And just like that, I knew it was true.

In that moment, I was flooded with deep emotion. It was as if I
was sitting by a beautiful lake surrounded by woods and mountains
and blue sky in absolute quiet, and I experienced complete peace. It
was like all the puzzle pieces of life had fallen into place, and I *knew*
Jesus was my friend. I started to cry. I knew it was real because I knew
it was not me, it was him. This was my new birth. Supernatural.

Now a couple things happened after this to confirm a change
had taken place. I obviously wanted to share what had happened.
I wanted other people to get to enjoy the peace and comfort I had
received. I can tell you that declaring joyfully that your life is surrendered to God will elicit some strange reactions, usually not what you
were hoping for. But I just had to, and I did. It turned out to be the
start of a sort of mini revival within my family. Very soon after my
born-again moment, our church sponsored an evangelizing meeting,
and my parents and a couple of brothers became born-again too.

I began to share my faith quite openly at school. Our church
was bringing in a music group and I went to the principal to ask if
I could hang up posters at school for this event. I ended up talking
to him for about forty-five minutes and telling him about what had
happened to me. Not long after, he asked me to come to his office
to talk by phone to the principal of Mentor High School who was
trying to decide whether to let some students there (also from our
youth group) start a Bible study in school. I hope that means he took
what I had told him to heart.

The other thing that happened was that I began to want to read
the Bible. There were a lot of big questions in life, and I suddenly
wanted to know what God's answers were for them. If God is good,
why is the world so not? How could God condemn someone to hell

if he has not heard about Jesus? How does God want me to live, that is, what am I allowed to do and what am I to avoid? What's all this about spiritual gifts?

When a person surrenders to God and the Holy Spirit wakes up inside, reading the Bible becomes an adventure. My experience with God is that when he wants to communicate something to me, he will often use something I encounter in the Bible to let me know. I may have read a passage ten times before, but now when I read it, I suddenly understand how it is to be applied to the certain circumstance God wants me to hear from him about. That's just how it works for me, and I consider that supernatural.

After my conversion, attending the youth group meetings at my church became central to my growth as a Christian. While there had been a kind of revival in the adults of our church, it was in the youth group that God really cut loose. I believe part of the reason for this is that we were walking in worship in a way that is just very hard to achieve in Sunday worship, even if you know enough to try, which my Lutheran church did not. I remember the first time I raised my hands to worship. It was in a normal youth group meeting, and we were singing, and I just raised my hands. I had never seen or heard of doing this, but I just somehow knew I wanted to do it. Supernatural.

As soon as revival comes, so does Satan. And he was so subtle. When you start to read the Bible with an open heart and the help of the Holy Spirit, you will begin to run across things that run counter to what you're used to. One of those for me was the detailed information regarding baptism of the Holy Spirit and spiritual gifts. If you take God at his word, and I did, it became hard to understand why the church I was in did not also take him at his word on these issues. Others in the youth group did too. And pretty soon, teenagers in the Lutheran church were speaking in tongues.

Now as soon as that happened, there began to be all kinds of consequences. The adults wanted to know what was going on. The kids wanted to run with it ninety miles an hour. The ones who spoke in tongues were pretty sure those who didn't were not baptized in the Spirit and, in fact, might not even be saved. The pastors were truly trying to be open to God, but...see what I mean about Satan?

One of the people who spoke in tongues fairly early on was Martin (see chapter *On Martin*). One who didn't was me. This was not a giant source of conflict between us, but it tended to make someone like me wonder. I did everything they said to do to receive this gift, and I just didn't. Meanwhile, people were praying for healing. Crowds of kids were attending the youth group and being saved. One night during the prayer time around the altar, a girl began to manifest signs of demonic activity. And our Lutheran pastors were right there, wrestling with Satan in the darkened sanctuary. Some of us sat on the other side, scared, and suddenly I said, "Let's sing!" And we did. As I have said elsewhere, some pretty not-Lutheran things were happening. Supernatural

Eventually, these activities were shut down, and the revival in the youth group petered out as they always do. Many lives were permanently changed though. In the meantime, I graduated from high school and prepared to attend college. I had decided to go to Concordia in Ann Arbor, a Lutheran college for pastors and teachers. Attending a church college seemed like a good idea. Not sure it was the best place for a spiritually awake person to go, but there I was.

In college, I spent an embarrassing amount of time determining that my classmates were not where I was spiritually. And of course, soon I really wasn't in such a great place anymore. My relationship with Martin pulled me further and further from doing right. It was weird to me that even as we entered into sexual sin, what I consider to be the most sinful period of my life, we still talked about our faith.

One night, not long after we took that plunge, Martin asked me if I had received the gift of tongues yet. And I declared with some heat that I had not and did not care if I ever did. I went to bed and fell asleep and woke up out of a sound sleep with words pouring out of my mouth. In tongues. I almost had to gasp to catch enough breath to say what was pouring into the top of my head and out of my mouth without ever going through my brain. Supernatural.

It seems so like God to wait until then, when I was at my worst, to give me that gift and to do it in a way that could never be me but could only be him. I mean, I was asleep. Why did he do that? Why was he not condemning me as I deserved to be? I think because he knew what was to come later, and he needed me to know that he would forgive me. That kind of love is…supernatural.

Do I think there were inescapable consequences for that sin? I know there were, and I have suffered them. I hope I have worked through them all by now, but they were real and substantial. And if there is more, I deserve it. But in the midst of my worst, he gave me his best. God is good.

My marriage with Jack had its roots firmly in his belief that my entry into his life was orchestrated by God. Supernatural. When I met him, I had to be sure he was a Christian, and that his divorce was biblically acceptable. While both those things were true, it has taken me until now to realize he was not yet born-again there at the beginning. For the first few years of our marriage, he wanted to return to Catholicism, and I was a Lutheran. Oil/water. After I submitted to his headship regarding church, I was out of the way enough that he was able to begin to seek God in the Bible. That was when he entered into a born-again state. And that state eventually led us back out of Catholicism.

After Jack and I were married, we embarked on a spiritual journey together that is chronicled in other places (see *Our Spiritual Journey*). We saw and participated in miraculous healings. We saw evil spirits removed from tormenting people. We heard and received prophetic utterances more than once. We were attacked by Satan often and in very harmful ways, but God kept us safe and together. We never suffered want nor serious illness or injury during our child-rearing days. All our material needs were always met.

I have a learned a few things along the way.

It is my opinion that the best way to do a thing is God's way to the degree one can determine what that is. For example, when I became a mother, I believed that the way God intended infants to eat was from their mother's breast. So though I had never known anyone who had done this, I determined that that was how our babies would eat. It was only later that I learned the benefits to both mother and child of breastfeeding. I did it because it's God's way. That is why I did not use artificial birth control during my childbearing years. It is also why I would never use female hormones after menopause.

Clearly, God intends for that to end, so for me, end it did. I am satisfied with the fruits of these efforts in my life.

One of the things I've learned is to be very careful about the ministry I commit to. I have got myself committed to things that were me, not God. That is a short road to drudgery.

When someone hurts you, tell them. Sometimes, they have no idea that the thing they said or did made you react in such a negative way. They deserve the opportunity to explain and, if necessary, apologize. Hoarding up your hurt, declaring to yourself you will never, ever let them know how hurt you are is simply dumb. I know this because I have done it. Fortunately, Jack pointed out my dumbness, and I learned from it.

When you make a mistake, own it and apologize, even if it's embarrassing. Even if it's *really* embarrassing. Owning upfront is *always* better. Try to learn from it so you don't repeat it.

When someone offers you help or stuff, receive it with appreciation even if you don't want or need it. Giving is a spiritual gift. If no one will receive, the person's ministry of giving is stifled.

Be careful about the oaths you take. Even a cursory reading of the Old Testament will show you that things once said can't be unsaid. I remember once being in a church service where the flavor of the day was an elaborate daily prayer ritual around the Lord's Prayer. In the heat of the moment, the pastor asked everyone to stand up and vow before God that they would perform this prayer ritual *every day for the rest of their lives*. I think Jack and I were the only ones who didn't stand up. It's not that we didn't want to pray daily. We just were not going to make a vow like that, knowing we would fail to keep it. Vows and oaths are a big deal and require care and respect. That was one of the little nondenominational churches we had to walk away from.

Now here is the hard one. Wives, walk in submission to your husbands. Ladies, don't you just *hate* when you hear those words. Doesn't something just rise up in you that says, "Oh hell, no. I am as good, smart, spiritual, as he is. No, I am *more* spiritual than he is." Doesn't matter. God set the order of authority into place. In the Bible. Deny it if you dare. Now I will tell you something that puts it into a whole different light.

Go to the book of Exodus and read about when God sent Moses back to Egypt to bring his people out of captivity. Moses did not want to go. He was afraid. But he went, and he took his pagan family with him. And there you will encounter a little nugget that, for me (who am *not* a Bible scholar), changes the whole dynamic of submission.

It says God was going to intercept Moses on his way to fulfill what God wanted to accomplish, and God was going to kill him. The reason God was going to kill—yes, *kill*—Moses was because his son was not circumcised. Why had Moses's son not been circumcised? Almost certainly because his pagan wife did not want him to be.

To fix the situation, *Moses's wife* circumcised their son and placed the severed foreskin at Moses's feet, saying, "Surely you are a bridegroom of blood to me!" Pretty sure she was not happy about having to circumcise her baby. Maybe it was against her religion or tradition. Maybe she thought she was better, smarter, and more spiritual than Moses. But when she submitted to him, even so unwillingly, the act caused God to step back from his plan to kill Moses and allow him to continue the mission.

Ladies, it is in our act of submitting ourselves to our husbands and, therefore, to God that we make a way for God to accomplish his purposes. A man can never *make* his wife submit. Only she can make this choice. The control is totally in her hands. It is our gift, it is our glory, and it is our power to make or break the plans of God.

The other good thing about submission is if my husband has the final say, then whatever comes of it is on him, not me.

Be careful of the kind of church you attend. The denominational ones end up full of traditions and practices that make it very hard to be open to the working of God's spirit. (Although it can happen as it did in our Lutheran youth group.) On the other hand, be wary of nondenominational churches because they have no hierarchy or tradition to keep them on the path, and they can easily wander onto some pretty oddball rabbit trails. Church in these days of apostasy has become pretty tough.

Try to find a way to worship. The church in general really struggles with true worship. In my opinion, worship is to Christian practice what intimacy is to marriage. It is how you become open to God, which enables you to hear from him more clearly. It is how you experience ultimate closeness with him. Like intimacy in marriage, it should be done regularly and with enthusiasm, always with an ear tipped toward heaven for guidance.

It is my opinion that the best worship is pretty spontaneous. While you can try to be in God's will in planning the songs for Sunday, you have to stay open to the possibility that, in the moment, God wants to do something completely different. With what song you sing, with how many times you sing it, with pausing to see if he wants to bring out a word of tongues or scripture or prayer or a prophetic utterance. Learning to wait on God in worship is, again my opinion, crucial to letting there be true life in the worship. Some small nondenominational churches used to know how to do this. I have not found any where I live that still do yet...

As an aside, I believe worship should be done with excellence as a gift to God. Practice how to make a song really beautiful for God's sake. And then don't sing it if, in the moment, he takes you in a different direction.

One of the hardest truths to bear as a Christian is that you can lead a horse to water, but you can never make him drink. I tried really hard to lead our children into the sort of life-giving relationship with God that I have enjoyed for all these years. God will judge the fruits of that effort. If I have to die to make it possible for them to see Jesus as the friend to them that he is, Lord, take me today.

I need to publicly thank God here and now for his faithfulness to me for my whole life. He is the ground I stand on, the sun that unfailingly rises, the air to my gasping lungs, and water to my thirsting soul. He has never failed me. I honestly and truly do not understand how anyone can possibly bear to live in what our world is becoming without such certainty. With no context. With no eternal future. Thank you, thank you, Lord.

On Martin

While I enjoyed my high school years, there was not a lot of activity in terms of dating. I think my personality is strong enough, and my inability to even pretend I am something I'm not was too much for most high school boys to get past. I was quite interested in boys from an early age but lacked much of a sense of where to go with that.

As a result, my romantic life in high school consisted of a series of dead-end crushes. I was a bit of a stalker in that I could figure out where in my day I was likely to encounter the current interest and be sure to be there, but girly games were just not my thing.

I remember having a crush on a boy named Jeff in the seventh grade. At the time, I was friends with an older girl, all of thirteen, who advised me that the best way to catch his attention was to get somewhere where he was and say bad things about him and how much I hated him. I was utterly flummoxed by such advice, and I did not take it. Now that I have been around awhile, I understand the logic of her plan, but that is absolutely not who I am as a person in any relationship personal or professional. I am who I am, and what you see is what you get, like it or not. I do understand that for some people, this is off-putting, but Jack liked that about me, so it worked out.

Near the end of my junior year in high school, God was beginning a move of his Spirit in the youth group in my church. I didn't know this at the time. All I knew was that I was suddenly in contact with kids who had a different, and, at that time, puzzling way of relating to God. I had always believed in God and freely expressed this at times in my school life, so I apparently had some kind of reputation associated with that. But I wasn't like them.

I was peripherally aware of a senior named Martin. He had become involved with this same group of kids to the point that he had made a commitment to become a follower of Christ. At that point, his friends told him he needed to find a Christian girl to spend time with as opposed to the girls he had been hanging around with. I guess by reputation I became a candidate.

Out of the blue, one of this group, Anne, approached me and asked if I had a date for the prom. Now this was a big deal for me because I had never attended a formal dance during my high school years. (I was invited to homecoming once, and I accepted and then unaccepted the invitation. I am not proud of how I handled that.) So I told her I did not have a date and then waited to see what would happen.

That afternoon, Martin visited the restaurant where I worked, and we talked for a while, at the end of which, he asked, and I accepted. I was not particularly attracted to Martin. But I wasn't not attracted either. I didn't know anyone my age who drank coffee (duh, Finnish), so that was kind of interesting.

And that was the way Martin entered my life. The prom was a few weeks off, so we began to spend time together. I learned that Martin was smart, which was important to me. (He would say it was nice to talk to a girl who knew words of more than two syllables.) But he was kind of a slacker. He was the youngest child and only boy of his family, and his parents were in their sixties. Being there now myself, I can see they must have been tired. Success at school had always been important to me. It was not for him.

It would be hard to overestimate what a big deal it was to me to finally have a person in my life who was almost a boyfriend. (In truth, for the three years of our relationship, I doubt that Martin ever really considered himself my boyfriend or me his girlfriend. Despite his new faith, he was pretty determined to be nonconformist, and even in the midst of his time with God, he was already beginning to buy into the spirit of the age. The ponytail was a dead giveaway.) It made me feel that this type of relationship that I had been studying and hoping for since I was ten years old had finally come my way.

The being committed to each other that way was always bumpy for us, and he reacted to it by constantly approaching and withdrawing. This was confusing and very frustrating for me. He would call or drop in (I still remember the sound of his red Triumph gunning up the driveway). He would come to church or not (he used to say he was attending St. Mattress when he felt like skipping it). He would act like he liked me and then say the most crushing, rejecting kinds of things.

We dithered back and forth like this through the summer and into the fall. (One thing I got out of that time was that he taught me how to drive a stick shift. Martin was a full-on gearhead, knew a lot about cars, and had already owned several by the time I met him.) By then, he had graduated and begun working for Ohio Bell, the telephone company. Back then, you could get a job right out of high school that would allow you to begin your adult life. College was in no way the be-all and end-all it is today.

Sometime during the fall of my senior year, Martin and I were having yet another of our "sit out in the driveway for an hour" conversations, and as I listened to him talk, I realized that what he was really telling me was that he just wasn't all that into me. He was big on sharing details of time he spent with other girls, and I suddenly realized this was humiliating, and I didn't want to do it anymore. I guess he didn't either. I don't know if I told him to stay away from me or if he just chose to, but for the next three or four months, I did not see or hear from him, and I was okay with it.

In the meantime, things with the church youth group were really heating up, and some really not-Lutheran things were happening. Because of events relayed elsewhere (see chapter *On Faith*), I was now heavily involved in the youth group, and it was the focus of my social life. During the late winter, Martin apparently stepped away from hanging around the women of Lake Erie College and came back to church and, to some degree, to me.

I know there were things about me he appreciated. Obviously, the conversation. Some, at the time, shared values. I think he respected my singing ability. There must have been something because he kept coming back and going and coming back...

Martin's relationship with his spirituality was so schizophrenic. I was with him through that time of his life, and I know, I *know,* that what he experienced was genuine and deeply real to him. Yet during the time he tiptoed along with me and God, he was also drinking Chivas Regal with extremely worldly college women and smoking dope with homosexual professors. Inexplicable.

We continued to spend time together, and he participated in the goings on at the youth group until the middle of the summer after I graduated. I was working full-time and preparing to go to college at Concordia in Ann Arbor, Michigan, in the fall. And then out of the blue, he told me that he and his good friend Bruce Call were going on a camping road trip with two or three girls from the college. To Colorado. For weeks. Say what?

So the end of my summer was spent dating someone else whom I used most unkindly and whom I dropped the minute Martin unexpectedly returned just before my departure for school. I am *so glad* I had the chance to apologize to Gary many years later. He was a sweet and nice guy who did not deserve that…at all.

When I went to college, I was suddenly three hours away. My attention and interests were moving away from Martin and home. And this was when I learned that the old saying, "Absence makes the heart grow fonder," is actually true. Because all of a sudden, Martin was fonder. Still messing around with other girls but also really missing me. He came to visit or to drive me home quite often. He called *a lot*. I spent so, so many hours in the middle of the night perched on the desk by the pay phone in the lobby of my dorm because that was the only phone in the building.

It was weird to experience his insecurity for a change. And even more weirdly, he encouraged me to date other guys, but yet it bothered him when I did. And I did. I discovered that suddenly, we were all mature enough and self-confident enough that dating became easy for me. It was so nice to realize I could actually be attractive to guys who were attractive to me. I enjoyed it but was never really tempted away from Martin except once. There was one guy for whom I might have left Martin, but things just didn't go that way…which was good because—Jack.

In college, I got to do some of my favorite singing with the first string choir. I got to sing "Jesu, Joy of Man's Desiring" with a pipe organ, cello, and viola in a church with awesome acoustics. I grew up singing sacred choral music, and that is where a big part of my musical heart lies, which caused Jack to occasionally accuse me of being a musical snob. Pardon me if I think people should sing in tune (I'm looking at you, Bob Dylan), preferably with harmony.

Our choir sang pieces in Latin, in German, and in old English. We spent spring break touring Midwest Lutheran churches and colleges, and we brought a harpsichord and kettledrums along for the ride. During that time, I formed the conviction that the gift of singing God gave me was to be used for him, so I never tried to do anything else with it despite how much I enjoyed some of the folky-flavored pop music of the time. I also played Lucy in our college production of *You're a Good Man, Charlie Brown*, clearly a case of astute typecasting. Martin came up with my folks for one of the performances.

And now we come to the part of the story I regret the most. When I went home for Christmas, the time that Martin and I spent together was simply wonderful. He really loved me, and I really loved him. But I always wanted the full commitment, and he always withheld it. So because I wanted him to commit to me so much, my twisted thinking hatched a plot to get what I wanted by giving him what he wanted.

Now you have to understand that at that time in my life, my grasp of what motivates men was less than zero. I thought their thought life was just like mine. I had absolutely no understanding whatsoever about men and sex. I mean, I got that guys generally wanted to get their hands under your shirt. But I did not by any means extrapolate this as far as it needed to go. So I told Martin we could be together in that way, but that he needed to understand that in that act, I would consider us to be married.

How naive yet diabolically twisted is that? That way, he gets what he wants, I get what I want, and we're not really sinning egregiously at all. And not surprisingly, he totally agreed. He even said he wanted to marry me, you know, just not right now. Oh, how often I have wished to get that decision back.

And thus began the part of the journey that ultimately led to despair. Because, of course, we were not married. Though I think he loved me to the degree a nineteen-year-old boy too smart for his own good was capable of love, he was no more committed to me then than he had been before. And my only bargaining chip, along with my self-respect and my purity, was gone. For the next year, we went back and forth and back and forth, agreeing not to continue and then continuing over and over. The guilt was killing me.

I loved college, but I couldn't afford it. I had worked hard for two years to save money for college, and after one year of school, it was gone. And I owed $495 into the bargain. That was a lot of money back then. When I got home that summer, I immediately began looking for work but couldn't find anything because no one wanted to hire a temporary employee. There was no such thing as internships in those days. I eventually got a job working for the city directory, but it was way too little, way too late. And then Martin said to me, "Don't go back. I want you home." Deal sealed.

So I got a job at a bank and paid off my loan and, by December, was in an apartment on Watson Street in Painesville. Martin's parents loaned my roommate and me some furniture, and Martin let me use one of his cars until he helped me buy a car of my own. (As an aside, it never really occurred to me until just now how odd it was that I got an apartment as soon as I was able, literally $6 in the bank, and Martin continued to live at home even though he had been making adult wages for eighteen months.) And the toxic cycle continued.

I remember staying really late at his house one night and trying to get to some kind of sweet spot regarding the sin we were in and a fix for it. You know, besides the obvious one. Eventually I got into my car and started for home. I remember the late night quiet of Hine Avenue. Looking around, I said to myself, "This is never going to work." I was right. It *was* never going to work. That was one of very few points in my life that I could say I was in utterly hopeless despair.

The sad reality was that we were two people in two completely different and wholly incompatible places in life. I was ready to be married, and Martin emphatically was not. It was late winter, and in March, I made an attempt to break up with him. But though he did not want a girlfriend, much less to be married, he also did not want me to break up with him. How many, many guys have performed that BS maneuver? You know, "I want you, but I don't want you, but I want you." On more than one occasion, I received calls at 2:00 a.m. where he would say something like, "How can you be a Christian and just walk away like that?"

Seriously. So I took him back. Yikes. And almost immediately, I was back to square one. I was also pretty sure he was seeing someone from the college, as well as me. Without saying anything to him, I started looking around for other opportunities.

When Jack came into my life, he was such a refreshment to me. Honest, mature, no games. That was when I began to see the difference between being with a boy and being with a man. The first time Jack called me honey, I almost dropped my teeth. All this and endearments too?

So I took my heart back from Martin, and I gave it to Jack. One day, not long before the wedding, I started to feel kind of badly about having dropped Martin pretty precipitously. I picked up the phone at work and called him. He seemed *completely* fine. In fact, afterward, I kind of felt like he might as well have said, "Linda who?" After the torture I had suffered trying to make an unworkable dynamic work. After throwing my integrity into the trash for him, he let me break up with him and was apparently unaffected. In that moment, my hatred for Martin was born. And I hated him freely and without guilt for the next seven years.

By that time, Jack and I had become Catholic, and I was reading a book by a priest on the subject of hate. Naturally, he frowned on it. I sat back and asked myself simply if there was anyone in my life I hated, and I thought of Martin. Because I still bitterly hated him.

So I purposed in my heart to forgive him and stop hating him. And I kind of did forgive him for letting me go without a backward glance. But through the next ten years, I still blamed him for dragging me without remorse into and never out of a sin that had scorched me so badly. Fortunately, God was not done with me yet.

One winter afternoon, I decided to take a walk in the woods by our house. It was one of those super quiet snows with giant flakes. I could literally hear the flakes hitting the top of my hood. And somehow God opened my eyes that day to *finally* be able to see my own deep and real sin. That I was the one who said yes. I was the one that did not make it stop as I should have. Furthermore, I was really the one, by saying yes, that dragged Martin into sin. What were the possible consequences of the sin in his life that began because of me?

I was able to really forgive him then and apologize, at least in my heart, for what I had done to him. And here's the funny thing. Though we both continued to live in the area but had never crossed paths, not long after my epiphany, I ran into Martin at the library in Painesville. It was the only real conversation we ever had after parting ways. I had the opportunity to ask his forgiveness for my part in what happened, and he was gracious in response. I think the whole issue was no big deal for him. By that time in his life, the word he used to describe himself was pagan. I absolutely believe that this moment in time was a gift from God to me, and I am so glad I did not waste it.

Because some years later, without my ever speaking to him again, Martin was killed in a motorcycle crash. Bruce Call called me at work, not as a friend, but because he wanted a ride to the calling hours. I went back and forth in my mind over whether to visit the funeral home. Ultimately, I decided not to. I did not want to be a distraction to his wife or his children. I still don't know if that was the right thing to do, but I hope there is some grace in having tried to be sensitive.

Imagine if I had not had that moment to confess and to give and receive forgiveness. It is such a relief to me. Though I did not escape the consequences, I no longer carry the burden of hatred or guilt for his and my messed up behavior. But I feel really sorry that he let his faith lapse. It's too bad for God and really too bad for Martin.

On Jack

Jack was born on June 23, 1947, at Corey Hospital in Chardon, Ohio. He was the firstborn of his father's second marriage. He never met the two half-brothers born of his father and the first wife though I learned that he exchanged a few emails with one of them after his father died. He grew up in Willoughby, Ohio, where his parents and grandmother shared in running the Willoughby Motel. His family lived in an apartment on the front part of the motel. His dad also had gas stations and a car wash over the years. When I came into his life, they had just sold their businesses and retired to Florida.

His father grew up in Cleveland, the eldest of two brothers born to Carl Burhenne and Mabel Crellin. Mabel, whom I always knew as Mike, was a Manx woman who emigrated from the Isle of Man in 1904. She lived with my in-laws for most of Jack's childhood and was a super important fixture in his life. You know how they say men marry women like their mothers? I think Jack married a woman like his grandmother. She was strong-willed and hardheaded and stubborn. Like me.

He liked to tell the story of how she decided to drive him and his brothers to see Washington, DC, but apparently did not use maps. When the boys told her she was going west and should be going east, she kept telling them that that is just how these new highways are, they take you all around before they take you where you want to be. When they reached the Indiana border, she asked the man at the tollbooth if they were getting toward Washington, and he burst out laughing and told her she was going the wrong way. That's when she finally turned around. Jack always felt she taught him to be truthful and generous, to work hard and have faith in God. He saw her as a stronger influence on him than his parents. He loved her stories of the Isle of Man and the little people. He absolutely identified much more with his Celtic side than the German or Slavic parts.

Jack's dad was an alcoholic, a serious, thrashing on the floor with DTs alcoholic. Jack lived with and saw this play out until he was about twelve. He saw the final ultimatum when his mother stalked to the door and threw her wedding ring out into the yard. Either Don was going to quit drinking, or she was leaving. Can you imagine what that must have been like for Jack and his brothers?

Jack told me his mother had made a deal with God that if Don quit drinking, she would see to it that the boys became Catholic. His dad joined AA and straightened out. Jack and his brothers became Catholic. As a kid, he loved the church, especially the sense of history and continuity from being part of such an old tradition. He loved the majesty of it. I don't think at that time he really thought of faith in terms of a relationship with the person of Jesus. That came much later.

His mother was born in Denver, Colorado, to Joseph Plute and Christine Frank. She had a sister from these parents, and then they were divorced. She was shifted around from pillar to post with aunts and uncles etc. because her mother remarried and started a new family that did not include Florence and because her father was generally a terrible person. She had a pretty rough upbringing that included an elopement at sixteen that was quickly annulled. She was taken on by some nuns, and she really appreciated that. Don, in the air force, was posted to Denver during the war where their relationship began. He was ten years older than her.

Don's marriage was on the rocks by the time he met Florence, but the divorce was not finalized until April 1948. Well after his discharge and return to Willoughby and Florence's following him to Ohio and well after Jack's birth.

Jack's mother was ninety-three when she died. She did not go into assisted living until shortly before that. By then the family was seeking the records needed for her to apply for veterans' benefits to help pay for her care. That was when we learned that Jack was born out of wedlock. He was taken aback and kind of angry that he learned this about himself at age seventy-two. It led to a long conversation with his mother where she revealed a lot more about her life before she met Don, which helped him have more sympathy for her situation. Still, that generation sure did know how to cover things up. I'm so glad they had that conversation because days later, she fell and broke her hip. Her heart stopped during the surgery to repair it.

Jack often expressed that he felt his parents kind of left him and his brothers to raise themselves. That they left the culture or the church to supply his moral upbringing. I think sometimes that's why he was so bent on shaping our children. There is absolutely no doubt whatsoever that Jack's fatherhood was of paramount importance to him. He really, really cared. That may be why so often he sat them all down for a good lecture that could leave them in tears. I hope that someday they can approach God in their own ways and learn to know him as the friend he has always been to me.

Jack was an engineer-hearted typical firstborn. You can see it in his stance in the many pictures of him growing up. Kind of stiff with hands clasped in front and top button buttoned. He was the most deeply analytical person I have ever known. As a child, he was responsible; his report cards show it. His first-grade teacher actually commented that he might be a tad too mature. I wonder if the situation with his dad's drinking contributed to Jack's maturity. Or if it was the grounding for his lifelong burden of outsized worry.

His mom kept a lot of records for him, report cards, event programs, newspaper clippings. His parents were clearly proud of him, as they should have been. He excelled in school and, I think, socially. When we met, he was still friends with guys he grew up with, and I got messages from more than one school friend when he died. One thing his mom kept that I particularly treasure is an autobiography he wrote in the eighth grade. So ordered, so meticulous, so revealing. It shows he was a bit of a wise guy even then, something all of us really enjoyed in him. I did not know he had been bullied in the second grade. It explains why his grades were less stellar that year.

You know how puberty can take a pretty cute little kid and turn them into something just okay? (I put myself into this category.) For Jack, the change was the opposite. He was a cute little boy, but puberty changed him into something really special. When I look at late-teen pictures of him with his family, I wonder where he came from. The perfect symmetry of his features, the deep chest, and strong shoulders. I still think he was one of the best-looking men I have ever seen.

Jack, on the other hand, never thought he was a big deal. Though he worked hard to excel, he was not ambitious to lead or supervise. When Eaton made him a supervisor, he did not like it and took the opportunity to get out of that role when it came. He was fairly diffident in high school though I know he was proud of being valedictorian, which status is not reflected in the records his mom kept because his GPA exceeded the so-called valedictorian's only in the last grading period after everything for year-end had already been printed. So he was advertised as the salutatorian, but his class rank was number one.

I believe what pride he took in his academic success was based on how hard he worked because the grades came as a result of hard, hard work. He wasn't a gadfly like me, learn for the test and quickly forget. Throughout our years together, he would often come out with snippets of poetry he had memorized in elementary school so long ago. How did he remember? The poems were always apropos and beautiful. I *loved* that about him. After his death, I found a large folder of poetry on his computer. I think he could still have done calculus on his deathbed. Once learned, things stayed with him. In later life, he expressed the wish that he would have worked less on school and more on following his interests. What we wish we knew then but didn't…

As he was diffident about his abilities, he was also diffident with girls. He never saw himself as especially attractive or desirable and was remarkably tone-deaf regarding women who eyed him. And yet he managed at one point in high school to have a serious girlfriend. More about that elsewhere (see chapter *On Elayne*).

During high school, Jack began to pursue an appointment to the Air Force Academy. His dad had been a flight instructor during the war and used to take the boys on joyrides from a nearby airfield. His mom kept copies of the many letters he wrote and the replies. Eventually, he was named an alternate. He told me that one day, he was called out of class by the principal to be told he could have the appointment, but he had to decide right then and there. He was a seventeen-year-old boy, and they didn't even invite his parents into the discussion.

By then, he had made plans to attend Oberlin College and, in the moment, decided to stay with that plan. So, so many things that came later hinged on that one single instant of his life. He shared with me that he thought his folks should have been called, but he also said he did not regret the decision. Even so, I think he kind of did. Though if it had gone the other way, we would probably never have met.

In high school, Jack was the same sort of anomaly that some of our kids were, the smart kid who was also athletic. He participated in several sports, but I think his real love was baseball. He played baseball every summer as a kid. He also got to play at Oberlin, and I think that meant a lot to him.

I think he started to do more physically as a result of having pudged up a little in adolescence. That formed in him the habit of working out that he continued for many, many years. If I had a dollar for every time I tripped over his weights lying around our living room through the years, well, I'd have a *lot* of dollars. He did one hundred sit-ups every day on the piece of thick insulation he'd snagged during the refit of the sub. (That exercise mat is now in the home of his firstborn son.) Only his illness brought it to a close.

Jack attended Oberlin for one year. That year was a kind of eye-opener for him. He was used to being a big fish in the little academic pond of Willoughby South High School. At Oberlin, he met students who made him feel really out of his league. It was at Oberlin that he met Mary, the daughter of a Buffalo, New York, gynecologist. I don't know exactly when that relationship became serious, but my impression is it was pretty quick. He also accelerated his dive into full-on atheism and rebellion while he was there. In later years, he never had anything nice to say about Oberlin and its influence in his life.

After that first year, due to circumstances explained elsewhere, Jack dropped out of Oberlin and enlisted in the US Navy's nuclear power program. It was a six-year commitment that he told me he made because there would be a lot of schools, and that interested him. I think school was a place he felt confident.

Jack found the experience of the navy to be a real mixed bag. He enjoyed the camaraderie but found the petty regulations grating. In the end, his fondness overcame his irritation, and he made sure I knew that having his military plaque was important to him. It is affixed to the back of our gravestone today.

I have learned in reading things he wrote to other people over the years that at this time in his life, he was much more pagan than I ever realized. I knew there was drinking, but I didn't know it started in high school and was what he described as "heavy." I knew he supported typical liberal causes with his heart and his money. But I did not really grasp the depth of his rebellion and antipathy toward God during that time. It was ultimately his divorce that drove him to his knees.

He went into the navy in February of 1967, and he and Mary got married that fall. Wherever they were, she tried to get a job, and they either lived in some truly terrible military housing or got apartments while he went from school to school on the way to becoming a nuclear trained electrician and reactor operator. I think he went to school for a couple of years before he got on a boat. During this time, Jack and Mary gathered around them a group of close friends who would hang out at their house.

Somewhere in there, Jack got his first motorcycle. At one point, he crashed it, and one of his injuries was a split lip. He had a little bump there ever after. He always had a love for motorcycles and owned several over the years. To the very end, he would look after them when they passed with a kind of longing.

The kind of submarine Jack was assigned to was a boomer, a missile sub. Its job was to roam around and be ready to defend the country by firing missiles. Those boats would go out on two-month long deployments where they would be out of communication for long periods. Even when they could send and receive messages, the message had to be very, very short. You know, "it's a boy," pretty much. Then they would be home for a while.

During deployments like this, it was hard to build the foundation for a marriage because the person left behind was living like a single person during that time. In addition, Mary's value system was what I would term liberal. There was no fear of the Lord, and Jack always said she was strongly aligned with what then was called women's liberation, something that bore bitter fruit when we were raising our family. Those were the days when such women would say, "A woman needs a man like a fish needs a bicycle."

In fairness, Jack was not a Christian then either. His Catholicism was left in the dust. Yet he was already developing the generosity that characterized his giving later, as well as the burden of wanting the world to be right. He and Mary donated to various causes, one being Zero Population Growth, ironically for the man who ultimately fathered seven children.

After a couple rotations, Jack's boat needed to come in to be refitted. During the extended period of time when this took place, Jack had to work long and difficult hours. He told me that it made him hard to live with, that he took a deep dive into himself that he called survival mode. Having been with Jack through fifteen years of rotating shifts when he was in survival mode, I am sure it *was* hard. Nevertheless, around that time, Jack and Mary decided they were going to start a family. I am so relieved that never happened.

It was only a short while later that Mary sat Jack down and told him, completely out of the blue for him, that she wanted a divorce. She had fallen in love with one of the men on Jack's crew, a part of the close-knit group that used Jack's home as a gathering place. The announcement sent him reeling.

He asked her to go away with him for a few days to see if the marriage could be saved. She went, but her heart was not in it. Her heart had already moved on. Once he knew she would not change her mind, he asked her what she would have done had she become pregnant. Her reply, which I have the impression was a bit offhand, was that her dad would have arranged an abortion. Even in his pagan state, he was shocked and asked her if she would have even told him to which she replied she would not. I think that might have been the lowest moment of the divorce experience for him.

The other man was a member of Jack's crew, and the captain of the boat asked Jack which crew he wanted Bob to be assigned to. The captain thought Jack would want him on the same crew so he would not be wondering all the time what was going on at home if Bob went to the alternate crew. Jack told him no, put him on the other crew, or he might go after him with a hammer.

Ultimately, Jack cooperated with the divorce process and became a single man once more. Mary married and then divorced the other guy. As far as I know, that was her last attempt at marriage.

Jack's last apartment during his time in the navy was shared with a crewmate. He and Jim Peterson were workout buddies both on and off the boat. They both had 450cc Honda motorcycles, so I'm sure they must have done some riding together. He even briefly dated Jim's sister.

Jack was kind enough to say more than once over the years that he wished we could have been together during his time in the navy. He knew how much I would have enjoyed the adventure. I think he also knew that I might have been a steadying influence for him. He even took me to Charleston once because he wanted to share his love for a city the navy had brought him to. In any case, he was six years older than me so…

During a leave around that time, Jack came home for a visit. His brother Bob had recently given his life to God during a time in America that was called the Jesus Movement. Bob and his friends talked long and hard to Jack about their faith, and as a result, Jack began his turn toward faith in God.

When I met him, he would say he loved God but hated the Bible. This was inexplicable to me because without the Bible, you can't know God. He said he had read it, and it was too contradictory for him. And he's right. Without the Holy Spirit to illuminate your reading, it seems like a hot mess. After a lot of reading and thought, I have concluded that Jack was not yet born-again when we met though at the time; I thought he was. It was actually several years into our marriage before that happened. It was then that he came to love the Bible as the key to a life of faith. His love for scripture became a passion, and he wielded the Word of God like a broadsword.

One night, when he was trying to sleep on the couch in our living room on South Street, Jack had an experience with God. I don't know if it was a dream or a vision, but his experience was that he was like a little child that God was throwing into the air and catching. He felt the way you imagine a trusting little child feels when their daddy throws them up, and they know he will catch them. He knew that his Father was delighting in him in the same way he delighted in his children when he threw them up and caught them. I think that was Jack's born-again moment. He certainly always regarded this experience as a turning point in his relationship with God.

Jack spent his career at the Eaton Telecomputer Center in Eastlake. His work evolved through many iterations over thirty years. He was ultimately a lead network analyst. He configured routers and pulled cable under computer room floors and did a lot of internal customer service assisting Eaton facilities all over the world. When the corporate environment became so much less friendly to work-life balance, with my encouragement, he took early retirement. It cost us financially, but it gave him sixteen years of getting to follow his passion for discourse. It probably saved his mental health.

One of Jack's legacies is the record he kept of an amazingly broad correspondence. He wrote to a man in prison faithfully for almost thirty years and, having saved what he wrote in a file, has thereby enabled me to see a record of the everyday happenings of our household through the years, the kinds of things that dissolve in the haze if not recorded. When I read this record, what comes through in a way that I assure you was not clear to me at the time was how much his job was drudgery to him, the "load" he would occasionally accuse me of adding to. It was one of the big sources of the depression that hauled him down into the abyss regularly.

He never in all his life actively acknowledged his depression, and, to be honest, neither did I. He had formed a strong distrust for psychology and psychiatry, so he would never have considered getting that type of help, much less medication. He would not even talk to a pastor, a friend, or his wife about it. Hence, my ignorance about *why* he was so hard to be with sometimes. The one tiny glimpse I had of what might have been came late in life when I brought him home after a hernia surgery while he was still under the influence of whatever he had got drugwise. He was so upbeat and enthusiastic about doing projects etc., so unJacklike. By the next day, "bouncy" Jack was gone.

Jack always said moving to Leroy felt like coming home to him. In our house on Callow Road, we had lived in sight of the Teare Farm for twenty years before we learned those Teares were descended from the same Teares that are his Manx ancestors. Leroy had received a large influx of settlers from the Isle of Man in the 1820s. Today, I live in one of the old Crellin farmhouses. Jack's grandma's maiden name was Mabel Crellin.

One of his quirks was how hard it was to give him gifts. Gifting is an expression of love for me but not for Jack. He was not that interested in receiving gifts, did not place a lot of value on material things, did not wear clothes I gave him, often seemed at sea in coming up with gifts for me. (He expressed love through affirming words. He also was generous with hugs, backrubs, and hand-holding.) When he was older, one of the girls gave him a card that was a cartoon of a Buddhist monk holding an empty box and saying, "Just what I always wanted, nothing!" I will say he hit a home run on our twenty-fifth anniversary when he bought us matching silver rings with Hebrew lettering that said, "I am my Beloved's, and my Beloved is mine." He wore his until the end of his life when the letters were nearly worn off.

One thing I really appreciated about Jack was how easy he was to sleep with. By that, I mean he was a very quiet sleeper. He would roll himself up into his favorite thick quilt and fall asleep. It took about ten seconds. Really, I watched him fall asleep with deep envy many a time. He seldom snored, and if he did, a quick poke would roll him over, and he was quiet again. Conversely, I am a restless and active sleeper. To be fair, once one is a mother, sleep is light at best. Now that I am retired, it is less of a problem because sleep lost at night can be made up during the day. I do miss having someone to wake with out of bad dreams or to snuggle with when it's cold, which it often is. We always said, "We like a cold bedroom," which is fine when there are two of you. Not so much alone.

Where food is concerned, Jack had a propensity for salt on his food. In fact, I never saw him approach a meal without the saltshaker in his hand. The man salted hot dogs! He used to be pretty so-so about my cooking because he felt it was underseasoned. No, he just really liked to taste salt. It took me years to figure out that I am actually a pretty good cook. But then I season it to my taste.

In all our life together, he was never big on eating fruit until his final months. For a while, he wanted to drink citrus juice. Then he wanted to eat grapefruit. He would get up every morning and fix himself a grapefruit. "It's so refreshing," he would say. One morning, near the end of his ability to do this for himself, I had had very poor sleep, and as he was cutting the grapefruit, I dozed off on the couch. The crashing of the garbage cans during pickup startled me awake, and I thought he had fallen. I jumped up and ran to check on him in the kitchen. "Take it easy, old girl," he said, and I started to cry.

When he was younger, Jack was attracted to several kinds of artistic expression. I still have a sketchbook with drawings he did. There were a couple of really good pen and ink drawings I framed. He never drew after we met. When he retired, we gave him paper and pen and ink, but he never touched them. After his death, I gave them to his grandson, Noah. He had purchased good camera equipment and liked to use it. He and I also always shared a strong love for language. He could really pull out a pithy phrase. He used to say my mom "played a strong hand weak." Of our son Mike, he would say he lived his life like "a tornado in a phone booth." We both dabbled with playing guitar. Over the years, he would pick it up fairly regularly and go through his repertoire.

Jack's love of music also expressed itself in the many, many mixed CDs he made where he married songs he liked together for different purposes. Worship mixes, Christmas medleys, music for my mom, and for friends who were grieving, and of course, at the end, music to say thank you, music to say goodbye. His taste was eclectic, and his recollection of pieces was impressive. He also liked to just sit and listen.

I never did that. I liked to have music to cook by, music to clean by, music to hang Christmas ornaments by. My busy brain always wanted to do, as well as hear. And sing. I always sang with whatever was on. Always added my own harmonies. And now that I am alone, I realize that always singing meant not really hearing. Now I do sit and listen and hear words I have missed and harmonies of other singers. This has deepened my appreciation for Jack's heart as he mixed so many songs into so many groups. It's like getting to visit with him and touch the tender heart he often kept so deeply hidden. It is gift.

As I have read Jack's many writings and remembered our interactions with various people, I have concluded that Jack was not very good at reading certain things in other people. He always thought other people were just like him, integritywise, no matter how often I assured him that was emphatically not the case. In particular, he was remarkably blind to women coming on to him. He had a note in his yearbook where a young lady invited him to "come out and play", which he in no way read as the proffer it was. When Julie, our thirteen-year-old foster child, developed a crush on him, he was completely clueless, did not accept it when I told him, and only believed it when the counselor backed me up. And in all his interactions with Elayne over the years, he never could see that she still carried a torch for him. He did not initiate these contacts, but he responded as he did to other contacts he got from high school friends, openly and interestedly. Even now I have to wonder, was he really as clueless as he seems? What was really in his heart when he got these missives from her? I wonder how he'd have felt had I been corresponding with Martin...

In younger days, we socialized mostly with friends from church. We spent time with a number of people over the years, even taking weekend trips with a few couples. But over time, especially as his illness progressed, Jack became less and less social. Date nights and road trips fell by the wayside long before his death. In his last few years, I think Facebook provided all the social interaction he needed or wanted. His condition lent itself to just staying home, and he was happy to do it. Then to top it off, we went through his final months in the midst of a pandemic. And now that he's gone but the pandemic remains, I have to try to build some kind of social network with both hands tied behind my back. Sigh...

One of the hallmarks of Jack's walk with God was giving. Both I and my children learned by his example. We supported people and missions all over the world, some of them our friends. I don't know what my kids do as adults, but their father set an unfailing example of financial generosity throughout his life both to churched and unchurched people.

In early 2015, Jack began feeling poorly. One day, after shoveling snow, he came in and threw up. He said it was from the snow shoveling. What? Over some weeks, he just did not get better but stubbornly refused to go to the doctor. Really, both I and our daughter the nurse bugged him pretty steadily to get checked out. My conscience is clear in that respect. When he finally went, the upshot of a long day was that his enlarged prostate had so blocked the flow of urine that he was in full-on kidney failure. He ended up spending four days in the hospital.

This was the beginning of five years of progressively unpleasant and invasive interactions with the medical community. He had surgeries and repeated and sometimes awful UTIs. After a year and a half, it became evident that his bladder was no longer functional, and he had to begin self-catheterization. Men, do not ignore your prostate until you are irreparably damaged because it can kill you.

In January of 2019, I thought the Lord spoke to my heart, saying, "Last Christmas was your last Christmas." So I spent all of 2019 quietly wondering just what that meant because I was pretty sure if someone were going to go, it would be me. When Jack started to decline in the fall to the point that he did not go to Thanksgiving or Christmas family gatherings and winter deepened with the realization that he was not going to seek further treatment, I knew that that Christmas had been, in fact, *our* last Christmas.

As his kidneys slowly failed, Jack had to decide what, if anything, he wanted to do. He could try for a transplant or begin dialysis, or he could do nothing. Had my blood type been right, without a doubt, I'd have given him a kidney, and I'm pretty sure he would have accepted it. One of our kids who was a match made the offer, but neither Jack nor I felt good about accepting it. Though I have suffered a lot of guilt over it, I was determined not to try to influence his decision one way or the other because he hated his "medicalized" life. I told him firmly that he could do whatever he truly wanted to do, and whatever he chose, I would help him. Eventually he chose to let his life come to a close.

He wanted to let each of the kids have a conversation with him. He wanted to be sure to share whatever memories he had that interested them, much as he tried so hard to do with his own father. In particular, he wanted to let them "have their say." As I began to arrange these talks, he kind of protested. He actually thought he might be like the old Indian in *Little Big Man*; maybe he wasn't really going to die. But I knew what would come and wanted his mind to still be clear for these conversations. We had them all. Each lasted around five hours. They were arduous.

As I work through his prodigious writings and the poems and quotes and bits of prose he saved and look at the pictures he took and listen to the many music mixes he left behind, sometimes I feel I know him better now than I did through all the years we were together. In a way, it makes me sadder to have been so dense, but I know if he had not gone home, nothing would have changed in my perceptions of him as the person I lived with. One thing that helps is that I feel God has spoken to my heart that Jack was not going to get better or happier or less angry with the moral decline of the world. That the unexplained slow decline of his kidney function was God's mercy to him, to let him shake off everything here that grated on him so badly. That it was his time.

During those few months, we talked together a lot about our life and how grateful we were for how God had always cared for us. We truly believed that we had had the very best of what life has to offer, from our relationship, to our family, to our work, and to our faith. He repeatedly expressed concern that I would be all right. I promised him I would. He looked at me out of the blue once with the saddest expression and said, "I just don't want to leave you." I feel we tried hard not to leave anything on the table with each other.

As he approached death and his mind became more and more fuzzy, I feel that he kind of returned to his Catholic heart. He wondered if he really was going to be with Jesus, whether he was good enough. I got to remind him that he is saved by grace through faith, which is a gift of God. I reminded him of his vision of God tossing him into the air and catching him.

The day before he died, we were up at six in the morning, and I asked if he would like to watch Mass on TV, and we did. Then I played a couple of his worship mix CDs. That afternoon at about two, he suddenly said he wanted to brush his teeth. He removed the lower denture and carefully and thoroughly scrubbed it as I had never seen him do before, and then he put it away in the case. Done. Sometime later that day, he took off his watch and just dropped it on the floor. Done. That night, when he was so restless and kept trying to drag himself up off the hospital bed, I knelt close and sang to him some of the old worship songs, there, just the two of us in the dark. My hope and prayer is that these final things helped him on the way.

In the morning, Becca came over and, by observing, told me he was actively dying. His breathing had been labored for about a week and continued to be that day. She helped me settle him more comfortably in the bed, and with advice from the hospice nurse we called, we finally were able to give him some medicine to calm him, the sort of comfort he had refused until then. As we did, I thanked him again for our good life together and reminded him he had been a good husband and father. He slept through those final hours. His breath began to gurgle in his throat because he was no longer swallowing. I thought we still had hours, perhaps even days. But he chose to leave us at midday during a few moments when Becca and I were out in the garage. We came back to find him gone. The weirdest thing in that moment was watching for his chest to rise, and it didn't. It didn't. As we broke out crying, I suddenly cried, "He's in heaven right now!"

I truly believe that my Jack was a remarkable and unusually special person. The combination of heart and mind, body and spirit, insight and intellect, art and humor was so far beyond the norm. It always broke my heart that till the very end, he could never see, much less accept, that about himself. I always felt *so lucky* to be with someone so exceptional. I do not anticipate encountering his like again in this life.

Every now and then, I like to imagine him up there in heaven, sitting around with his former workmates, Matt Logies and Jim Fisher, drinking coffee and shooting the breeze. I like to think what a relief it must be to him to not have to worry about the world or me or the kids anymore. I like to think that the mansion that Jesus prepared for him is the farm he always hoped for, and he can stand and feel the sun on his face and listen to the wind and just be.

On Marriage

I have often pondered the question of how much of who a person is, is who a person is and how much is who a person is with. I could never have become the person I am had I not been married to Jack. And he would not have been who he was had he not been with me. We spent forty-seven years shaping one another, iron sharpening iron.

I was barely twenty when we got married. I had been in a three-year relationship that had been slowly dying for some time (see the chapter *On Martin*). I had actually tried to end it three months before meeting Jack but succumbed to the late-night phone calls when a glimmer of hope showed through the darkness. You know, oh, if he still cares like this, maybe he really does love me and want to be with me. Sadly, over time (a long time…years), I realized it was more like, oh, if he still cares like this, it's because of the friendly benefits he will no longer enjoy…yeah.

When I met Jack, he was a year out from the finalization of his divorce. He always said it was the most civilized divorce a couple could possibly have, and yet it was the worst thing he ever endured. He was working nights at a food warehouse on the west side of Cleveland, and the sole focus of his social contact consisted of his brother and the old lady he rented a room from. He was newly reconciled with God. One day, he knelt down beside his bed and told him he was lonely and would appreciate it if God would send someone for him to spend time with. Enter me.

Jack's mother and I had worked together at the bank where their business had accounts. She had told the young tellers about him, but we never got to meet him before she left her job with the bank. Then one day, a handsome, longhaired, bearded fellow pulled up to my auto teller window, and I noted who he was. A few days later, I mentioned to my customer, his dad, that he had been to my window, and that "he's pretty cute." Long story short, he called me, and we planned a date for my day off when he was free. I'm pretty sure he had absolutely no idea whatsoever who I was or what I looked like.

He arrived on time on a big Honda motorcycle on a beautiful summer morning. From the upstairs front room window, I watched him take off his helmet and shake out that hair, and I thought, *He is cute.* When he walked into the living room of my apartment, he took in the couch-sized poster on the wall and said, "Oh, *Lord of the Rings.*" And I thought, *Oh, kindred spirit.*

The *Lord of the Rings* saga stirs something down inside some people, and Jack and I were both that kind of person. Before we ever met, we both were deeply moved by the place, the characters, the language, and the story. Many years later, when the movies came out, we played a game in our church small group with each person saying which character he or she most identified with. Jack's was Frodo. He was the guy who carried the unbearable burden. He was the one with the unfixable scars. And without a doubt, I was his Sam.

(As an aside, our first date was on June 14, Flag Day. For the entire remainder of our time together, Jack always considered June 14 as our anniversary and remembered it more faithfully than the actual day we married.)

We spent that whole day together, and by day's end, I was already half in love. He was so handsome and smart and funny and truly sincere. Good, good talk, all day long. Riding the motorcycle and hiking in parks and talking. We had so much in common, most especially our Christian faith. He was kind enough to say he really loved my candor. Not everyone likes that, but he did. If a soulmate is someone with whom you feel an immediate and deep affinity, I am confident we were that for one another.

He told me about his marriage and divorce that first day. He said it was his fault. Even then as he related the details, I asked myself how exactly he could think his wife cheating on him was *his* fault. To his credit, he never said a bad thing about her. But he let his bitterness over her values and beliefs taint his opinions about women generally and his daughters specifically till the end of his days.

The next time Martin came around, I spent the whole time telling him about Jack. I thought he understood what I was telling him. I thought he understood my heart was moving on. When he stood up and started to unbutton his shirt (yeah, he really did that), I knew this was a moment of decision for me. Though Jack had made no commitments to me, how could I be with Martin when I already knew I wanted to be with Jack? I told him I did not want him to stay. Then he got it. He buttoned his shirt back up and walked out. He never called me again.

Jack was registered to go to Kent State on the GI bill that fall. Once we decided we wanted to be together, it didn't make much sense for me to be in Painesville while he was in Kent, so we figured we'd just get married. The date we picked was September first, ten weeks after we met. It would let us have a bit of a honeymoon before school started. As it turned out, he did not go to Kent. Instead, we bought a van and drove all over the country throughout that fall (see *On Honeymoon Trip*), camping and looking for a town with a school to call home. Three months camping out of a van makes up in large measure for no courtship.

His parents had retired to Florida right around that time. I often wondered what they thought when we bought an engagement ring eighteen days after our first date. Neither his parents nor mine ever said a word to us about what we had decided to do. I guess they figured we were adults, and it was ours to do. But I do wonder about his folks especially. I know in later years, when the marriage was apparently working, Jack's dad liked to take credit for bringing us together by having relayed my teller window comment to his son.

One day, not long before we married, Jack sat me down and said to me very seriously, "If there's ever something you want me to do, just tell me." I think he was trying to avoid a repeat of what he thought were his failings the first time around. I also think he felt Mary had not communicated her unhappiness to him in time for him to try to fix things. I said, "Well, there is one thing. Could you take your wedding ring off your key ring?" I thought he could put it away in the tin with his navy dolphins. Instead, he immediately removed the ring, walked to the nearest door, and chucked it. Nice.

I had cause to remind him of what he'd asked me to do in this regard on occasion over the years. He could get so balled up down inside himself that he could be remarkably unkind and selfish. I don't think I ever abused his invitation. I'm also not sure he was always able to access the reasons he had extended it. Either way, I never forgot what he'd said that day and, through me, neither did he.

Once I got to know him better, I realized that his jump into marriage with me was completely out of character for him. He was an engineer at heart and a nuclear-trained electrician into the bargain. (Do *not* get me started on what the navy does to a man's ability to make decisions.) When I expressed to him this realization, his response was that he did it in faith. He always truly believed that I was the answer to his prayer and felt it was one of the foundations of our marriage.

Because there is a chapter on Jack, you know that he came to me deeply scarred by his divorce. You will feel appropriately sorry for me when I tell you it was only *after* he died, almost forty-seven years later, that I actually realized the true depth of his hurt, and that he never really recovered. So much of our relationship was colored by what had gone before.

Because, of course, I was going to fix the wicked thing Mary had done. I was going to show him, and I really did know it would take time, that I would be faithful to him, unlike her, and he would eventually be okay. My actual theory (okay, I *was* twenty) was that, when we passed the five-year mark that mirrored the end of the first marriage, he would see that I was still there. That I had not cheated on him with his best friend. That I was still loving him and serving our family. That I was *not her*.

It's funny because, for long stretches, I could feel that it worked. *He* probably even thought it worked. But every once in a while, something would happen that would stir it all up inside him again. Like the couple times we left churches we had thought we were committed to. It was like ending that commitment took him right back to having to end his commitment to Mary. And he would somehow find reason to say, "You're here now, but you could always leave," as he did several times over the course of our marriage. It was teeth-grittingly irritating.

Even in his very last days, he brought out the old complaint, "You're revolving in a separate universe. You and the nurse get off in the other room and decide things." Yes, really. By then, of course, I just let it roll off because, you know, very last days. Plus, in fairness, kidney failure eventually messes with your thinking and perceptions. I mean, this is the guy who told me one morning that there had been little spiders on his face the night before. He saw them.

One of the very best things about my husband was his faith-fulness. A few years in, I told him that because I knew looks were not my strong suit, I was not confident in that area, and that I had been watching him during our time together and noted that he never looked at women. You know, the way guys look. He looked startled, and then he said, "When I married you, I made a covenant with my eyes that I wouldn't do that." And he didn't do that. I promise you, not ever. You can forgive a lot from a man who contracts with his eyes to be faithful to his wife and then is for forty-seven years.

One of the convictions Jack made his own over the years was a phrase he adopted from a book he read by Jay Adams. He considered marriage to be what he called a "covenant of companionship." We both came to embrace the concept because it really encapsulated a core quality of our relationship. I was his companion, and he was mine. One of the things I knew I would miss the most was having someone who cared about you right there all the time. Someone to talk to, someone to laugh with, someone to hug. Near the end but before he could no longer safely stand, I was hugging him in the kitchen one day, and he was perfunctory. "Don't go cheap," I said. "These have to last me a long time." So he hugged me good and hard.

I am still processing the inner workings of Jack's and my rela-tionship. It was so complicated. On one hand, he would say how smart and competent I am, and yet he could really make a person feel, I don't know, so not good enough. Usually in the areas of spirituality and current affairs. I will admit, maybe even brag, that Jack was very insightful and a deep thinker. I am a much shallower person than he was, on purpose (see chapter *On Mental Health*). Nevertheless, I stayed up on current affairs, and we talked about the state of the world often and with sorrow. In later years, we would say, probably once a week, how glad we were that we're old because times seem to be going in such a bad direction. So he always went deeper than just about everyone. And it was easy to see the validity of what he said. Even when he said outrageous things, as he often did, you had to at least consider the nugget of truth that was usually there.

Jack was a misogynist, which did not do his daughters any good. (Thank you, Mary.) He took it way too far and would never back down. But at the same time, he was supportive of my walking in roles that were directly the opposite of his views, such as holding elective office as I did for twenty years. It was weird. Sometimes, when he would say something especially egregious, I would say, "Yeah, but *I'm* a woman."

And he would say, "You're not a woman, you're my wife."

And I would say, "Still a woman."

Sometimes I would pull up my shirt to prove it, which made him laugh. I think his point was that because I was a Christian woman under authority to my husband that that negated my evil femaleness. Again, outrageous yet with a nugget of truth that ought to be considered.

Once I told him that I think in every couple, there's one who feels lucky to be there. He *immediately* said, "That's me." I was totally taken aback because clearly that's *me.* I mean, I was so happy the day we got married, the photographer said, "I've had a lot of crying brides, but I've never had one hysterically laughing." You can begin to see, I hope, how schizophrenic his treatment of me could be. And how confusing for a purposely shallow person like myself.

Doing home projects together became increasingly challenging as the years went by. He *had* to be in charge. He had to make the decisions. Always. Fine, but you're a turtle, and I'm a hare. Sitting and waiting for you to decide what bolt to buy or how to wire the room is *boring.* Sometimes I would get up and go do something else while he thought through whatever he was thinking through. That irritated him beyond bearing. Being yelled at for it was ditto for me. Yet we did a lot of projects together. And we did good work even into our latter years. That said, now that he is gone, I don't mind getting to decide some things.

It is common knowledge that there are certain areas within a marriage that cause conflict. Money, sex, power, children. For us, the only thing we ever truly fought about was the upbringing of our children.

Regarding money, we were about equal in our frugality. You can't raise six kids on a modest single income without being pretty inventive and without having really low expectations about what stuff you have to have. Fortunately smoking and drinking were not vices for either of us, and that saved a lot of money. We were lucky to be on the same page financially throughout our life together, and it paid off in that we came to the end with ample resources to see us through.

He always regarded everything we had as ours. So did I. Except when I received an inheritance from a distant cousin. He did not appreciate that I wanted to consider it something of my own. He protested that he would never consider a thing like that as his rather than ours. "I would," was my reply. "If you got an inheritance, I would regard it as yours to do with what you want." In the end, the inheritance was spent on the kids and the house and a car down payment. I did get my trip to England out of it.

I've already said what I have to say about sex (see chapter *On Sex*).

By power, I mean who gets to be the boss. I am a boss kind of person. That was why I was able to do well as an elected official. It was why I rose pretty high in the pecking order in Geauga County. I understand authority, both having authority and being under authority. At home, Jack was the boss. And in the main, he and I were in agreement about what the Bible says regarding the chain of command within the home and how to carry that out in practical ways within our marriage. He actually only went too far when something had roused the sleeping bear of his Mary experience. Then his need for control was very hard to live with.

Where we did struggle was in raising our kids together. I always felt his expectations about what they should be doing, saying, thinking regarding faith in God were unreasonable, perhaps unattainable. I used to say, "You can't even make yourself what you think you should be. What makes you think you can make them?" Sometimes I felt his standards were higher than God's. Hence, the conflict. That conflict never subsided, not even at the end.

When Jack retired at fifty-seven and I took up the mantle of breadwinner, it was with the understanding that we were trading roles. I would work, and he would keep house. At the time, I worked full-time for a bank and part-time as a township trustee. So when I noticed that the house was dirty and the meals were not great, I waited awhile, and then we had a chat. I explained that he was not meeting expectations, which would be reflected in his quarterly review (just kidding, I didn't really do reviews, though I could have). He literally asked what he needed to do so I wouldn't be mad. I told him, and he mostly did it.

You know how in marriage, you begin to delegate certain tasks to each other? Whether by interest or competency, things fall one way or the other. For instance, Jack mowed the lawn and took care of the cars. (In forty-six-plus years of marriage, I never had a flat tire.) I paid the bills, made and tended the gardens, took care of the house and the kids, including homeschooling. He did the technology, the computers, and TVs. I did the decorating, painting, and hanging wallpaper. (The first time I hung wallpaper, he watched in amazement and shook his head saying, "I could never do that.") And he did the investments.

As his health began its final decline and he moved inexorably to the decisions that led to his death, he worried about me. A lot. He said over and over, "I just want you to be all right." And I would say, "I will be. I'll be all right." And people who know me would shake their heads, wondering how he could even imagine me, me! Not being all right. What he actually meant was he worried that I would struggle with the things I had always delegated to him. He was right to be concerned because these are not areas that I have managed before. And it *is* hard. He could not have predicted the house would be struck by lightning two months after his death. Or that I would suddenly become allergic, like really allergic to beestings. Or that letting the toilet run for two hours would cause our water to become cloudy. All these are things I have had to rectify alone obviously.

I have lately begun to suspect he may have understood better than me that I would grieve his loss as painfully as I have. I honestly did not see it coming, but I think maybe he did. Self-awareness has never been a strong suit of mine. I am working through it, but it has been way harder than I imagined. It doesn't help that I never expected to outlive him.

As far as technology goes, within three days of his death, my TV became confused and stopped behaving, the battery in my laptop finally died, and my cellphone started screaming at people. I think it is fair to suggest he threw me some curveballs on his way out the door. My solution was to replace them all. If I have to learn how to do this stuff, I would like to only have to learn once. Of course, I know I probably have enough time left in this world that I will have to learn again, but getting new now makes me hope it will be a while before I have to.

During the last few months of his illness, the things I did to care for my dear one were increasingly challenging, especially because the pandemic meant that ordinary hospice care was truncated at best. Several times, he said he was so sorry I had to care for him in that way. The very first time he said this, I replied, "Dude, this is the deal we made, to take care of each other until the end. If the roles were reversed, you would be doing the same for me." And that was no bull, I really felt and feel that way. Which is probably why when the level of intimacy rose to its ultimate, it truly did not bother me the way it had when I cared for my mother.

When Jack finally acknowledged that his kidneys were truly failing and determined he did not want to pursue a transplant or dialysis, he began to make some mixed music CDs. Music was something we enjoyed for all our years together. Way back in the beginning, the fact that he loved the same popular music I did was one of the things that made me trust my heart to him on such short notice. Like me, he wanted to listen to Cat Stevens, not Burt Bacharach. He called his end-of-life collections "Death Mixes." Because it's a little bit funny.

These mixes have been an aid to my grieving because I believe I can hear the echo of his heart in the choices he made. One of them, Death Mix III is, he told me, a tribute to me. His words. The songs are almost all soft and romantic. And I said to myself, "Oh, Jacky, I'm so glad you think this is how you feel about me, but that is not how you treat me." How I wish I had known he had these things in his heart. How I wish they had been manifested to me in some way I could grasp and believe.

Because believing Jack loved me was always a challenge for me. You know, love has two sides, the side you give and the side you receive. Sometimes being able to receive someone's love might be even more important to them than the love you give to them. It must have been so hard for him to be married to someone who struggled so much with receiving love. (As it turns out, inability to receive love is an absolute hallmark of the presence of the spirit of rejection. See chapter *On Grief.*)

After he finished Death Mix I, he brought it into the living room and played it. While it played, he stood with his back to me, looking out the front window at the soybean field across the street, swaying and singing along. I sat weeping on the couch as I listened to the music he chose to say goodbye to the things he loved about this world. He loved God and nature and reading and thinking and music and poetry and his wife and his children. He *so* wanted the world to be how he thought it should be, and that was never going to happen. And though leaving made him sad, I think a part of him was relieved at the prospect of getting out.

One thing I began to notice after he was gone was how often he included a particular Simon and Garfunkel song, "April Come She Will", in a mix. He used it a lot. As I have meditated on this song choice, I think that was his song for Mary. He never talked about her with me after the beginning when he first told me what she did and how it was his fault, and that he had destroyed all his pictures of her. (The thing with the pictures should have been so much more revealing to me than it was at the time. Why could I not see the true depth of his wreckedness?)

Though he never talked about her, I have to believe he thought about her because I know how occasionally I think about Martin even now, even though he, too, is gone. I think the song popping up so often may be proof of that. He must have wondered where she is and how she's doing and if she ever thinks about him and if she regrets what happened…because I have about Martin.

What I think I know, now that it's too late, is that with her betrayal, Mary broke something in Jack. That the sweet, innocent boy in his passionate first love got crushed like a cigarette when you throw it down and stomp it to kill the ember. She heedlessly destroyed his young, sweet boy heart, and what I loved and lived with for the rest of his life was what he could cobble together from the ashes.

In Death Mix III, he repeatedly laid out the depth and strength of his love for me. And I believe him. But it is the truth when I say that is not how he acted toward me. It may be that in the end, he was able to rediscover and/or articulate it as a remembrance and keepsake for me, and thank God he did. It means everything to me when he blesses the broken road that led him to me. But he and I both know that road was really broken for him.

So I will qualify what I wrote above to say that what was broken was not his ability to love. It was his ability to ever completely trust and expect faithfulness from a wife. He has said that he went into his first marriage with the lessons of his parents' faithfulness as his example. He fully expected to marry once and be with Mary for the rest of his life. He was a pagan then, and at the time, he felt the marriage was the only good thing he had, and everything else was built on it. When it collapsed, he could never really trust in that ideal ever again. Those are the graveclothes I wore for forty-seven years.

He was a good, good man but not an easy one. As I look at the pictures from when he was a boy and a sailor, before she wrecked him, there is a softness about him that was gone when I met him. I loved the beautiful hard planes of his face, but, oh, don't I wonder what it could have been like to know and love and live with the young Jack, the sweet Jack, the "before Mary" Jack. Oh, don't I?

On Honeymoon Trip

When Jack and I married in 1973, we had known each other for ten weeks. We had bought a van and embarked on a twelve thousand-mile drive around the country to find a town with a college where I could get a job, and Jack could attend school on the GI bill. Below is a daily log he kept of a good portion of that trip. Ultimately, we ended up back where we started.

Wednesday, September 5
  Drove across Indiana and Illinois, crossed Mississippi and Missouri Rivers

Thursday, September 6
  Crossed state of Missouri. Went through Kansas City. Saw KC Sports Complex. Camped on a small lake, fifty miles from Lebanon, Kansas, geographical center of US. Kansas has superroads and lots of sunflowers.

Friday, September 7
Mileage: 3977. Finish 4285.5 Malone Lake Rec. Area, Nebraska.
  Went to Concordia College, Seward Nebraska. (We stopped to visit with some of my college friends who had transferred there after two years in Ann Arbor. This is when I learned again that those types of friendships, for me at least, end up being transitory.) Started to cross Nebraska on I-80. Stopped for night near North

Platte. No Coors 'til Colorado Oly, however, will suffice. Starting to see hills. Weather nice and cool.

Saturday, September 8

Went remainder of way through Nebraska. Went through Cheyenne, Wyoming, a town of house trailers. Finally made it to Colorado and Rocky Mountain National Park. Van started acting up around Loveland, Colorado. Needs repairs, we're afraid. Selected nice, secluded campsite (A108) at Moraine Campground.

Sunday, September 9

As fine a day as we've ever spent together. Hiked up to visitor center for Moraine Park. Saw some movies, slides, and exhibits there. Trucked on back to our little tent paradise where we spent the afternoon doing whatever we wanted (again and again). Were treated to a mountain thunderstorm. Hail as big as marbles covered the ground. Looks like rain for the evening. Back to doing whatever we want. What a life!

Monday, September 10

Got up early and went horseback riding. Rode up to Cub Lake. Horseback riding not too bad until you sit down later. After the ride, we drove to Bear Lake and hiked up to Nymph Lake. Then we went into Estes Park for gas, etc. Coors turned out to be as good as everyone said. Rained in the afternoon but cleared up in the evening. Looks like a cold night coming up with much huddling together for warmth and what not.

Tuesday, September 11

In the morning, rain kept us in the tent for reading and letter writing. When it cleared up, we went to Glacier Gorge and hiked up to Alberta Falls. Spent the afternoon trying to get our tent and sleeping gear dried out. We've had good luck seeing animals. The ground squirrels and chipmunks around our campsite are super tame. We've seen a couple coyotes and a rabbit and two deer on the way up to Glacier Gorge. Tonight, as we were eating dinner something similar to a green olive plopped onto the table. We looked up and in the ponderosa pine next to our table was a big porcupine who provided us with the quills taped onto the page above.

Wednesday 12 September

Left Rocky Mountain National Park. Drove into Denver where we went to Bob and Bev Ficco's house. Went to Chevy Dealer to have van worked on. Timing advanced to eight degrees BTOC and carb set for more gas. Went to Lafayette, Colorado, where we got a motel room. Cleaned up and then went to see *Little Big Man* in North Denver. Denver's really grown.

Thursday, September 13

Spent day visiting with relatives. Saw Bob, Bev, Diane, Mel, Nicky, Kathy, and the kids. Stayed overnight at Grandma's house. These people are the real "American Sportsmen." Working for post office sounds good.

Friday, September 14

Drove south from Denver. Saw Royal Gorge. Gorge okay, but whole thing sickeningly commercial. Lot of air pollution over Colorado Springs. Next stop, Sand Dunes National Monument where we spent the night. Heard coyotes howling at night there. Golden Eagle pass proving worthwhile… Have used it three times so far and will use it again tonight at Black Canyon of the Gunnison.

Saturday, September 15
    Drove from Sand Dunes to Black Canyon of Gunnison. Crossed continental divide at N. Cochetopa Pass. Beautiful scenery between Saquache and Gunnison. Country much drier than expected. Black Canyon of Gunnison most spectacular thing seen thus far. Saw a herd of five deer at dusk.

Sunday, September 16
    Left Black Canyon of Gunnison for Salt Lake City. Drove through a good part of Utah today. Utah very barren, the closer to Idaho we get the better Utah looks. Got nice campsite north of Logan, Utah. Broke down and bought some steaks. Salt Lake City disappointing.

Monday, September 17

Tuesday and Wednesday, September 18 and 19
    Tuesday drove to Blackfoot, Idaho, to see Jim Peterson and LuAnn. Went out plinking with .22s outside of town. Went to drive-in that night. Slept on Peterson's living room floor. Next day changed oil and filter and rotated tires on van thusly (diagram of tire rotation). Broke down and did our laundry. Spent evening lying around reading.

Thursday, Friday, Saturday, Sunday, Monday

Have spent the last few days fighting off colds and sore throats and gaining weight. Monday went to Craters of the Moon National Monument, which was pretty unusual. Saw some fine lava caves. Washed and waxed van. Went into Pocatello to Waremart for food.

Tuesday, September 25
Total $237.06

Wednesday, September 26, 1973

Left Blackfoot for Tetons. Took backroads over Teton Pass in Wyoming. Beautiful scenery. Teton Pass covered with snow. Set up tent at Jenny Lake in Grand Teton National Park. Lake unbelievably clear. Will be cold tonight. (It was frost on the ground in morning.) Night was beautiful, clear with so many stars…it was almost as bright as a full moon.

Thursday, September 27

Finally at Yellowstone. Camped at Bridge Bay—good site. Lots of snow coming into Park from south. Saw a whole lot of things—geysers, mudpots, waterfalls, and animals. At Mud Volcano saw Dragon's mouth and dragon's cauldron. Saw 5 bison and 2 moose, Canadian geese. Bison were really close to us in one little picnic area. They're huge! Took trail to upper falls of Yellowstone River and went to Artists' Point for fine view of Grand Canyon of Yellowstone. Fantastic weather today. Sky was so blue it looked fake and temp. Must have been up in the sixties. Will stay in Yellowstone for a while, as long as weather holds out. Looking forward to another cold night. Warned to keep a clean campsite—guess this grizzly bear country.

Friday, September 28

Spent day hiking and driving in Yellowstone. Started off with five-mile hike to Lone Star Geyser. Then went to Old Faithful area where we hiked another 2, 3 miles looking at various geysers. Saw Morning Glory Pool. Old Faithful didn't erupt while we were there. After Old Faithful we completed loop in middle of park in the van and ended up back at Bridge Bay. Saw Virginia Cascades and Gibbon Falls. Have continued to see animals. Today: four elk (to which we came super close), one bison, and a coyote or wolf. Weather couldn't have been better these last couple days, though the nights were cold enough to cover the tent with frost. Van is running just fine and except for a cold and cough things couldn't be much better.

Saturday, September 29

Went to Mammoth Hot Springs to camp. Took good hike into river valley and drove to Tower Falls. Saw three buffalo, five to six deer, and coyote.

Sunday, September 30

On the road again. Spent morning rearranging inside of van, washed the little beauty. Stopped at Lewis and Clark Caverns in Montana for the night. Montana is good-looking state so far, and Montana State U. At Bozeman might not be a bad place to go to school. Took 1 1/2 hr. Tour of caverns. Beautiful caves! Ride back on train pulled by converted Jeep.

Monday, October 1

Spent most of the day driving through Montana and eastern Washington. Not much unusual happened. Eastern Wash. Very dry despite Washington's claiming to be "The Evergreen State." Camped tonight in Sun Lakes State Park not too far from Grand Coulee Dam. Dam has huge reservoir backed up behind it edged by spooky-looking black cliffs. Linda said water looks dead, and that is a good description of it. Lots of Canadian geese.

Tuesday, October 2

Left Sun Lakes and traveled to dark, dank rain forest of Mount Rainier National Park. Mount Rainier dominates all other mountains. It's over fourteen thousand feet and has great deal of snow on it. Trees are huge. Checked out Ellensburg, not bad, small but campus had new, good-looking buildings, and country was pretty nice.

Wednesday, October 3

Drove from Mount Rainier to Seattle. Went up in Space Needle. Air pollution spoiled view. Seattle not much better than any other big city buildings at city center interesting. Electric elevated train system in city. Went through Tacoma, Olympia, and up Olympic peninsula to Port Angeles on strait of Juan de Fuca. Broke down and spent night in motel and ate out in restaurant.

Thursday, October 4

Drove from Port Angeles to Pacific Coast section of Olympic National Park. Camped in Mora campground there. Pretty damp and chilly.

Coast and ocean beautiful. Spent afternoon searching rocks after tide went out for shells, animals, etc. Found weird plants, starfish, crab shells, and rocks. Beach covered with all kinds of huge logs and driftwood. "Seastacks" (islands) are just like you see in the pictures.

Friday, October 5

Spent most of day driving down coast of Wash and Oregon. Spent a wet, rainy night at Camp Lookout, Oregon. Slept in Van. Campground nice but pretty developed.

Saturday, October 6

Rained all night and all day. Headed inland to Portland to try and get out of rain. Gave up and got motel room for the night. Snow in mountains down to about four thousand feet. Trouble ahead? Oregon sorta strange. Can't get beverages in tab top cans, big on recycling, $100 fine for having weed, energy crisis causing people to cut back on lighting etc. Lots of old people here it seems. Portland pretty nice.

Sunday, October 7

Drove from Portland to Eugene, Oregon, through Corvallis. OSU at Corvallis pretty nice.

Monday, October 8

A rip-off on snow tires/rims. Spent day walking around Eugene and UO Campus. Could be our future home. City center has fine mall. UO seems like a place I could enjoy. "Don't Californicate Oregon."

Tuesday, October 9

Headed south through Oregon to north-west corner of California. A 450-mile strip on Oregon/California coasts suitable for redwoods, and you see plenty of them here. Really beautiful. Just can't seem to fully realize how huge they are. Camping stuff finally drying out. Field by our campsite had large herd of elk. Trivia note: layer of vegetation on forest floor called "duff." Learned this on revelation trail in park, trail for blind. Also, root systems of redwoods penetrate usually less than ten feet into soil, no taproot.

Wednesday and Thursday, October 10 and 11

Left Prairie Creek Redwood area and drove and drove and drove...all the way to the Grand Canyon, about twenty-five hours straight. California is one long state. Drove all Wednesday evening and arrived at the canyon about 11:00 a.m. Too tired to do much, except set up the tent and conk out. Wednesday the tenth, we were somewhere near Redding, California, when we first heard of Agnew's resignation.

This is the end of the journal Jack kept though it was not by any means the end of the trip. We had decided to make Eugene our home, but it was the middle of the semester, so to pass the time, we decided to head back to Ohio for a last visit. For some reason, he decided to drive straight through the entire length of California in a day. I have to say I have always regretted the hurry through that state as I would have liked to take a closer look while we were there. I do think we were getting tired of being nomads.

We spent a few days at the Grand Canyon. He wanted to hike down into the canyon, but as I looked over the edge into that gigantic slash in the ground, I told him I was pretty sure I could make it down, but not so sure I could make it back up. From there, by reasonable hops, we made our way east through New Mexico and Texas. I remember finding Arkansas a much prettier place than I would have expected. Up through Tennessee and Kentucky and back home to Ohio.

We stayed in Painesville for a week or two. It was pretty weird sharing my old bedroom with my new husband. Then because Jack had a number of personal items stored with his parents in Florida, we decided to head there. There is a picture of us from that visit. The clothes we were wearing in it, funnily enough, were exactly the same clothes we both wore on our first date.

I had never been to Florida, so it was a bit of a revelation, especially when a good sized palmetto bug (let's be honest, that's Florida speak for cockroach) fell out of the speaker box, and no matter how hard Jack stomped him into the carpet, he just kept getting up and walking away! I do think I enjoyed the summer weather in November. After another week or two, we decided that, instead of returning to Eugene, we would return to Ohio. I honestly don't remember why except we might have just been tired of traveling, and it was a much shorter trip.

I know we stayed with my folks again but not for very long. We had kept back enough money to get a start someplace and, on our first day back, went to Lake County National Bank to open some accounts. I know I had my hair in braids and was wearing cutoffs and saddle shoes. I happened to ask our teller if the bank was hiring and mentioned I was an experienced teller. I was immediately whisked upstairs, saddle shoes and all, filled out some papers, and voila, I had a job.

We only looked at two apartments, one in Painesville and one in Willoughby. It became clear to me that Jack really expected to stay in his hometown, and to be honest, I didn't care where I was as long as it was with him, so we went for the one in Willoughby. It was in the right hand half of a big house on Ridge Road. We had two bedrooms and a garage/utility area in the basement and a woodburning fireplace in the living room. So it was pretty nice.

Jack started his own job search, and once again, God had his hand on my husband. The search took a few weeks, which I think made him feel kind of pressured since I was already going to work every day. He had applied for a job with a company in Mentor that made some kind crystals. He had also applied for a job in the print shop at the Eaton Telecomputer Center in Eastlake. The crystal guys offered Jack a job, but he wasn't sure he should take it. He was literally kneeling in prayer, asking for direction from God, when the phone rang. It was Eaton. They felt he was overqualified for the print shop, but they hoped he would consider a job in their office services department. Boy, did they get a deal! He worked for them at the telecomputer center for thirty years, ending as a senior network analyst. Not bad for a print shop applicant.

On Sex

Some things are meant to be private.

On Elayne

When Jack was in high school, he had a girlfriend named Elayne. It seems they went together for a pretty long time and sometime during that time became intimate. There was a bit about blankets in the field behind the junior high and what it was like to sweat out pregnancy fears as a sixteen-year-old boy. I know she broke up with him because she became interested in someone else. I know they were not together during his senior year. He would later say of this relationship that it warped his school experience, his life, and his future. That he paid the price for his lack of character in this area.

I remember when he first told me the most significant thing about his relationship with her. It was during the few weeks between our engagement and the wedding. We had decided to go to a baseball game in Cleveland. We had parked in one of the municipal parking lots and were making the long trek to the stadium, and he began telling me the story.

He reminded me about the relationship, and I was thinking, okay, my background was not spotless, and I had already accepted that there was an ex-wife. He gave me some context by saying that during the fall of 1965 at Oberlin, he had met Mary, but they had not yet become exclusive, and he went home for Christmas. While at home, he ran into Elayne, and they ended up having sex. And I thought, *That's kind of cheesy.*

So he went back to school, and he and Mary became exclusive, and along about March, he got a frenzied phone call from his dad that Jack was to get himself home, and he didn't care how. Jack had to hitchhike. When he got home, he was confronted by his parents and her parents and Elayne and informed that she was pregnant.

93

I have a sense that there was talk of him marrying Elayne. I also have a sense she might have liked that. But he had given his heart to Mary, and he didn't want to marry Elayne. In addition, he thought she was dating other guys around the time she got pregnant, and he was not sure the child was his. Long story short, he refused to marry her. He went back to school, continued his relationship with Mary, and Elayne stayed behind and, by September, gave birth to a little girl. At some point, he became aware that Elayne was going to take him to court for child support.

That was why he dropped out of Oberlin and enlisted in the navy. Apparently, at that time, if you were in the military, a suit like that was suspended until the end of your service, in his case, six years. By the time he got out, Elayne was married, and her little girl had been adopted by her husband. The suit was settled for a nominal amount not long after he was discharged from the service.

And this was the story that he told me on the trek through the dust to the stadium. As it began to dawn on me just what it was he was telling me, I remember thinking, *Okay, there's not only a wife but an illegitimate child, a child to whom he has not been very honorable.* I give him credit that he wanted to tell me everything while there was time to back out.

We married in September, took our twelve-thousand-mile journey around the country, and ended up by December in an apartment in Willoughby. Along about that time, Jack's mom sent him a big fat letter that had gone to their former address at the motel, been forwarded to them in Florida, and then on to us in Ohio. It was twelve pages long with pictures of Jolie from Elayne. "I was standing at the sink washing dishes the other day, and I got to thinking about you…" It made me wonder if she had heard about his divorce.

He read it, and I read it, and he put it on the end table in our living room, and there it sat. For days. I asked him what he was going to do, and it eventually became apparent he was doing it.

I was twenty years old and newly married. The letter read to me like regret. It read to me like maybe she thought it was the start of a correspondence. So being the bull in a china shop I am, I took the letter and the pictures, wrote a brief cover note, and sent it back to her. I said, "Jack is married." I reminded her that her daughter had been adopted by her husband, and *he* was now her father. I probably said I didn't expect we would hear from her anymore. Because I was not going to have my husband getting letters from a former girlfriend with whom he had made a legal settlement and who was or was not the mother of his child. Not having it.

I do not recall Jack objecting to my having done this. When I became a mother myself, I felt a little bad about it. And a few years later, when she called our house using a fake accent and representing herself as a workmate who needed to talk to him but did not know his work phone number, I knew it was her but gave her the number.

When Jack got home from work, he told me she had called him because Jolie had been having some health problems, and she wanted to know if there were any similar issues in his family, which there were not. As far as I know, that was the only contact they had at that time. I seem to recall years later his telling me they emailed a bit and asking if it bothered me. After he died, I found the emails on his computer, and in fact, it did bother me. Not because of him but because of her. She never could get herself to leave him alone. I will say I think he was always appreciative that she not only gave Jolie life but also raised her.

We never hid this chapter of Jack's life from our family. In a way, it was a cautionary tale for them though it didn't prevent us from having a similar experience with one of our kids. When my kids were curious, I did not stand in the way of their getting to know Jolie. After all, it was certainly not her fault that her beginnings were less than ideal. As a result, my girls have met her, though neither Jack nor I ever did. They shared that she seems a kindred spirit and just as driven and type A as they are. In my exchanges with her, my impression of Jolie is that she is a truly nice girl and a good person who has been stuck in a tough position her whole life. I still send her our little Christmas letter every year so she can know what our family is up to.

I know Jack felt badly about that episode of his life and his less-than-stellar behavior After he retired, he reached out to Jolie, and they exchanged emails and letters over an extended period of time though eventually it petered out. During those exchanges, it is clear he was accepting her as his daughter. While he was declining, I asked if he wanted me to contact her, but he said no. I think he thought there was no redeeming himself in a relationship he had bungled so badly.

After his death, I found a file in the drawer where he kept her letters and the pictures she had sent. Another file in the computer had her emails and the letters he sent to her. She is a very talented artist and a serious animal lover. She ultimately became a nurse, just like Mike and Florence and Becca. She married someone quite a bit older than her. She never had children.

On How My Mother Quit Smoking

Both of my parents were fairly heavy smokers throughout my years growing up. I think my dad started in his early teens and my mom in her late teens. As I have said elsewhere, this was perfectly socially acceptable in those years.

My dad had his first heart attack at the age of forty-seven. He had had a blowout on the freeway in Cleveland. The attack struck as he was changing the tire. He was sprawled across the open trunk when an empty ambulance went by. The guys stopped and saved my dad. He had a triple bypass shortly thereafter. He immediately quit smoking.

My mom said then and for some years after that she was not the one who had a heart attack. She saw no reason to give up a habit she enjoyed. As an aside, my mother was super-sedentary and over-weight her whole life. Despite this, she enjoyed remarkably good health physically pretty much the whole time, except for diabetes. Her cognition gave up long before her body did.

After about fifteen years, years in which smoking became less and less acceptable and many of my mom's smoker friends quit, my mom continued to smoke. I guess those smoker friends, like many converts, got after her fairly regularly about quitting. Eventually, one too many times, someone said, "Joanne, when are you going to quit smoking?"

She snapped and said (I am not kidding), "If God wants me to quit smoking, he's going to have to make me really sick!" What!?

Within a week, she was in the hospital with Legionnaires' Disease, a particularly virulent form of pneumonia. I guess God wanted her to quit. While she was delirious in the hospital, my dad took the opportunity to throw away all the ashtrays. He strongly admonished all his kids that they were under no circumstances to furnish their mother with cigarettes.

And that is how my mother quit smoking.

On Our Spiritual History

This history was a file I found in a folder on Jack's computer after his death. It is obviously his story rather than mine, and I have not edited it much. But it is a pretty faithful recounting of where we went and why during a good part of our marriage.

Early Years

God seemed to have his hand on my heart from the time I was very young. As a child of five or six, I distinctly remember a direct answer to prayer about our dog, Nubby, who had turned up missing. I was walking around the yard crying and prayed for the Lord to help us find him. I heard a muffled bark from one of the buildings we had on the property; the dog had somehow gotten closed up in one of them. I immediately recognized it as an answer to prayer and was amazed at how fast God had responded.

I knew about Jesus from early childhood, especially through Christmas events. Our family had a large oil painting of Mary holding the baby Jesus, and I remember one Christmas our putting the picture in one of the big front picture windows of the new motel and cutting out colored tissue paper to make a stained glass window to surround the picture.

I think we were baptized at Willoughby Methodist Church, but not as infants. Mike had belonged to the Methodist Church in the Isle of Man. I think Mom (or maybe my brother Bob) has her Bible from when she was a girl. At some point, when we were young, I remember going to a vacation Bible school at the Willoughby Methodist Church and doing a project where we covered a coffee can with a concoction made from a paste of pastel-colored Ivory Flakes

99

and water. Many years later, I would learn other things about our Methodist roots and how they involved Leroy, Ohio, where our family would move in 1987.

When I was about in the fifth grade (1957?), Mom made a vow that if Dad would quit drinking, she would send the kids to catechism classes. We had not been active in the Catholic Church to that point because Dad was divorced when he married Mom, and the Catholic rules excommunicated her.

About the time we started catechism classes, Mom subscribed to Maryknoll Sisters' Publication, which was a series of booklets covering the books of the Bible and what they were about. I read them cover to cover during the course of the summer. As we took religious instruction, I was impressed by the stories of the courage and faithfulness of the different saints and the miracles God had performed through their intercession. I have always believed that God performs miracles in answer to prayer and considered such things to be a normal part of the Christian faith.

Eventually Tom, Bob, and I were baptized, received first communion, and were confirmed in the Roman Catholic Church. I think Joe O'Donnell (a friend of Dad's from AA) was my confirmation sponsor. I took the name "Francis" at confirmation time because I related strongly to Saint Francis of Assisi.

Navy Years

I think the worst thing I ever did occurred during this time. I believe it happened while I was stationed in Charleston, South Carolina, and if so, it would probably have been in the summer of 1969 after I had returned from my first patrol on the Nathaniel Greene. Mary and I were out riding on the 305cc Honda Super Hawk motorcycle I had, and as we came over a hill, there was a big billboard with scripture verses on it having do with salvation. I think one was "Jesus said, 'I am the way, the truth, and the life.'" I raised my left arm and made an obscene gesture toward the billboard in defiance. Even Mary recognized the seriousness of what I had done and made some kind of protest.

Summer of 1971, Mary asked for a divorce. Shortly before this, we had discussed her going off birth control pills so we could have children. In the middle of the conflict that summer, I asked her what she would have done if she had gotten pregnant. She said she would have just gone off somewhere without my knowledge and had an abortion. Even in my pagan condition at that time, I knew this was terribly wrong, and I was shocked that something as important as that could happen without any kind of input from me.

Somewhere prior to the time I was getting out of the navy in December of 1972, I went home on leave, and my brother Bob and Mark Hartman (his mother was an old lady who had a Christian bookstore in her house on Lakeshore Boulevard) collared me and witnessed to me about Jesus. I remember that Mark had been recently divorced, and I thought I could see the Lord's hand in this coincidence. I think I may have also gone with them down to the Chagrin River downstream of the dam at Daniels Park at night at this time to be baptized. Something must have happened when Bob and Mark shared with me because I returned to the ship and must have been outspoken about the change in my life. I remember the sub's executive officer (Lieutenant Commander Browder) asking me something about how "our group" conducted Sunday services.

Roman Catholic/Vatican II/ Catholic Charismatic Years

In May/June of 1973, I prayed that the Lord would find me someone to go out with, and soon after that, I met Linda, discovered she was a Christian, and immediately recognized that as the answer to my prayer. We met on Flag Day (June 14) and were married by Pr. Ottomar Bickel, September 1, at Zion Lutheran Church in Painesville, Ohio.

Her dad, when he found out I was a Catholic, said he would rather see her married to someone with no faith at all than to marry a Catholic. I appreciated his honesty and commitment to his faith, even at the time he said it.

(This actually happened in response to our decision to join the Catholic Church several years after we married. What my dad said was he would rather we attend no church than the Catholic Church. By that time, I had been in no church for four years. Being in some church, even the Catholic Church, was better. Having been raised Missouri Synod Lutheran, my position on a lot of Catholic doctrine was that it was clearly not scriptural. I did not want to be Catholic, and Jack did not want to be Lutheran, so we were at an impasse. Someone he worked with, maybe Jim Fisher, gave him a book called *Our Lady Comes to Garabandal* about one of those visitations that happen with Catholics from time to time. I read the book and saw the evidence of supernatural happenings, and I also came to grips with what the Bible says about who is the spiritual head of the home. So I went to Jack and told him that I was willing to take instruction in the Catholic faith as long as and until I came up against something that I just couldn't live with. Which is how we came to spend five years in the Catholic Church.)

We were married in a Roman Catholic ceremony at Immaculate Conception Church by Fr. Frank Godic, March 26, 1977. This was possible because my first marriage was a civil ceremony and thus was never recognized as an official marriage by the Catholic church. Linda was *very* pregnant with Jeff at the time. Ed and Dorothy Slavick were Jeff's godparents.

We had a lunchtime prayer group at Eaton led by Jim Fisher. Lyle Stusek came to us for prayer for his infant son Charley. Charley had some condition where the bones on the side of his skull were not expanding as his head grew, causing his head to become skewed. He was due to go into Cleveland Clinic for surgery to cut the skull bones. Lyle knelt down in the conference room, and we laid hands on him by proxy for his son and prayed for healing. When he and Joni went in for pre-op work, the doctors came to them and told them something had happened, and Charley no longer needed surgery.

We (our charismatic prayer group) offered to hold a preconfirmation Spirit Day for kids at Immaculate Conception Parish. Debbie Bell and Margie Miller received the Lord at that time, and a youth group began as a result of that day. Matt Logies was instrumental in the group. He and Linda became very close with Margie and Debbie, and a longtime relationship was formed. Linda eventually spent a lot of hard time in counseling with Margie after she graduated from high school. Her life was coming apart, and Linda helped her literally to hang on to life. Debbie, too, had some real problems, and we had a difficult deliverance prayer session with her. Satan had convinced her that she had committed the unforgivable sin. I think this occurred later when we were going to New Testament Fellowship.

Life in the Spirit weekend at St. Joseph Christian Life Center, inner healing where no one came through the door when Jutta Edwards had us mentally bring our parents into the room for reconciliation. When I tried to picture this with my father, no one came through the door. I suddenly realized how little my dad had seemed to have been there in my life as I was growing up. This was a revelation to me, but when I shared this with my folks, they were hurt and offended.

Delores Winder healing service, a demon-possessed man brought by a priest for deliverance. I was asked by Jim Fisher to be part of a group to pray deliverance with him prior to the actual service. I can remember him becoming very agitated when Delores Winder just walked up behind him without him even seeing her and noticed how tongues just seemed to flow out of me in that situation. Delores Winder has an incredible testimony of healing.

There were also some interesting things going on at Eaton at that time (very early eighties). Phil Vollman had gotten dramatically saved while he was in a St. Luke's Hospital mental ward through the ministry of a Nazarene pastor who visited him there. As he always does, he hit the street running and preached to Wayne Bileci, who also trusted in Christ. Wayne, in turn, shared with Bernadette who I worked with in the computer tape library, and Bernadette was saved and left the Catholic Church. This was interesting because both she and I had recently been involved in Catholic men's and women's renewals (Christ Renews His Parish) in our parishes, and her leaving Catholicism so abruptly was disturbing to me.

(One of the things that led to our leaving the Catholic church was when we both read a book called *Radical Christianity*, which was, I think, by Ralph Martin, a well-known Catholic charismatic. As

Jack wrestled with what he was learning about scripture and holding Catholic faith and practice up to it, something had to give.)

New Testament Fellowship (NTF) Years

We started going to NTF, at the suggestion of three different people (Lyle Stusek was one of them) about six weeks before the time Tim was born (1981). We had decided we had to leave the Catholic Church because we felt there was nothing more we could do there, and that we had to go somewhere that was faithful to God's Word, and Catholic doctrine clearly was not biblical. I had to choose between Catholicism and God's Word. Input into this decision probably involved materials from and exposure to Jimmy Swaggart Ministries and Last Days Ministries (Keith and Melody Green).

When we decided we had to leave Roman Catholicism, we started praying. As I saw it the choice was between God's Word in scripture and Roman Catholic doctrine and practice. Within a short period of time, we decided to try New Testament Fellowship. We went there one Sunday, walked in the door, and when the worship started, we both felt we had found the place for us.

About this time, Tim was just a baby. I can remember one afternoon, I was sitting in a chair in the living room in the house on South and Summit Street with Tim sleeping on my lap. I laid hands on him and silently prayed that even from the time he was an infant that he'd be filled with the Holy Spirit. To my surprise, I no sooner finished the prayer when he opened up his big blue eyes real wide and actually started to laugh out loud. I remember thinking "Boy, God really must have heard *that* prayer!"

The pastors at NTF when we got there were George Loper, Chuck Grant, and Greg DeMeolo. Bob Meek also was an informal part of the leadership. Since it was trying to be a "New Testament" church, one of the things they believed in was having a plurality of elders/leadership. Some time later, George Loper was removed as a disciplinary measure, and Paul Coumos became an elder to replace him.

Somewhere in this time frame, when Becky was about six, one of her breasts began to mature prematurely. Linda took her to the doctor at Kaiser and began praying for the process to be reversed with the promise to God that if the prayers were answered, she would take Becky in again and tell what had happened. The prayer was answered, and the doctor said that it was unusual for the process to be reversed.

The day of Linda's and my baptism (in the very early eighties) at NTF on Ridge Road in Willoughby was interesting. We had been warned that Satan doesn't like believers standing up for their faith in Christ at baptism and were told to expect hindrances or problems. Sure enough, on the March, Sunday, we were to be baptized, as we got out of the car, we saw Deacon Dale Rhodes grinning. We asked him why, and he said the thermocouple in the heating system for the baptismal font water was broken, and the water was very cold. He asked us if we wanted to wait until another Sunday, and we said no. The water was so cold it took your breath away when you were submerged in it. I think I was baptized by Greg DeMeolo. Prior to the baptism, Linda said the Lord had her "mend fences" with the Schwanns next door to go into baptism with a clear conscience.

Prophecy by Lattie McDonough. He had just prophesied about Phil Vollman and had been right on the money. He must have seen tears in Linda's and my eyes. He came over and prophesied over the two of us about us weeping together in the meetings and having power as we brought things before him with our tears. He also prophesied that God was going in time to give me the understanding and wisdom and courage to share his word.

While at Eaton, working in computer operations, Roy Hepler and I had a chance to share with an Inroads student named Dennis Lopez. When he first got there, he was very undisciplined, but Roy had some good talks with him, and eventually Dennis came to trust in Christ. I also had some good talks with him where I tried to give him direction and encouragement. He really appreciated what we had shared and came to have a special place in his heart for us. I recently found a Christmas card from him where he wrote, "I strongly believe the only reason that I got my job during the summer was just to meet you and Roy. I won't forget Lynece either. I also pray that I will see you and Roy again." I did get to see him again when he came to visit the TCC some time later, and he was still walking with the Lord.

Linda and I were home group leaders. I remember Tom and Melinda Shimrock, Frank and Sue Prijatel, Tom and Mary Oboczky, Jim and Mary Lou Harmon, Ruth Madden in our group. I think Paul and Jane Coumos may have been in the group too.

(During our years at NTF, we began to support Hope Ministries, a children's ministry in India. We continued to support this ministry all the way until I retired in 2018, at which point we had to curtail some of our giving. We also met Peter and Sharon Georges at NTF. They eventually became missionaries with the Greek Orthodox Church and are still in Uganda today. My entire tithe for now goes to the St. Nicholas Uganda Children's Fund. The Georges support themselves with their own funds and 100 percent of donations go to educating Ugandan children. In addition, through all these years, we supported Pam and her husband's Christian camp ministries, even after Pam died. We only stopped that support in 2018 as well.)

Scott Duey

At some point in these years, when Tim was about five years old, a best friend of mine from high school, Scott Duey, showed up on our doorstep on a cold February morning. He had checked himself out of a mental health facility in Akron and was in real bad shape from drug usage. He was borderline insane, and eventually our conversation shifted over from cosmic baseball to witchcraft. When I told him such things were satanic and dangerous, we ended up discussing whether Satan was more powerful than Christ. I told him Jesus was more powerful since he had created Satan, and when he asked me where I had gotten that information, I read scriptures from John 1 and Colossians to him. As I read the words out of Colossians, he grabbed his head in his hands and said the words were like someone hitting him with a hammer. This was an awesome demonstration of the power of God's Word that I have never forgotten. Linda picked up on what was happening and came over into the dining room where we were talking, and we laid hands on him and prayed for him to be delivered. As we prayed, he coughed up a wad of green phlegm and spit it into an ashtray on the table. (This is a common manifestation of spiritual deliverance.) As we prayed, he became more peaceful and told us he was very tired, and we settled him on the couch in the living room where he quickly fell asleep. (Scott ended up staying with us for about three weeks. His behaviors could be pretty weird, like when he fished an empty peanut butter jar from the trash so he could drink his coffee from it. While shoveling snow, I saw him put a walnut into his cap and return the cap to his head. Eventually, he got annoyed with Tim and hit our boy with a fly swatter, at which point I told Jack I no longer felt safe alone in the house with him, and Jack and Matt Logies took him back to Akron.)

We left NTF after about five years over the issue of how authority was being exercised by the leaders. By this time, Phil Vollman and Peter and Sharon Georges were active in the Church. The incident that pushed us over the edge was a meeting where a number of people in leadership roles came together to discuss whether or not to build a new church. When Chuck Grant said that it was the place of the elders to hear the Holy Spirit for the people rather than having a situation where the Holy Spirit could be leading everyone in the body, I felt we had to part company. We tried to do this as biblically as possible, making an appeal and explaining our position. (Jack refused to descend into anger or bitterness over this occasion and would not let me do that either. I am *so* grateful for that.)

Home Fellowship at O'Keefes' Years

After we left NTF, we eventually were invited to meet with Jack and Sue O'Keefe at a church meeting in their home. Richard and Sharon Chappini also went, as did Joe and Rita Galfidi. Mary Oboczky and her family also ended up meeting with us. March 1989, I was arrested for blocking entrance to an abortion clinic in the University Circle area of Cleveland. I remember Patricia Blackmon, prosecutor for the city of Cleveland, standing around in jeans, laughing with one of the abortion clinic's directors as we were carried to the vans. Blackmon eventually became a judge of some kind on the Cleveland Municipal Court. Bill Tuscano was sitting beside me in front of the "clinic", and we were hauled off to the police vans together and taken to the fifth precinct jail. The police treated us very well. We spent the remainder of the summer going through the municipal court system. I can remember us walking in a big circle in front of the Justice Center praying and singing our Christian battle songs, especially "Our God Is an Awesome God."

Initially we all came before Judge Shirley S...S..., who seemed completely off the wall and on some kind of power trip. We were not allowed to retain Ed Heban as our lawyer and be tried as a group. We were not allowed to use the "necessity defense", that we were doing what we did to save lives. We were split up into smaller groups and came before different judges. I was tried by Judge George Trumbo, a decent, reserved, respectful Black man. His wife, Sarah Harper, was also a judge. He seemed genuinely attentive as he gave us the opportunity to speak before he sentenced us. I mentioned that I had six children (and heard murmurs of surprise from the spectators), and I tried to speak to the issue of how concerned I was about how wrong it was that the justice system allowed and protected the shedding of innocent blood. I remember Greg DeMeolo nodding his approval after I spoke. I was judged guilty of disorderly conduct and some other charge (possibly resisting arrest) and received fines and court costs totaling about $200. Bill Tuscano had the misfortune to come up before Judge S and received large fines and hundreds of hours of community service.

(This little home fellowship slowly died of attrition right about the time I was running for the school board for the first time in late 1993. I remember feeling rather abandoned at a time when I really felt the need for support. But that was God's timing so what can you do?)

Painesville Christian Center Church/Rising Star Years

(This was an African-American congregation in which we were the only white family.)

Somewhere in this time frame (1992). I began writing to Ric W, a friend of Lynece Dawson's who was sent to prison for killing his wife.

Pr. Willie Shaw was interviewed by the News Herald about his son's death in the Desert Storm war in Saudi Arabia. I was impressed by his honest answers and his faith, and as our home-fellowship was looking like it was going to disperse before too long, I cut out the article, and posted it on the refrigerator so we could consider going to Pastor Shaw's church when that time came. When it came time to attend Sunday services at Pastor Shaw's church for the first time (possibly in the autumn of 1993), early on that Sunday morning, I was up praying and asked the question of the Lord, "What is it I'm looking for, or hope to find, in the church we go to?" I have always thought the picture of Adam and the Lord walking together in the Garden of Eden, talking with each other, is what I want from a Church, close, simple fellowship with the Lord. When Pastor Shaw preached his sermon that first Sunday, one of the things he said was that the purpose of being saved wasn't to restore you to fellowship with God based on Moses, it was supposed to restore you all the way back to the relationship Adam had with God in the garden. What an amazing answer to prayer! Of all the things Pastor Shaw could have said, he picked that very specific thing! I felt this was a sign that we were at the right place because it lined up so exactly with what I had prayed earlier that morning.

As members of Rising Star Church, we had some very encouraging experiences holding Christmas services for male and female inmates at the Lake County jail for about three years. Pastor Shaw and Ella ministered at the jail, and that opened up doors for us. We also worked with Kent Morgan and Jim Porostoski in this. One time, I was asked to share from scripture, and I spoke from the Prodigal Son parable of Luke 15. When I asked the group of men how many wanted to return, like the son in the story, to their Heavenly Father, I was blessed and amazed when they all stood and came forward. The song "Jesus, Jesus, O What a Wonderful Child!" led by Ella Shaw, was something that really got everyone in the spirit of the holiday.

In the summer of 1994, Pastor Shaw, Embry Jackson, and Kevin Boswell baptized our five oldest children in Lake Erie at a baptism service held at the Metro Parks beach in Fairport Harbor. It was a very special time. At some point around this time, Linda's Dad had bladder cancer, so we laid hands on him as he was sitting on the foot stool in our living room and prayed for him for healing and relief. I remember him being deeply touched, and we all, especially Linda, felt it was a powerful time of prayer. He had no further problems with bladder cancer.

(This event was what led me to understand about faith and prayer. Before we ever prayed for my dad, I knew the prayer would be heard. We are taught that it is our faith that causes prayers to be answered. But what we are not reminded of in this context is that faith is a gift from God. I learned to wait to pray after being led by faith. Faithless prayer is useless. We have to let God tell us what to pray for and *then* pray. Now I approach God with the words, *God, what do you want me to pray for today?*)

We sadly left Rising Star Church due to a dispute over what the proper response for a believer was to be to Clinton's affair with Monica Lewinski. Pastor Shaw and nearly all the Black clergy took a "loving," nonjudgmental approach to what he had done. When I told Pastor Shaw that I found this strange by Blacks pastors since sexual immorality was doing more damage in the Black community than acts of racism by Whites, he got very upset and called me a racist and just couldn't see what I was trying to say. We just couldn't seem to reconcile, and we felt the best course of action was to leave. We still maintained friendships we had made over the five years we were there and saw the people at different events, mostly funerals.

Leroy Community Chapel Years

We went to Leroy Community Chapel after leaving Rising Star because it was a church in our own community and because we knew it to be a solid, Bible-believing church. We were looking for a measure of stability for our kids after the cross-cultural experiences of the previous five to six years.

God closes some doors hard sometimes! Around the Fourth of July, 1998, during the course of one week, Mike broke his kneecap at Bayshore Campground, playing basketball. Becky totaled her Honda Civic when she put it in a ditch going around a curve on Girdled

Road on a rainy day, Linda's dad died after a heart procedure, and my mom was diagnosed with cancer on her tongue and needed surgery. At this time, we were actively pursuing packing up and heading off to New Mexico to be houseparents for a ministry called The Ranches. My job at Eaton was really making me miserable, and when all these things happened, it was clear that the life change to New Mexico wasn't what the Lord wanted to happen. I was disappointed. Looking back, we see this as a definite no from the Lord, and it was good that we didn't go. Becky just would not have been able to afford to be on her own living in Memphis and working as a nurse at St. Jude's hospital. She was in sad shape coming out of college. Her friend (boyfriend?) Dave probably had much to do with it, and the months she ultimately spent living with us at home helped get her back on her feet. We began attending Leroy Community Chapel regularly in about January of 1999. The pastors were Jeff Allem and Tom Chapman, and there was a search going on for a youth pastor, a position which was filled later in the year by Jeff Pierce.

(Over the years, Jack slowly became convinced that he just did not fit in in the different places we tried to fellowship. And to some degree, he was right. He had a prophetic heart, and the things he saw burned in him, demanding to be expressed. He was a son of Issachar, gifted to see the signs of the times that others couldn't. I remember our being in a small meeting once. I was seated next to our young pastor. I don't remember the subject of the discussion, but I remember Jack talking for a bit, and he just took my breath away with how insightful and articulate he was.

When he was done, I said, "And I get to be married to this man!"

And my baby pastor said, "Better you than me."

Just imagine trying to be under the headship of that. Eventually Jack gave up. Till the end, two songs he consistently added to his mixes were Fernando Ortega's "Don't Let Me Come Home a Stranger" and Chris Tomlin's "Will There Ever Be a Place Where I Belong?")

Our first home group, headed up by Tom Chapman, met in the spring of 1999 at the home of Bud and Patty Lors. People I remember were Roy and Ethel Nelson and Frank and Barb Francosky.

The second home group we were part of met in the home of elder Lynn Stephens and his wife Tina. This was in the fall and winter of 1999/2000. We had reservations about Lynn Stephens because he seemed pretty "by the book" and because he taught the class for prospective new members, and we anticipated awkwardness because we knew our charismatic beliefs probably didn't line up with Moody theology. Those fears proved unfounded. When Lynn said, "I was/am a Swaggart man!" at one of our home group meetings, it was a real shot in the arm for my hope of really being part of a body of believers where I/we could fit in. It showed that he was someone who could think for himself and admit that God had used Swaggart despite his problems. This was a real turning point.

In October, I began attending a men's fellowship meeting at six o'clock on Saturday mornings at the Cornerstone. They were using Henry Blackaby's book *Experiencing God* as a study guide, and I found it to be *exactly* what I needed for this time. It seemed the events of my life were running exactly in parallel with the material covered. The section about the Gilgal stones and setting up landmarks to be used as guides for future direction led to the starting of this spiritual history. As I started identifying spiritual markers in our lives, things kept turning up that I had forgotten, and remembering them showed how active and faithful God has been in our lives. This helped to restore the excitement and expectancy of earlier years. In January of 2000, at the exact time when I was trying to muster up the obedience to pursue ministry at the Lake County Jail, the section we were studying was the one about how God's invitation to work with him will lead to a crisis of faith, which requires both a decision and action.

December 17, 1999, we went to the Christmas outreach at the jail. Linda invited Lynn and Tina, and they accepted, even though it was something totally new to them. We had a great night. The Holy Spirit really put the whole thing together, and we left rejoicing. Kent Morgan invited me to come and share whenever I wanted. I began seriously considering that the Lord was actually calling me to pursue some kind of jail outreach. (Jack's jail outreach ended up being confined to his thirty-year correspondence with Ric White.) Summer of 2000, June 28 to July 11, Linda, Mike, and I went on a short-term mission trip to Aiquile, Bolivia. The impact of this trip was very important in our lives. It began relationships with Eric and Shirley Bender and with Cliff Peters, missionaries we worked with in Bolivia. In 2002/2003, home fellowship group with Levi and Dyann Beckner, Circle the Wagon(s). In Blazing Saddles, when they holler, "Circle the Wagons!", the one Black family forms a circle all by itself. Our home group was so small, we identified with the Black family. Ray van der Laan's *That the World May Know* videos and John Eldredge's *Wild at Heart* book were resources we used that made an impact on us.

Memorial Day weekend of 2003. We went to Michigan to help Kevin and Beth move into their new house in Marshall. While we were there, Beth told us about how she and Kevin had been attending a small nondenominational church (The Family Altar). I was so happy to hear Beth say, "It's good to be back." They had been participating in a home group, and at some point, they both got up in front of the congregation and told of dedicating their lives to Christ. The pastor of the church comes from a Roman Catholic background, and the things he said must have made sense to Kevin.

Summer of 2003 (end of July to beginning of August), Mike and Rachel Williamson went on a short-term mission trip to Mexico with a group from Trinity Baptist Church; Jim and Cheryl Eberline hosted them. While they were there, I saw a big hawk carrying a snake flying over our yard in Leroy, which is strange since the symbol for Mexico is an eagle perching on a cactus holding a snake in one of its feet.

November 22, 2003, through Barb Rottas (a distant Manx cousin), I learned that one of my Manx ancestors, John Tear(e) had been a follower of John Wesley. We found his gravesite at the Brakeman Cemetery here in Leroy, and the inscription on his tombstone read,

John Tear
Follower of John Wesley
Sat under his ministry
Born on the Isle of Man July 1760
Migrated 1826
Died 1841

I also learned that a granddaughter (or great granddaughter) of John Tear's was Clara Tear Williams, who was a Methodist evangelist and who had written the words for the well-known hymn "Satisfied."

May 2004, I spent nearly two weeks in Florida with my parents. I had the opportunity to pray and fellowship with my mother, something I had never done before. She had a tendency to shy away from growth through Bible study and really got angry about my strong antiabortion beliefs. I had a hard time reconciling this with her claims to be a believer. My dad remained hardened to the truth of the gospel, but I shared it with him as simply and directly as I could. I came away from that visit worn out and burdened by the death and decay and unbelief I ran into.

Summer of 2004, we continued to grow closer to Beckners via home group. Moved on to John Eldredge's book, *Waking the Dead*, which was a more scriptural expansion of the concept of the goodness of the redeemed human heart presented in his *Wild at Heart* book. Dyann Beckner had been deeply hurt by her treatment by people at Leroy Community Chapel as she tried to head up the music ministry. The conflict resulting from this caused Beckners to drop out of Leroy Chapel.

In this time frame, Becky and Abby became regular members of our home group with Abby making very good progress in seeking the Lord. In July, the Holy Spirit seemed to be directing us into spiritual warfare as we were called to pray for deliverance with families of Denise Ball and Susan Schaeffer. Our "Circle the Wagon(s)" group started becoming the "Ones who Bump Back" group. Books used were *Pigs in the Parlor*, *The Bondage Breaker* (Neil Anderson), and *The Believer's Authority* (Kenneth Hagin). We were pointed to the scriptures speaking to the authority believers in Christ have over Satan and demons.

In July of 2004, Beckners, who were looking for a church to attend, asked us if we knew of any charismatic churches to go to. We called Sue O'Keefe about their church, Faith Victory Center at Cricket Lane School off Route 6 in Willoughby Hills, and we attended this church with Beckners. We called it the "Crazy Church" because it was so much more unstructured than things were at Leroy. We continued to attend there during the rest of the summer, and we were blessed by what went on. The freedom and use of the gifts of the Holy Spirit was refreshing, but I was troubled by how some scriptures were treated and by the issue of prophets like Rick Joyner being looked to for direction. The pastor, Joe Hayes, had a real gift for teaching, and I still remember his definition of "grace", the power of God working in you to be able to do what the truth requires. I really like that way of putting it.

On Sunday, August 15, 2004, a girl named Linda prayed/prophesied over me and said I had a kind/sweet heart, but that I was an "irritant", especially to those who had a religious spirit, and that this was their problem. She gave me Ephesians 1 as a scripture, said I had been writing, and that I loved truth. I was amazed at how accurate she had been in her discernment and was comforted to hear that God, at least, could see my heart's attitude, even if my family and others misunderstood me.

During this summer (2004), at a church picnic, Abby was baptized by Levi Beckner and Mark Antonelli in the swimming pool of a family who were members of the Faith Victory Center Church.

Beckners did not seem to feel at home here, and they moved on to other churches. I could just not accept how the church handled scripture, especially on things like women pastors, Paul's thorn in the flesh, God always wanting to heal people, etc. We eventually stopped attending services here, and for several months, we simply did not attend church anywhere on Sundays. Beckners and we seemed to be heading in different directions. Levi's job was taking a heavy toll on him, and they continued investigating the possibility of selling their house and moving, perhaps even out of state. Our home group continued to meet infrequently, and finally in the spring of 2005, we had a blowup that offended them, and we agreed to put off meeting in the summer. I think we all realized that our home group had reached the end of the line.

Throughout 2004 to 2005, I spent a good deal of time blogging in the World Magazine blog site, and I sent numerous emails to various columnists on the WorldNetDaily website. I actually received some replies from the columnists. The volume of writing I did was significant.

October 2, 2004, my dad died on this date. During the summer and fall of 2004, he had to be evacuated to shelters because of four hurricanes that hit Florida, and I think the physical stress was finally too much for him.

In October of 2004, we began supporting the ministry of Lad and Crystal Chapman who were working with Bruce Wilkinson's Dream for Africa program in Swaziland. This ended early in 2007 when they changed ministry groups. In 2005, we saw our tithe support of both Eric and Shirley Bender and the Cliff Peters family come to an end when they left the mission field.

By August of 2005, I had reached the point where I just could not justify not belonging to a church somewhere, and Linda was feeling the same way. We decided to return to Leroy Community Chapel and to try to make the best of it. We signed up for their home group program, and we were put in a group led by Elder Dave Ortiz.

Late in October of 2005, Linda and I went on a vacation to the Williamsburg, Virginia area. On the Sunday, we visited Jamestown. We participated in a short prayer service that had begun all the way back in 1607 when Jamestown was first settled.

(It's hard to believe it's been this long since we have been in a church, especially when we know better. Since Jack's passing, I have spent many Sundays on the Internet livestreaming services from various places and waiting for God to show me where the cloud is for me to follow and what work there may yet be for me in his kingdom. Right now, I attend The Experience Community in Murfreesboro, Tennessee, online every week. I know this is not a long-term solution. I am still looking for direction to someplace local. I have learned the hard way; it does not pay to get out in front of God's purposes. So for now, I wait.)

On Motherhood

When our oldest child was about eighteen months old, she threw up in her bed in the middle of the night. This was not like the infant spit-up that goes down your shirt. This was the big gag followed by the big splash. The sound woke me up, and my first thought was *Somebody is going to have to clean that up. Oh wait, somebody is me. I'm the mom.* In that moment, the real mantle of motherhood became mine.

If there is an aspect of my life that is most foundational to my sense of myself, it is my motherhood. I always expected to be a mother. It never occurred to me for a moment that I might not be, as has happened to two of my daughters-in-law. In fact, due to having formed a principle that I did not want to use artificial birth control, it was trying *not* to be a mother too often that became an issue.

I loved being a mother. As I have considered what it is about mothering that pleased me so, I have come to think it may be because the love between mother and infant is so pure and uncomplicated. As I have shared elsewhere, Jack's and my love was complicated for me. In addition, I don't seem to be able to sustain the love of friendship. But I never had to wonder if my babies loved me. I knew they did.

To me, one of the most fulfilling actions in life is to pick up a crying baby in the middle of the night and be the one and only thing they want. To nurse them and soothe them and put them back to bed clean and happy was ultimate satisfaction to me. In retrospect, I should have let Jack be more active in their care. I probably stole that from him a bit.

Of course, as time passes, things can't stay so simple and sweet. Nevertheless, I gave the best of all that I am to the best of my ability to be a good mother. Any ambitions I may have had for myself were absorbed into my hopes and dreams for my children. I tried to protect them, I taught them useful and beautiful things, read to them my favorite stories (the fruit trees I planted suffered the fate of the orcs in *Lord of the Rings*), and then had to painstakingly peel my fingers off them over and over until I was able to let them go and be what they wanted to be.

I'd like to take a minute to say here that we were wonderfully blessed in the natural gifts God gave to our children. Jack was really smart, and so am I, and the smartness we each had encompassed a broad range of ways to think and reason. Some of our kids are more like his way of smartness, and some are more like mine, but in their combinations of our skill sets, I think each of our kids ended up smarter than either of us. In addition to intelligence, our kids have so many talents, including the arts and the ability to be managers. Jack liked to say he felt like he was the father of the Village People in their variety. They are kindhearted and hardworking. Not one of them unduly harms themselves or others. I am so, so proud of them. My great sorrow is they mostly do not seem ready to let God be the boss.

As an aside, I have always felt being a mother was good preparation for being an elected official. Mothering, especially when the hands-on aspects of it stretched out through fifteen years of homeschooling, was an absolute exercise in conflict resolution and general decision-making.

Maybe that's why I became hyperdecisive. You read a situation, hold it up to basic principles, and decide. While there are a few decisions I wish I could get back, I am mostly satisfied with the choices I have made, even the ones made on the fly.

Becca was born eight days early in February of 1975 in the midst of a snowstorm. It was our first journey through childbirth, and though we had taken the Lamaze classes and I had read and read, it was still long and hard. My water broke at two in the morning, and she was born at ten thirty that night. Her poor little face was so mashed by her journey. She was our smallest baby weighing in at six pounds fifteen ounces.

Becca was not an easy baby. She had a *lot* of ear infections, a tendency she got from her dad. In childhood, he had suffered repeated ear infections, several broken eardrums, and a couple tries at removing tonsils and adenoids. In fact, he had ear infections well into adulthood and ultimately another surgery that involved a complete reconfiguring of the little bones in his left ear. Becca was on a similar path.

She would go to bed and, a couple hours later, wake up crying from the pain in her ear. I eventually developed the practice of just getting up and taking her in to the Kaiser emergency room in Cleveland where we had our health care. I wasn't going to sleep anyway, so doing that let me get to the amoxicillin a little sooner. So many bottles of pink medicine.

Her issues with her ears finally cleared up when she had tubes put in at around six years old. I still remember her asking me after the surgery why everyone was talking so loudly. Because all the thick, gross, infected fluid that had lived behind her ears for years had been drawn out during the operation. On the drive home, I had to pull over in Euclid to let her throw up in the snow at the side of the road. But once those ears had a chance to really dry up and heal, she never had a lot of trouble with them anymore. I often wondered why the doctor waited so long before giving her relief.

Becca was just a cranky baby. I can honestly say I don't think she was awake and not crying for more than about fifteen minutes at any time during the first year of her life. During that time, we bought a fixer house requiring a lot of effort to repair. Jack was working full-time and going to school. Consequently, he was also cranky. I almost walked out once. He almost hit me once, the only time he ever raised a hand in my direction. Good times.

Despite being crabby, Becca was a bright little girl. She talked early and paid attention to what went on around her. She never crawled but got around by scooting on her butt. She got into everything, including Crisco. At eighteen months, she could spell *Burhenne*, having heard me spell it on the phone. Our neighbors used to come and get her to show off to their company and have her perform this feat like a ventriloquist's dummy.

When Becca was a toddler, I went back to work a couple days a week as a bank teller. Our neighbor, Mrs. Posey, an old friend of

Jack's family, agreed to babysit. After a while, Becca was talking to me one day and said something about getting a "byag."

I said, "What?"

She said, "Byag." She meant bag. She was learning to talk from Mrs. Posey who had a pretty pronounced southern accent. I thought *someone else is teaching my child how to talk*. I immediately quit. What is the point of having children if someone else is going to raise them? Becca remained friends with the Poseys until into her teens and would walk over for a visit regularly.

Becca was always really smart and independent. When it was time for her to go to school, we were in our Catholic phase, so that first day, I loaded up the stroller, and we all walked her the four blocks to the Catholic school. Later in the day, we loaded up again to go and meet her and walk her home. When she came out of the building and saw us, she said, "What are you doing here?" Her tone was just what it sounds like.

"I came to walk you home," I replied.

"I know the way." Also, just what it sounds like.

Okay then. From then on, she toddled her little five-year-old self off to school and back again every day by herself.

In September of 1976, I suffered a miscarriage at about six weeks along. By then, I was taking instruction to become Catholic. I do think this decision had led us to a happier environment at home. We were working with Father Frank who had become a friend. He came to our house and took away the marble-sized little sac with the underdeveloped baby inside. I guess there is a place for such things in Catholic cemeteries. Two weeks later, I became pregnant with Jeff.

My pregnancy with Jeff was shadowed by the miscarriage. My Kaiser obstetrician told me I was more disposed to lose this pregnancy after having just lost one, not the best thing to tell a fearful expectant mother. I prayed my way through until I was far enough along to hope that an early labor would still leave me with a living child. I have often wondered if this fact rubbed off on him in utero, as he was a careful and cautious child.

Dr. T also thought I had got pregnant later than I did. I told him Jeff would be born in the last week of May or the first week of

June, but he set the due date at June 25. When I was in labor, they had an incubator ready. I looked at the giant lump of my belly and asked the nurse how anyone could possibly think someone small was going to come out. He was born June 3, weighing over eight pounds.

At that time, we were in the process of selling our first little fixer house and moving to a larger one around the corner. I had a lot of false labor with Jeff. One night, it seemed real, so I called the OB nurse for advice. She told me to drink an ounce of something alcoholic and lie down. If the labor were false, it would stop. I did as instructed, and the pains stopped.

My real labor cranked up on the day we were supposed to sign the final papers for the purchase of our new house. We went to the bank in the early afternoon on the way to the hospital. The bank guy brought out the papers for me to sign in the parking lot. Once again, we had a long, hard labor. Jeff wasn't born until about six the next morning. I remember thinking on the way to the delivery room that I had forgotten how bad giving birth is. Duh.

We moved when Jeff was two weeks old. By the late afternoon of moving day, we were in, everything put away, and I was folding a load of clean laundry upstairs on our bed when for the first time in my life, I hit the wall. There was just nothing left in the tank, and I laid down. The laundry had to wait a minute while I rested.

Jeff was a completely different kind of baby from his sister. I used to wonder if he was autistic. He sat in his little seat and watched the world, ate when he was hungry, went to bed when he was tired, no three/act play to get him to sleep. It was pretty awesome. And I have to say, Jeff never really gave us a minute of trouble in all his upbringing. He is a righteous man, always trying to do the right thing. It is one of my chief bones to pick with God that he has never been allowed the joys and challenges of fatherhood.

He ran away once when he was about three. Something had happened to offend his sense of justice, and the only solution was to strike out on his own. I did not try to dissuade him. I helped him put on his little green plaid coat and told him how sorry we would all be not to see him anymore. He set off down the street, making his way along the sidewalk between the piles of snow. He walked slower and slower, and he started to cry. He turned around about three houses down and came back.

I nursed him for almost a year. One of the weird things with him was he decided at some point that he was not going to nurse on the right side. Now anyone who has nursed a baby knows you nurse on both sides because both sides produce milk, duh. But he resolutely would not nurse on the right side no matter how I held him or quickly switched. Very painful for me until the one side kind of dried up. My left breast has ever after been a little larger than the right. Thanks, Jeff.

After I brought him home, Becca began to have screaming nightmares a couple times a night. Between getting up twice with her and up twice with him for several nights, I was just about losing it. One night, I did. I jumped up and said to Jack I just couldn't do it anymore. I ran out and jumped into our van and drove down to Daniels Park. I laid down and slept in the back of the van for about three hours and then went home. It's the only time I was ever pushed to that point. Poor Jack.

One day, I was walking Becca and Jeff to the playground and encountered a big rock at the end of someone's driveway.

"Look at the big wock," he said.

"Rrrrock," I said.

"Wock," said Jeff.

After we went around about four times, he said, "Look at the big stone," and kept walking down the sidewalk.

I remember one day, I had set him up outside in the playpen. (Why is it that playpens have gone out of fashion? They worked so well!) I would check on him and Becca through the window every few minutes. I looked out once and burst out laughing. Jeff's entire head was shiny and black. His sister had found a pan of used motor oil in the garage and, naturally thought the best thing to do with it was to coat her brother's dome with oil.

One of his quirks was that he liked to chew on plastic and rubbery things. He bit the knees and elbows and eyelashes off a significant number of Barbie dolls. He chewed off the hands and feet of plastic soldiers. He had a little toy guy, dressed as a camp counselor, that he especially liked to play with. His name was Jimmy. I bet if I mentioned Jimmy today, Jeff would remember him. He creeped me out pretty well one day when he told me about the tiny, tiny lady he saw in his room. I never did figure that one out.

When he was about six, he was playing outside one day, and he had a flat, round magnet with a hole in the center to which he had attached a piece of string. He would swing the magnet by the string and flip it onto one of the cars. He was innocently amusing himself. But once when he flipped the magnet, instead of hitting the metal, it hit the window. It didn't even hit very hard. But it broke the window. I remember a sort of *tick, tick, tick, tick* sound as that whole window cracked into at least a million pieces and collapsed into the car. He turned and looked at me, horrified. I was kind of horrified too. But, you know, stuff happens.

At around this time, we began the process of becoming foster parents. There were some hoops to jump through, and then we had the placement of Julie, a thirteen-year-old girl. She was my size and borrowed my clothes. We used the money received for her care to pay for her to attend Catholic school and buy her a bike. We also used it to buy her a savings bond in her name every month she lived with us, so she would have something of her own. I was twenty-four.

Julie was interesting because having her with us forced me to develop child-rearing standards for a much older child long before my children were that age. The first time she asked me what time I wanted her to come home from a friend's house, I was at a loss. What time *did* I want her to come home?

From Julie, I learned that foster children will always tell you everything would be fine if they were just with their *real* mother. And who can blame them? Eventually, after a year, she went back to the foster home she had lived in before coming to us. It was in our neighborhood, so she kept in touch. Ultimately, she went to live with relatives in the south. When their house burned down, her savings bonds were lost in the fire.

When she came to us, she shared a room with Jeff. She had hearing problems and had an ear operation while she lived with us. After the operation, she was supposed to cover a cotton ball with

Vaseline and put it in her ear before showering. One day, instead of napping, eighteen-month-old Jeff climbed out of the crib and up to the top of the closet shelves to get that jar of Vaseline. Because what you do with Vaseline is you wipe it all. over. everything.

While Julie lived with us and in the midst of weaning Jeff, I became pregnant with our Elizabeth. Surprise! Another pregnancy with no start date. I had had some trouble losing baby weight after Jeff. I'd joined the Y and exercised and ran faithfully and dropped fifteen pounds. Just in time to do it all again. Sigh…

So Beth was supposed to be born at around the turn of the year. They based her due date on the ultrasounds and the size of her head. Except that besides being bald (my dad could always pick out our babies in the nursery by their baldness), our children always had big heads, you know, to house those big brains. She was not born until January 30. That last month was *so long*. I used to walk around the house, singing, "In his time, in his time, he makes all things beautiful in his time…" It didn't really help. Everyone who knows me knows I do not wait well.

Once again, we had a long, hard labor. This time, I was given drugs during labor that completely destroyed my self-control. It was pretty bad. After twenty hours, she was born, another eight pounder. She had a large ridge from ear to ear across the top of her head, and her fingers stuffed into her mouth. She was a baby who did not need to be taught how to nurse. She knew what to do. She was possibly even easier than Jeff had been. Just a sunny, pleasant, nice little girl. She could entertain herself for an hour with a block and a Weeble. She is the only one of my babies where the pediatrician said she was too fat. Funnily, she is one of my kids who is very disciplined about her weight as an adult.

Beth got her picture on the front page of our local newspaper as a five-year-old. A photographer was cruising our neighborhood one day and saw her playing on the rope swing we had put in one of our trees. He took her picture hanging upside down with all her jelly bracelets up her arm and her jelly shoes on her feet. Her face is so serious, as if there is a right way to do this, and that is what she's doing. Hilarious.

Beth and Jeff are only nineteen months apart and were always close growing up. They played together really well, and even now, I would say they are friends. One day, they had got the rope swing caught up in the tree, and Jeff was throwing up a board to try to knock it down. He kept telling Beth to get out of the way, and Beth kept being in the way until the board came down and caught her right by her eye. It is always heart-stopping when a child runs into the house with blood running out from between their fingers. I would just like to take a minute to point out that stubbornness can get you hurt or even dead. Those were our first stitches.

They are the ones that managed to get Barbie stuck up in the garage gutter. They are the ones, I learned much later, who liked to climb up in the garage and walk across the two by four that stretched from the top of the door to the beginning of the attic floor. You know, above the concrete floor. Yikes!

When *she* ran away, there was no reverse psychology that would turn her around. Her mind was made up, her plan was solid, and she was done with us. She would go wait on Grandma's porch till Grandma got home from work, and there she would stay. I finally had to just tell her to turn around; she was not allowed to run away. She was three and a half.

Beth is the only one of our kids who is left-handed like her dad. She was more than three years old before we were sure because, also like her dad, she uses her right hand for a lot of things. Interestingly, two of our five biological grandchildren are also left-handed.

Once when we had company, the guys had been riding motorcycles. Beth walked up to one and, for whatever reason, wrapped her little hands around that shiny, shiny exhaust pipe and burned the bejebbus out of both palms. Poor little thing. I was right there. I watched her do it.

During this time, we had our second and final foster placement, a nine-year-old boy named Chuck. He had been removed from his home by being taken from school. He had two black eyes, burn marks on his arms, and bumps on his head from being struck with the business end of a high-heeled shoe by his alcoholic stepmother. She had bitten both his thumbs hard enough to turn both nails black. I could only wonder what took people so long to notice the abuse he had been suffering.

He lived with us for four months until he could be returned to his mother's home. What kind of father lets his child be hurt like that and does nothing? And why did neither he nor the wife ever reap consequences for what Chuck suffered? Chuck was very controlled, as abused children often are. It is their survival mechanism. He resolutely refused to tell anyone who had hurt him. His stepmother had promised death to him if he did and he had good reason to believe her. Eventually I explained to him that a person who does those things is sick and needs help. Then he told.

Once free of danger, it is common for such children to act out, and Chuck did, mostly at school rather than at home. He seemed to get along well enough with our kids and the kids in the neighborhood. After he left and I became pregnant with Tim, we withdrew from foster parenting. Our house was full.

But some years later, when Julie aged out of foster care and had nowhere to go, we told her that she could stay with us. It was just as we were moving to Leroy and we made a room for her in the basement. She had her own car and worked as a nurse's aide in a nursing home. Five months after she came to us, we got a call from the hospital. Julie had sat in her car in the parking lot at work and taken a whole bottle of aspirin with a Coke. She walked into the building and told her supervisor what she had done, and they sent her to the ER. We found her on a gurney in the hospital hallway smoking a cigarette after her stomach had been pumped—an experience she found quite unpleasant. She said they were sending her to a psychiatric hospital and we could follow the ambulance.

We replied, "No, Julie. We have five children at home, and we are not going with you to the hospital. When you are released, please make plans to live somewhere else because this is more than we can handle."

I suppose this seems cruel, but we had to protect our kids. After her release, she went to California and finally got her wish to live with her "real" mother.

When Tim was almost ready to be born, we had found our way to New Testament Fellowship, the group of believers we thought, at the time, would be our section of the wall for life. I had been a mother for six years. I thought, based on the general ease of managing Jeff and Beth, that I had a handle on this whole child-rearing thing. And then came Tim.

My labor with Tim was the shortest, only sixteen hours. He was delivered by an African-American doctor whose treatment of me was so cold and physically abusive that I contacted the hospital after I got home to lodge a complaint. It was racially based as I had seen his manner with my African-American roommate, and he was completely appropriate with her. By the time I called, only a week or so after Tim's birth, that doctor was no longer employed there, so I must not have been the only one who noticed.

I eventually formed the habit of describing my kids as easy or hard. I had three of each. Becca clearly was hard, not just because of her health issues but because she had determined that she was going to break down her parents' resistance on behalf of her siblings. She often fought us on things based on this principle more than the issue itself. As I have shared, Jeff and Beth were easy. Tim was hard, uber hard.

From an early age, it was a real battle to deal with his determination to do whatever it was he wanted to do. In addition, he had a propensity for screaming when things did not go his way. Serious full-on bloodcurdling screams. You should hear a scream like that echo through a mall.

When he was eight months old, he had decided it would be fun to fiddle with the knobs on the stereo. I would pick him up, pull down the diaper, give him two or three swats, tell him no, and set him down, and he would crawl straight back to those knobs. One day, we went through that scenario *eight times* before he would leave the stereo alone. I remember so many times when I *wanted* to say, "I hate you!" but instead, I said, "I hate what you do!"

During those years, I was a stay-at-home mom with four little kids and no road map. There were times when I would pound the wall to keep from pounding kids. Though I had an instinctive knowledge that I needed to keep the upper hand, I had no framework in principle to aid in the work. Tim was about eighteen months old when I read the book *What the Bible Says about Child Training* by J. Richard Fugate. It may have saved Tim's life. It certainly saved my sanity and my relationship with my little boy.

The book lays out an orderly rationale for the purpose of parenting, which is for parents to train a child in self-control by bringing the child's will into submission to godly authority so that, as an adult, he/she will know how to submit to God. The procedure for training a child's will is a combination of corporal punishment and application of Scripture followed by explanation and reconciliation. Corporal punishment was administered with a paddle that hung on a nail in our living room.

Based on what I learned from this book, I was able to construct a mental process that let me judge a behavior against a clear standard and then respond appropriately. The hardest challenge was to maintain consistency. With Tim, I used to carry the paddle with me everywhere we went.

I am well aware that spanking is out of favor today. Some people want to liken it to child abuse. The way we did it was not abusive. In fact, one of the first principles of the book is that you give a requirement to a child exactly once. If the child does not obey, the process was to quote the Scripture, "Folly is bound up in the heart of a child, but the rod of correction will drive it far from him." Then a couple of swats followed by an explanation of the infraction, what should have happened, and then love and hugs. I freely admit it did not always go this way.

This once-and-done approach has many benefits. There is no endless negotiation. There are no arguments. There is no buildup of irritation toward rage. There is no pounding of walls to keep from pounding children. No sore throat at the end of the day from the yelling. I always knew I had dropped the ball when my throat hurt by bedtime. For the child, the benefit is certain requirements and certain consequences. If she wants to do what she wants to do anyway, she can count the cost by considering what she can be sure will happen.

Much later in life, I had a coworker ask me once with consternation, "Did you *spank* your children?"

I said, "Yes, it's the only thing that made it stop."

"Didn't they mind?"

I was flummoxed. "I don't know. I'll ask them."

When I asked my children if they had minded being spanked, they replied without exception, "No, I always deserved it. But you should ask Tim."

Tim had to be disciplined with the rod of correction very faithfully. Exhaustingly. He was so hardheaded, so easily irritated. When he played in the yard, the neighbor kids tormented him just to hear that earsplitting scream. I would go out and collect him and bring him in and administer correction. We were trying to teach him self-control, and screaming is not that. I used to scold the kids outside.

"Why do you do that? You know when you make him scream I have to bring him in and spank him!"

The only time my dad ever questioned my child-rearing was what I did with Tim. When we were kids, it was the fashion to ignore temper tantrums. He said to me once, "If you just ignore him, he'll stop."

I replied, "Dad, it doesn't say anything in the Bible about ignoring sin." He stayed out of it after that.

Sensitive skin was an issue in my siblings and also in some of my children. For Tim, it was a particular challenge. He was troubled with eczema quite a bit. I wondered later if that might have contributed to how irritable he was. I guess if you were itchy all over all the time, you'd be irritable too.

He also was the only one of the kids that objected with fury to the application of scripture with his training. I believe in demons, as well as angels, and I feel confident that Satan was at work in Tim until we recognized the issue and took authority over it through prayer.

When I asked Tim if he minded being spanked, his answer was the same as his siblings. The Bible says that the parent who does not discipline his child hates him. It also says that all discipline is hard to go through, but it yields the peaceful fruit of doing right. Tim as an adult is hardworking, not at all ruled by money or things, and kind-hearted. The discipline he received has yielded peaceful fruit. He is another one who had to have stitches because he cut himself carving a pumpkin. Two years in a row.

After Tim, I was ready to call our family complete. Two boys and two girls seemed just right. As I always do, I scouted out a book to help me manage fertility. Thus, began a couple of years of very faithfully taking and charting my temperature every morning to discern ovulation to avoid pregnancy. It worked quite well as I was pretty regular.

When Tim was about eight months old, one night when Jack was on the night shift and I was alone, I clearly heard the Lord speak to my heart.

He said, "You're going to have another child. It will be a son. You are to name him Michael."

I did not say a word to anyone because it was my plan to be done. I did my temperature and marked the chart, and every month, I ovulated on the thirteenth or fourteenth day. So after quite a long time of consistent results, I stopped taking my temperature and just steered clear of those days. It worked great until the month when I ovulated on the seventeenth day.

When I learned I was pregnant, I was not happy. All my pregnancies had been hard on me, and the labors *never* got any easier. Jack was also not thrilled. He was almost forty and starting over again dragged both of us down. I was seven months pregnant before we repented of our poor attitude toward having a fifth child. We sat down together in our living room one day and laid hands on my belly and apologized to God and the baby and asked for forgiveness.

During this pregnancy, I had many prayers raised for me regarding my labor being easier, but I never had any faith that it would happen. And it didn't. It did not help that Michael was born eleven days after his due date and came in at a whopping nine pounds, thirteen ounces. After twenty-two hours, he was born by Cesarean.

Interestingly, while I recovered at the hospital, someone came in and asked if they could take a picture of him for a nursing textbook. They placed his little bed next to the bed of an African-American little boy who had been born weighing four to five pounds at thirty-six weeks. The point was to show how the size of full-term babies can be very different. Mike made almost two of that little boy.

Mike was interesting in that he was the only one of our kids who really had a preference in terms of who he loved the most. For his first few years, he really loved me. I so enjoyed that time with him. He was enough younger than Tim that I had a good bit of time with just him. We started to home school in Willoughby when he was about eighteen months old.

During that year of homeschooling, we spent a lot of time with another homeschooling family whose four children mirrored, in age and gender, our four oldest. Maggie and I also sang together at church. We were at their house one day. They had installed a wood-stove in front of the living room fireplace for supplemental heat, and once again, I watched a child inexplicably walk up to a very hot thing and put hands to it.

Poor Michael. At the doctor's office, they had me keep his hands immersed in ice water while they decided what to do. To distract him, I was asking him the sounds that different animals make. You know, what does the cow say, *moo*, and all that.

Then I asked, "What does a bunny say?"

He did not miss a beat. "What's up, doc," he replied. He was two years old.

Sometime around that time, I was sitting out on our front steps. Mike walked up to the taxus bush beside me, plucked off a few of the berries, and popped them into his mouth. Taxus is poisonous. So I called poison control and, as instructed, administered ipecac. Now the thing to know about ipecac is that it is not a sure thing regarding when it will take effect. So I put Mike in the tub and let him play there until he threw up. I pulled him out and took him to get cleaned up and dressed. When I came back, there in the tub drain, right next to the remains of the berries, were two marbles. Well…

When we moved to Leroy, we were able to send the four older kids to the Lutheran school in Painesville for a couple of years. I took over the management of the school library on a volunteer basis for those years. They had given us quite a break on tuition, so I felt I owed them what I could do to help. Michael would go with me to the school and hang out with me while I worked. He was less than three when we started this practice, and I still remember him leaning back in the big librarian's chair, crossing his feet, and saying, "It's so nice to relax in a comfortable chair." I just stared. Less than three!

I am not sure Mike ever forgave me for having Abby. It would be interesting to ask. He was four when she surprised us, and I think it was just hard on him not to have me to himself anymore. In addition, having her caused me to have to give up the part-time cleaning I did to pay the school tuition, so it meant that we were back to home-schooling. For the next fourteen years, homeschool was my career.

Right around that time, we embarked on one of our attempts to have a dog. We got a black lab mutt, and that dog attracted fleas like it was her job. The house was soon infested. We didn't have the handy little drops on the back of the neck back then. We had insecticide bombs you fogged the house with, and we did. Two days later, Becca started having trouble breathing. She literally could not walk down the steps without stopping to catch her breath.

I called the doctor to tell them we had a problem, and they started to tell me I could bring her in the afternoon.

"No, you don't understand. She *can't breathe*. I am just calling to let you know we are coming *right now*."

After several hours of tests and breathing treatments, our doctor decided to send her to Rainbow Babies and Children's Hospital in an ambulance. Rainbow is big guns territory.

Becca was eleven, and though she had always been kind of allergy prone, she had never had asthma. But now she was in the middle of a full blown, life-threatening asthma attack.

She ended up being in the hospital for a couple of days until her breathing was restored and stabilized. The weird thing is it's the only asthma attack she ever had. I am pretty convinced it was caused by the flea bomb. Sheesh.

When I began to suspect I was pregnant yet again, my husband said those fateful words husbands are *never* supposed to say, "How could you let this happen?" Yes, he did. "You were there," I replied after overcoming a natural inclination to slap him. This time, it was really only a few days before we came to peace about it. I felt the Lord had assured me he would provide for all our needs, and he would take away all my fears. And he did.

In the way of needs, we needed baby stuff because we had given everything of that type away…again. We were done. Our quiver was full. God provided for that need through our friends who were coming to the end of several years of fostering infants. They gave us everything—furniture, clothes, the works.

In terms of fears, we knew, having had a section the last time, that she would be born by Cesarean. I remember when that decision was made. I was about six months pregnant, and my doctor said, "You've had four natural births. Would you like to try going natural?" I looked at him like he was crazy. "I am thirty-six years old. I have gray hair. I want to go into labor, come into the hospital, and have you take the baby out." Seriously, does anyone *want* to endure twenty hours of labor? For the sixth time?

In addition, we began to pray about having my tubes tied since they were going to be in there anyway. We ultimately did that, and let me tell you, even though you have peace about a thing, it doesn't mean it isn't a really big deal. Many times, I had to sit down with myself and work through having made myself *sterile* until I turned forty. For some reason, after forty, I was pretty well over it.

Abby was another of what I would consider an easy baby. It could be it seemed that way because her biggest sister was so happy she was there. It was like having a nanny in the house. Being the littlest by a good bit and kind of having to make a place for herself, she was a pretty forceful little kid. Once when she was about four and her sisters had developed the habit of locking her out of their room, she was leaving the room but paused at the door to say, hands on hips, "And don't even, *even* lock this door, girls!" before stomping out.

A few days before her first birthday, I was with the kids at our homeschool co-op, and Abby was just not acting right. I grew concerned enough that I called the doctor though it was late in the day, and they said I could bring her in. My doctor said, "This is an experienced mother. Let them come."

When we got there, she had a fever and was lethargic but had no ear infection, nothing in her lungs. So we got this little stick/on bag to try for a urine sample. We got the sample, and they started her on antibiotics and sent us home. She did not improve overnight, and in the morning, the doctor's office called to say she had a urinary tract infection, and they wanted her in the hospital. We had to go into Cleveland, something I always find nerve-racking.

Abby ended up being in the hospital for five days, and I had to be with her because she was still nursing. It was awful. The infection was in her kidneys, and the germ was pseudomonas. At the time, it was a thing they said could only be treated intravenously. We would give her Tylenol, and she would throw it up. She had no appetite. They kept doing tests that were so invasive I was afraid she would be scarred for life. Eventually, the vein they were using collapsed, and despite several awful attempts, they could not get another line in. They sent us home with a plan to send a nurse daily to give her a shot of the antibiotic. I wanted to slap them. Had I known we could treat her illness in that way, we'd have been home much sooner. Either way, she recovered. She has never had anything like that again, and no one knows why it happened that one time. It did push her development back by a couple of months, but otherwise, thank you, Lord, it was a onetime thing.

One of her little quirks even until she got pretty old was that she liked to stuff little things into the various orifices on her head. A BB in her ear. A popcorn kernel up her nose. It's *really* hard sometimes to get these things out, and we hauled her to the doctor more than once to deal with it. In the end, it was the BB that cured her. She did *not* like having a waterpik squirted into her ear to flush out a BB.

When our kids were old enough and as opportunity arose, we encouraged them to work. Becca started in junior high by babysitting for my sister for a couple hours every day after school. She was able to help us pay for her braces in that way. She's the only one that had braces. She was a mouth-breather, which lets a kid's teeth get pretty scraggly.

She was the one who taught me that a fourteen-year-old is capable of doing her own laundry. She thought everything she touched had to go into the wash to the point that I told her she could do her own. After I saw how that worked out, they all learned to do their own at around that age.

Jeff did haying in the summer. He also started pretty early with landscaping with a family up the street who had a side business. He was always athletic and competitive. I still remember him out behind the house with a Wiffle ball bat, chunking carpenter bees. Hitting one will give you a good hard *thwack*. He also liked to try to catch these little hovery flies we got every summer with a bare hand.

The kids pitched in every week with cleaning. Everyone learned how to dust and wash windows and clean the bathroom and mop the kitchen and run the vacuum. I had to have household help in order to do school. Over time, I taught them to cook though generally food was something I managed.

Beth's first job was working for a local nursery she could walk to. She had an interest in growing things and had made a garden of wild things in our woods. I think it was a good fit though the lady she worked for was a bit of an odd duck.

Once they were able to drive, several of the kids worked fast food. Mike worked for a small local grocery and then for a hardware store where I had to take him and pick him up. Beth worked in a pro shop for a while. Tim caddied. In fact, Tim's scholarship grew from his caddying for which I am very grateful. Abby went to the local community college for her last couple years of high school and worked at a fabric store near there.

The point of all this is that our kids knew if they wanted some of the things they wanted, there was a good chance they would need to work for them. So they did. I am confident this has led to the good work ethic they all have now.

The kids were homeschooled through the eighth grade and then were enrolled in the local public high school. That way, they were able to grow socially and do extracurricular things to broaden their interests. Some chose sports and some the arts. Choirs and plays and track meets and football games. All but Becca also participated in Leroy softball every summer. One year, five of them were playing. I would go from field to field to try to catch some part of each game.

One really interesting thing is that Beth got to serve as a congressional page. Our local representative put an ad in the paper, and forty kids applied. When I went to turn in her application packet, as I handed it over, I said, "This one is the best." And the office guy gave me a smirky smile. "No, really," I said. "The best." And she was.

She was one of about sixty kids who spent their entire junior year of high school in Washington, working for the 435 members of Congress. And those kids worked. They went to school in the attic of the Library of Congress from six thirty until noon and spent the rest of the day running around for all those congressmen. One of the jobs was to be the door page. That was where you opened the doors for people entering the house floor. When she was going to be the door page, she would call and let me know, so I could watch the house session on cable TV and get a glimpse of her.

Beth's older sister and brother had both been very successful high school students. Both were National Merit Finalists, and both were valedictorian of their class. She wanted to do the same. Our high school gives weighted credit for honors classes, but the congressional page school did not offer honors credit. So in order to stay at the head of her class here, she had to contract to do extra schoolwork in order to earn honors credit to be applied to her local high school credits. And she did it, which allowed her to also be a National Merit Finalist and valedictorian.

The headmaster of the congressional page school, possibly the most exclusive private school in the country at the time, said in his college letter of recommendation for Beth that he would rank her among the top three students he had ever taught. Wow.

She was in Washington the year Bob Dole ran for president, and the picture in her high school yearbook about her service shows her shaking his hand. She had a tough adjustment when she came home because she had been living like a college kid and suddenly she had to be a high school kid again. I asked her once how it was to be back at school. She said, "Well, when you have stayed late in the Republican cloakroom with Majority leader Dick Armey listening to him expound on foreign policy, it's a little hard to be back at Riverside."

As a sidebar, shortly after she came home, we got a phone call. It was during a scandal when it was discovered that the Clinton White House had got hold of some FBI files they had no business having. The guy said he was from the FBI, and that Beth's file was one that turned up at the White House, and he needed to talk to her. Turns out it was a congressman prank calling my daughter. Which was funny but, you know, a little weird.

While in Washington, against explicit instruction from me, she had had her ear cartilage pierced. When I took her for her senior pictures, I suggested she might want to remove the stud for the pictures. She tossed her hair and said, "This is who I am now." She went to twirl the stud in the hole and the top of the earring broke off in her hand.

She turned to me and said accusingly, "You prayed for that!"

"No, I didn't," I replied. "But God knew what I wanted."

About that time, Jeff was being recruited by some pretty nice colleges. He was a decent football player and went to state in track. Add that to his intellectual gifts, and he was a pretty complete package. I know he heard from Yale. He also heard from Carnegie Mellon. These types of schools do not offer athletic scholarships, but they still were interested in him as an athlete. He knew he wanted to be a chemical engineer, so Yale was not too tempting, but the other one... The football coach from Carnegie Mellon kept calling, and Jeff told me he didn't know what to say.

My brother Scott is an electrical engineer and was in the midst of a career with a local chemical company. I called and asked him how big a deal it was in engineering world in terms of where you go to school. He said right out of school, it might help for your first job, but after that, your success depends on how well you do.

The next time the coach called, I had Jeff give me the phone. I asked him what they were offering. Turns out, Jeff would have to go to school for engineering *and* play football *and* have to do work-study *and* would still have to borrow $6000 a year to go there.

So I said, "Coach, my son is the very best our country can produce. He can go to the University of Toledo, where they just finished a brand-new chemical engineering building, for free and be done in four years with no debt. Why would I send him to you to have to work that hard and end up with $25,000 in debt?"

He was a little flustered. "No one goes to Carnegie Mellon for free."

"Then please stop calling us."

I still think it was the right call. Jeff went on to have his senior project entered in a national contest and to come in first. He went straight from school to Avery Dennison and was a plant manager for them before he was forty. I feel like the education he got at UT prepared him adequately for the world of work.

As an aside, he called me once to say he wanted to walk on for football there. I absolutely forbade that. He weighed on a good day, maybe 150 pounds. (He had already had a broken arm when he fell in the gym at school in the sixth grade.) "The first time one of those Division I guys hits you, and you go down on that turf, you will be broken in pieces." He was disappointed but went on to participate in several intramural sports (and in fact managed to break his arm a second time playing touch football. You can't even imagine the complexities of paying doctor bills for a college kid!) Ultimately both he and Beth played lacrosse at UT.

By then, Becca had been at University of Toledo for four years. The three oldest kids all went there on full rides that were then available to National Merit scholars. Becca started out to be a high school history teacher but changed her major to nursing, which made her have to go to school for five years. She eventually became a nursing professor. She is Dr. Burhenne now and is on the national leadership team for one of the largest online nursing schools in the world.

Beth was awarded their presidential scholarship that gave her everything the others got and more, including an overseas trip with the president of the university. At the time, five students out five thousand were presidential scholars. Her major was business related. She also earned an MBA while working and raising a family. She has focused on human resources and currently works in public service. They are so lucky to have her. She got out of corporate executive life because it was too hard to get the work-life balance she wanted for her kids.

When Tim went to college, he went as an Evans scholar. I bet you didn't know that the largest private scholarship program in the country belongs to the Western Golf Association and is awarded to golf caddies. Golf takes care of its own. The scholarship was connected to specific state schools and included full tuition and about half of living expenses, but you had to live in their house. The one at Ohio State was located right near the Greek houses, and the deal was the boys were in charge. As a consequence, the state of cleanliness when I took him to school was about what you would expect. It was pretty hard to leave him in that pestilential abode.

He had to get a job because he needed to earn half of his room cost, all of his food and his books. I have so much respect for how hard Tim worked to earn his theater degree on time. I am pretty sure his share of a room for one semester was *under* the other two bunks. On the floor. Geez…the upside is that he started in restaurants while there, which has turned out to be his career. He has been a bar and restaurant general manager in Chicago for some years now. I don't expect he will ever move back to Ohio.

Mike and Abby both went to school at our local community college. Mike finished at Cleveland State with a degree in sociology. After graduation, he worked in medical sales and now is a logistics manager in Texas for an aerospace manufacturer. As an aside, while he was working in Akron, he briefly lived next door to LeBron James. I guess he and his buds had a party once, and one of the guests threw up in the hedge. LeBron was apparently cool about it. Mike and his wife have a side business making candles and bath products, which he hopes to make his full-time job eventually. He used to do a lot with music, and I am sorry he doesn't anymore. I think he has talent as a songwriter.

Abby has three years of college under her belt, but I don't know if she will ever finish. Now that she is married with a couple of little kids and still has to work full-time, I expect finishing school is pretty far down her priority list. She is a deputy clerk in the Geauga County courts system. That may end up being her career. She is quite artistic and follows that passion at home. She is also active on social media and, in my opinion, really funny.

All of our children are animal lovers, some more than they should be. Between myself and my kids, our family owns eight dogs and, I think, eighteen cats. Yikes!

As each of our children launched into life, Jack and I never really had trouble with empty nest syndrome. There were so many children, and it took so long to rear them. But when Abby got married, suddenly, I was filled with sadness. She and her husband came by the day after the wedding to say goodbye as they were leaving for his home in Virginia the following day. As I looked at them, I realized that the whole of all the good things of life lay before them. The whole of mine lay behind. I grieved the end of my motherhood then. It took quite a while to get over it.

I love being a mother, but I have learned that that does not necessarily translate to being a grandma. I have seven grandchildren, and they all live locally. That said, I am not the good grandma. I'm not the one skyping while they read to me or taking them out a lot (though I am trying to improve in this) or giving them giant stuffed animals. I am the one trying to be a person with them, and with the older ones, I *think* they may see me that way. With the little ones, I sing Jesus songs and scratch their backs and hope, hope, hope that some of this seed planting will grow a little faith plant.

I have tried to teach my grandkids worthwhile things with fairly limited success. In addition, after all I poured into mothering, I do not want to mother my grandkids. I don't really want to babysit a lot, and I am not asked to very often. When I am, I do, but my kids know it's not my favorite thing. I just don't tolerate little kids well anymore. Maybe I blew my wad with mine.

All I ever wanted as a parent and now as a grandparent was to see my dear ones come to faith. Still waiting on that.

On Homeschooling

When we started our family, I'm sure we expected to have a conventional experience. Though I don't remember discussing it, we assumed we would be together for the duration and that we would do the usual things: stable marriage, modest home in a safe neighborhood, and send the kids to public schools. The reality turned out to be quite different.

As our spiritual journey took us closer to what we thought God wanted from his people and as we held the devolution of American culture up to that standard, we began to worry for our children. We tried for six years to work within the public schools, but eventually the dissonance between them and us became unfixable.

In the last year our kids attended public school, our three oldest children were in first, third, and fifth grades. We were in the school eight times that year to discuss issues where we felt the schools were undermining our religious values.

For example, in the first-grade class, the teacher chose to read *James and the Giant Peach* to her class. The story begins with a little boy seeing his parents killed by zoo animals. Really? The fifth-grade teacher had a personal connection to substance abuse through a family member so spent an inordinate amount of class time focused on it to the point that ten-year-olds were learning just how all those nifty drugs work. It felt like laying the groundwork for future abuse. That year the school district brought in an outside family planning organization to teach the "maturation unit" again to ten-year-olds. When we spoke up at the parent meeting to object to an abortion provider being held up as someone to turn to for this type of information, we were told by an administrator, "Frankly, I don't think most parents care." The implication was "It's too bad for those of you who do." Under another program, all the kids in school were going to be required to stand up and declare, "I now believe education is the most powerful force in the universe." Uh…no. Our kids really began to object to being pulled out of class for so many activities, and we didn't blame them. We came to recognize that the world-view of these educators was so fundamentally different from ours that despite everyone's best intentions, there could be no end to the stuff they would do that we objected to.

On top of all that, the teaching method used to teach Beth how to read was destroying her. Beth is left-handed, and I have observed there can be a correlation between handedness and reading problems. At home, she had once written the entire alphabet backward, both letters and the order they belong in. Written English is a sound-based language as opposed to, say, Chinese or hieroglyphics, which are picture based. Reading English can be taught very easily; it is basically the right sounds in the right order. But our so-smart educators had decided to use a picture-based approach instead of phonics. A child had to memorize the entire language in the look-say method. Beth was drowning. She would stay in at recess to try to finish work that she struggled with. She declared once, quite stoutly, "Everyone in this family likes to read, but I don't!"

I replied, "You don't have to like to read. But you have to know how to do it."

Part of the impetus to homeschool was to save our little girl.

The year was 1986. Homeschool was just entering the awareness of educators. They usually assumed parents were not equipped to educate their children. There was also a lot of talk about whether homeschooled kids would be adequately socialized. I guess life in a multigenerational neighborhood or attending Sunday school and church don't count. As we began to explore homeschooling, we also became aware that there would be legal implications to taking this step.

Back then, there was no apparatus in place in law around home-school. The law was that children were compelled to attend school, for good reason. In the past, children sometimes had to go to work at an early age and compulsory education protected them from that.

Lawmakers were not prepared for the possibility that parents would want to educate their kids themselves. In Ohio, every school district could do what it wanted regarding home education. As a result, though I do not have a degree, our school district did not object to our plans or interfere with us in carrying them out. In the same school year, our friends in the Cleveland schools were taken to court despite the degree in education held by the mother. In legal terms, this is chaos.

Thank God for the Home School Legal Defense Association. Homeschoolers all over the country joined together under the protection of this organization. We not only received legal help when harassed by rogue districts, but this organization also worked tirelessly, for years, to get state governments to write laws codifying how homeschoolers were to be treated. We joined every year that we homeschooled, long after Ohio law was settled, because we believed in helping other homeschoolers enjoy the freedom to rear their children as they saw fit. Getting to meet, shake hands with, and thank founder Michael Farris was a real moment for me.

The practical effect of choosing homeschool is that, at the moment when the cost of obtaining teaching materials falls on a family, one parent is completely removed from the workforce. Opportunity cost is a big factor in choosing to homeschool.

In Ohio, homeschoolers were required to teach certain subjects and to have their children independently assessed annually to assure they were learning. We chose to have our kids take standardized tests since we knew we planned to enroll them in public school in the ninth grade. In order to do this, we had to find a certified teacher willing to administer the tests. Special thanks to Mrs. Beifuss for helping us with this for so many years.

Some of the subjects we had to teach, such as art, music, and physical education could be hard to get done in a homeschool setting. We might go to a nearby parcourse or go sledding. I would look at art books with the kids or play classical music and visit museums. We did piano lessons and the kids played softball. A couple of them sang for a while in a local children's choir. For a couple of years, we participated in a homeschool co-op where we met at a local church and different moms taught different specialized things. I taught Ohio history. My kids had a shop class at the co-op and built wooden projects.

Eventually, sometime in the early nineties, I decided to take it a step further. I called a local roller rink and worked with them to set up a regular homeschool skate. This let the kids socialize as well as learn a fun skill while helping the venue with a new income stream. I also contacted the local YMCA. They created a homeschool gym and swim class. As far as I know, local homeschoolers are still participating in these activities.

I would like to take a moment to talk about socializing and homeschool. I feel that this is actually a reasonable concern. I have been around families that did not take this issue seriously enough, and it is my opinion that they did not do their kids any favors. It is easy to declare (somewhat self-righteously) that we do not want our kids socialized by an apostate culture, but at some point, kids grow up and become responsible for themselves. I feel parents have an obligation to be sure they are not throwing their kids into the deep end unprepared.

I have also been around parents who did not take actually educating their kids seriously enough too. One of the hardest things about homeschooling is when you have to accept that this is what you do. It is your work—your career as it were. Anything less is a disservice to your children and the wider homeschool community.

We chose to use materials from multiple sources to do the actual schooling. Even as early as 1986, there was enough homeschool material available to make a novice feel utterly overwhelmed. I thought I would have a classroom and actually bought retired school desks for that purpose. I set up the classroom in the basement, but, in the end, everyone did their work in their rooms or at the dining room table.

I used a Life Pac system for most of our work. These were self-contained workbooks that taught and then tested different subjects within the book itself. I used Saxon for math. Saxon is not overtly Christian but, in my opinion, is simply really good math taught in a really good way. Years later, on the school board, I was able to persuade the district to give Saxon a try. We also went to the library a lot and, as I have shared elsewhere, I read to the kids frequently. The things I chose to read were based on my own interests and my desire to expose them to ways of thinking and acting that conformed to our belief about how people should behave in this world.

The nuts and bolts of how we did school consisted of me making sure a child could read and understand the basics of math. From there, they were mostly self-taught. I had an assignment book, and every morning, they got their assignments and turned them in when they were done. I graded the work every day so I could catch it if they missed or misunderstood something. After grading, I would write down the following day's assignments. We were usually done by around noon after which they could do whatever they wanted. I gave the kids regular report cards. I wanted them to be prepared for the accountability they would encounter later.

I did not have a lot of trouble teaching the younger kids to read. As I have shared, all my kids are very bright. I did have to adjust my approach based on personality, though, and over time I was able to do this. The first year we homeschooled, I was full of enthusiasm and excited for the adventure. By November, I was pretty burned-out. That's when I learned what I shared above. I had to adjust my attitude to the long haul. The long haul ended up covering seventeen school years, two of which were spent at a Lutheran school in Painesville when I cleaned houses to earn tuition. The rest was mine to do and I did it.

One thing I never did through all those years was to ever encourage or exhort others to homeschool. If someone made that choice, I was always available to help. But I would never hold homeschool up as a must-do for anyone. It's just too hard. Anyone who says differently is not being honest or is not dealing with the sort of strong-willed children Jack and I raised.

At the end of the day, we resorted to homeschool to try to protect our kids and to try to pass on our faith to them. I feel that the protecting aspect was worth everything because they were ultimately able to withstand many of the worst temptations available to kids then. As far as faith goes, as I have shared elsewhere, when a parent is done, the baton of responsibility before God passes to the child. Now it's on them.

This is my first grade school picture. I remember that blouse was red satin with white polka-dots and the jumper was blue denim.

Jack with Santa. What a sweet and pleasant little boy.

Jack at boot camp.

This picture of me was taken in the kitchen of our
first apartment in the summer of 1974.

Jack—same place, same time.

Our family on July 6, 2005. Clockwise from lower left; Rebecca, Michael, Abigail, Elizabeth, Timothy, Jeffrey. Jack and I in the center.

Rebecca and her two children, Cora and Alex.

Jeff and his wife, Kim.

Beth and her husband, Kevin.

Beth and Kevin's family—from left; Audrey, Kevin, Noah, Lauren, Beth.

Our Tim.

Mike and his wife, Krystal.

Abby and her husband, Brett.

Abby and Brett's kids, Ruby and James.

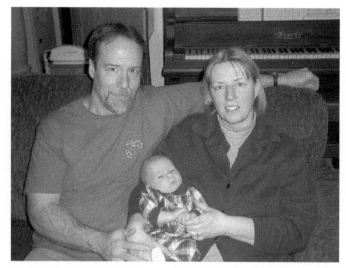

Jack and I with our first grandchild, Noah. He is now older
than I was when I got married. How can that be?

The Bolivia team ready to present a mime. Jack and I are in the front
and Mike is just behind us. Not sure why everyone was making faces.

My day in London.

One of the few times we could gather everyone together at one time.

This is the professional photo I had done for use on my campaign
literature when I ran for county commissioner in 2012.

Jack and I on Christmas in 2006. After that, most
family photos got trapped in phones.

On Mental Health

There is an issue with mental health in my family. I'm not sure why, but having been a genealogy hobbyist since my twenties, I see it running like a thread through the tapestry of our history. It sometimes manifests as suicide.

My grandfather died when I was nine years old. It was the first time I saw someone who was dead. I remember standing by the casket and looking at him and noting a smudge of makeup on the earpiece of his glasses and thinking that was strange. I was in my twenties before anyone told me that he had died by his own hand. He had gone down in the basement of the little house in Chagrin and shot himself.

Family members have speculated about what drove him to such an act. Was it the pain from breaking his back in a tractor accident so many years before? Was it fear of losing independence due to a traffic stop the day before?

Many years later, during my time directing the Geauga County Archives, I had the opportunity to look at the file on his suicide among the coroner's records. I did it alone one day after everyone had gone home. In the sadly slim little folder, there was a slip of paper with a nearly unreadable scrawl addressed to the "Boys." His message to his sons (interestingly, not his wife) was essentially that he just couldn't take it anymore. Whatever that meant to him in that desperate hour.

I was told my grandmother had not been that kind to him in life but wept over his grave many times in his death. I don't know if that's true. I can say now that widowhood is upon me, and I am talking to others similarly afflicted, very often, we are flooded with guilt, as well as sadness once our dear ones are gone. I guess there's a lesson to be learned here. As cliché as it is, it's pretty smart to be good to the ones we love while we can.

The day he died, it was my father who ended up cleaning the basement. After this event, my dad, the youngest of the boys, began to act strangely. He became paranoid and obsessed about keeping the doors and windows of our house locked. Finally, one Saturday, whatever was tormenting him drove him to walk up and down our driveway for several hours. We lived in a postwar subdivision, and our driveway in total was less than seventy-five feet long. Ultimately, he stumbled into the house and collapsed onto the living room floor. Actually, he fell on me where I sat in front of the TV. In our family, this event was called his nervous breakdown.

Back then, there were not a lot of resources for mental health issues. I remember the neighbors gathering with my mom and every-one trying to figure out what to do for him. You couldn't really go to the hospital. Eventually, he began to see a psychiatrist and to take tranquilizers. I remember he had a little pillbox he carried with him. It was gold and had green faux leather on the top.

As this issue unfolded, I remember standing in our bathroom one day, and my mother freely expressing to me her fears about how we were going to get through what was happening to my dad. I know I said something to her along the lines of, "Don't worry. Everything will be all right." And being fully aware in that ten-year-old moment that this was a reversal of roles.

Eventually things settled out with my dad. My recollection is that through it all, he continued to work and support our family. I'm not sure that's correct though it must be close to right, as I know he did not lose his job. I always thought it was true though and had a lot of respect for my dad for getting through a crisis like that while taking care of us.

When I began to research my family history in my twenties, I learned that there is also suicide in my father's mother's family. Her grandfather and uncle both killed themselves. One hung him-self from a bedpost, which, when you think about, must take a lot of resolve. The other walked out into the woods and shot himself. Much later, two of my first cousins died untimely. One died of a drug overdose, so it is fair to question whether he did it on purpose or not. The other straight-up shot himself.

Knowing these things and especially what I experienced with my father's nervous breakdown has led me to two actions. The first was to warn my children early and often that there is a weakness in this area in our family and to be wary of it. Jack also had a tendency toward inordinate worrying, which added that element along with my family black hole. I have seen anxiety as an issue in my kids and grandkids. But times are different now, and there is help, and I do think getting ahead of it has been a good thing.

The second thing I did was to choose to stay shallow. By that, I mean I have purposely chosen to avoid plumbing the depths of my own mind and emotions throughout my life. I don't want to fall down the hole. Even so, one time I almost did.

There was a period of several months in Jack's and my marriage that I have always referred to as "that bad time." Since his death, as I have delved into the writings of both Jack and myself, I have come to believe the root of it was unresolved issues from Jack's divorce. I think the trigger may have been the fact that we had entered into a period of unusual closeness and tenderness together. I think getting back into the sort of feelings I imagine he experienced in his first marriage may have taken him right back to that place of pain. I am very confident Satan had a hand in it to steal our joy.

Jack started picking really nasty fights. Every few days, he would start up, go after me, accuse me of thoughts and motives that he said were deep inside me. When I would deny or defend, he would just amp it up more. I needed to confess and repent, but how could I when I did not believe that what he said was true? There were occasions when he made me just about crazy. I can remember retreating to the woods once and banging my head against a tree. I pounded my head against the wall in our bedroom once too. It got to where I could not think straight about myself. "If I am what he says I am, then everything I think I know about myself must be wrong, and maybe I don't really know God at all and…" I know that I began to think of ways of harming myself. He was driving me mad.

One Saturday, unfortunately in front of the kids, he started up again, and I reached a breaking point. I felt all my strength just drain out of me, and I collapsed on the floor. I couldn't even get up. He picked me up by the back of my belt and dragged me into our bedroom. I believe this was my moment of nervous collapse, and I know I was standing on the edge of the black hole down inside myself.

It was the weirdest thing. That day, he talked and talked, but the only thing he said that I remember was something along the lines of "this is never going to change, so I am just going to stop." I don't know what he meant because I never knew what he was trying to accomplish with these fights. He seemed kind of resigned; he almost shrugged. But he did stop.

That was the end of "that bad time." Just in time, I think or I might have actually hurt myself. A few times during these fights, I was driven to tear at my hair. I think he thought this was just being dramatic. No, he was literally driving me crazy. And ever after, in certain circumstances, I could be sent immediately into self-harm mode. Kind of like how flesh, once frostbitten, is so much more sensitive to cold. My psyche was sensitive to that stimulus, and I really had to be careful to stay mentally healthy. I have come to believe he may have had the same kind of frostbitten tenderness that caused him to return to "you're just-like-Mary" mode repeatedly during our marriage when events took us close to that broken place.

So I have been to the edge of the black hole down inside myself and looked into the abyss, and I never want to go there again. That is why I say I am shallow. I want to stay up in the sunlight.

On Public Service

I had the privilege of working in public service for twenty-four years. My public service started when I was a forty-year-old homeschooling mother of six who decided to run for the school board. My desire to do so was precipitated by two things. In reading the local paper, it became obvious to me that the local board at that time was in total disarray. At the same time, the state board of education had begun to work toward a policy shift to something called "Outcome Based Education" that sounded perfectly fine until you drilled down into what it really meant, which was not good.

My local school board had obviously been in trouble for a while because I remember telling Jack two years before that I wanted to run. He thought Abby, at two, was too young for me to start outside work. By two years later, it was clear things were even worse. In fact, the hopelessly split board had had one member flip to the other side and vote to non-renew the superintendent's five-year contract just a couple of months after voting to grant it. That one vote eventually cost the school district about $500,000 by the time they bought out the old guy and hired on the new one. The community was very unhappy.

That spring, when I learned about the state's OBE educational plans, my friend Judie Keller and I began to hold parent meetings to try to let people know about this threat. Education was going to expand to encompass not just factual learning but emotional as well. The school mission would include becoming a "one-stop shop" for all social services. The school would decide what a child should know and be like. For people like us, this was not acceptable.

We decided to circulate a petition and ask other parents to join us in letting state government know of our concerns. We gathered three thousand signatures in three weeks under the auspices of something we called Ohio Freedom 2000 since we couldn't do it under "Judie and Linda." Ohio Freedom 2000 got noticed big time and was even mentioned in the National Education Association's national newsletter. It was a little embarrassing, when asked, to have to reply to "What is Ohio Freedom 2000?" with the words, "Uhh, Judie and Linda." We presented the petition to our local state rep at a large public meeting to address OBE. I am fairly certain it went straight to his wastebasket afterward. But the effort did launch both Judie and me into elected service as we both ended up running for our local school boards that fall.

Judie was a nineteen-year-veteran teacher, and her district was running smoothly, so she was clearly qualified and in a normal election cycle. My experience was quite different because I was running in a district that was in serious turmoil. Three and a half of five seats were up for the election and eleven people ran. In political terms, that's a scrum.

I had never been active in politics, except as a voter. And as a voter, I had always assumed people in office were qualified to be there. I will never forget when Judie and I went to our first political event. As I listened to the speakers and how inept and possibly not very smart they sounded, I thought, *No wonder things are so messed up.*

As I began attending the meetings of my local school board, the true depths of the dysfunction became apparent. Large numbers of interested citizens were attending the meetings, a sure sign of trouble for any board. The board was hopelessly split, and there was one board member who would get so upset that she would jump up and run out in tears in the middle of a meeting. People began to talk to me about the underlying shenanigans around the district to the point I began to wonder if maybe I actually lived in Peyton Place.

As I began my campaign, I figured the best way to proceed was to gather the people who wanted to help me and bring in somebody who knew what to do. I called a young man from our church who had experience in this area, and he came to my house to speak to my group. We learned about distributing literature, putting up signs, holding fundraisers, and sending mailings daily to those who had requested absentee ballots. Running for office is work!

Because there was so much discord in our district, various groups sponsored six candidate forums that fall. Six! The first was held at a church and sponsored by some of what I call school groupies. They are the parents who show up to help and seem like they don't want to question any school decisions. The purpose of this first gathering was to let the candidates know there were too many of us, and some needed to drop out or the vote would be so divided that the incumbents would be reelected. That was something everyone in the room (except the incumbents) agreed should not happen. Because all they knew about me was that I was a homeschooling homemaker, I'm sure I was high on the dropout list in the groupies' eyes.

The format of that event was to simply go around the candidates and let each introduce him or herself and say a little bit about what they would want to accomplish on the board. I spoke about OBE and fiscal responsibility, which seemed appropriate given the district was facing a deficit of more than $1 million. At the end of the evening, the hostess (more about her later) wrapped up by saying, "And Mrs. Burhenne turned out to be much more articulate than I expected." Is that the definition of a backhanded compliment? Needless to say, no one dropped out.

As the parade of campaign events marched on, the target on my back got bigger and bigger. Even though my children attended public school for high school, and in fact, my eldest child had graduated the year before as valedictorian and National Merit Finalist, I was considered an outsider and my faith-based home schooling an affront and disqualifier. I just kept talking about OBE and fiscal responsibility.

There was a pair of ladies who attended every event and sat right in front. At every opportunity, during audience questions, they would ask, "Mrs. Burhenne, how can you possibly be responsible for the elementary schools when your children do not attend them?" Seriously, I wasn't even the only candidate without kids in the elementary schools.

I would explain that our decision to homeschool was based on our desire to pass our religious convictions to our children, and that we enrolled them into public school in the ninth grade at a time we thought they would be able to handle peer pressures. Over and over, same ladies, same question.

At one forum, a well-bearded old guy shouted out, "Well, what religion are ya?"

"Uh, Christian."

At another, someone noted I had received a campaign contribution from a local well-known pro-life pastor. "Why would someone like *that* support your campaign?"

The moderator turned to me and said, "You don't have to answer that!"

I said, "No, it's okay. Before he was a pastor, Phil worked for many years with my husband at the Eaton Corp. I guess he just wanted to help me out." It was often fairly hostile, and I always kept my composure.

But the night I caught those same two ladies stealing the campaign literature my sons had just run down the street stuffing into newspaper boxes, I did lose my temper. I chased them down, passed and blocked their car, and jumped out to confront them. As I chewed them out, they stood by open car doors just staring at me like deer in the headlights. Maybe they knew, though I did not, that they could have gotten into a lot of trouble if I reported them. I didn't. But I did call their candidate and let her know to rein them in because, for my sons' sake, they needed to back off. Later that night, I planned to call and apologize for my outburst but did not get the chance. They came to my house and, with tears, apologized profusely for what they had done and actually offered to distribute my last precinct worth of literature. I let them. It reminded me of the scripture where God says he will make your enemies to be your friends.

A couple weeks before the election, the local paper sponsored a televised candidate forum for our district election. The number of candidates was so large, I think we were stacked three high on the platform. The purpose of the forum was to give voters another look at the candidates and issues and to help the paper in making endorsements. The paper ended up selecting me as one of the endorsed candidates.

On the Friday before the election, my phone rang in the middle of our school time. It was the editor of the local paper. He told me the paper had received a letter to the editor that was highly critical of their endorsement of me. Remember the school groupie lady from the first forum? Yeah, she and a former board member signed this missive. The editorial board had sat up until eleven o'clock the night before deciding whether or not to print it. He told me they were going to print it but thought it would only be fair to allow me to respond. He did not tell me much at all about the letter, but he told me I had two hours to drop off eight hundred words. I called the associate editor and asked if he would read me the letter. He did, and it was bruising. They had got hold of letters my husband had written to the high school principal over the years generally critical of public education and painted me with that brush.

I found someone to take the kids and sat down in front of the computer, and I prayed. After thinking and praying, I decided to pretty much ignore the letter and simply lay out what I had done to prepare myself for service on the school board. Things I had learned and what I thought should be done about it. Concerns about OBE and the need for someone on the board with knowledge of it. At the end, I thanked everyone involved and said, "It's been an enlightening experience." It was printed the Sunday before Election Day right next to their letter under the heading, "Most controversial school board election in county history." Really.

On Election Day, I had people holding my signs at every polling place all day long. That night, we met at the home of one of my helpers and had a helper at the school who called the results to us as they came in. Things were analog then, and the tabulation took several hours. I needed to be at least third among the nine running for three open seats. I ran second all evening until the second last precinct to report where I got walloped. I fell to third by only about one hundred votes. The only remaining precinct to report voted in the same location where I had run so poorly. It took about twenty minutes to get the final tally. A very long twenty minutes. When the number finally came in, it showed I had placed third and secured a seat on the school board.

The lady who was at the board of education for me called to say there was a large gathering of school people at a party in a rented space at the fairgrounds. We decided to go. When we arrived, there were a lot of people milling around, including the other people who were elected that night. We circulated around and received many congratulations. The ladies who had stolen my literature were there and were kind enough to say, "You ran a great campaign." The man and lady who wrote the nasty letter to the editor about me also spoke to me. The man had the grace to look a bit shamefaced, and I quickly assured him the campaign was over, and it was time to move forward. The lady didn't seem embarrassed at all.

After a decent amount of time, my friend said, "Well, the only one who hasn't spoken to you is Jane." Jane was the president of the teachers' union at the time. "She's right over there."

Rosetta started toward her and I said, "No, she comes to me, or we don't talk. And she has five minutes."

Rosetta looked at me in surprise. How could I explain to her what I knew by instinct? The position I now held was superior to an employee and should be respected as it represented the will of the people. I had to start out as I meant to go on, and that meant making sure people understood that I understood we all had to respect the position. Not me, per se, but the job. I am happy to say Jane made it over to me, and that began a professional, mutually respectful relationship.

Judie also won her election, and we were soon contacted by the Cleveland Plain Dealer for an in-depth interview at Judie's home. I have never read the resulting full-page story, but that experience taught me some hard lessons about dealing with the media. This reporter quickly established a rapport with us that made us more comfortable than we should have been in light of the generally unsupportive article she wrote. In addition, a photographer was present, and that was how I learned to always smile when there was a camera in the room. If you don't, they will print the least flattering and most menacing view of you they can capture. This article caused me to begin the practice of ignoring most of what was written about me due to its usually being only about 50 percent right. I actually started writing down what I planned to say and giving it to the reporter ahead of a meeting in hopes of being quoted accurately.

That election was a real turning point for our district because none of the incumbents was reelected. Four members of the five-member board would be new upon being sworn in in January. The superintendent who had been hired to replace the ousted one had his work cut out for him.

We were sent to new school board member school sponsored by the Ohio School Boards Association. Know who runs that organization? Ex-superintendents. Know what they want board members to learn? That "micromanaging" is very evil, and the only job of board members is to make policy and to hire and evaluate the superintendent and treasurer. My view was always, "If that is true, then why do we have to vote on everything else?"

When I went to my first board meeting, I carried a notebook on whose cover I had written some Scriptures to guide me. Don't think more highly of yourself than you ought. Treat others the way you want to be treated. The one who would lead must be the servant of all. Let there be no corruption found in you. Do your work as if you're doing it for God. Avoid the appearance of evil. I used that notebook for years and tried hard to model my service on those biblical principles.

I quickly learned how naive I had been to think I could go to a budget discussion with a pad of paper and a pen on which to write everything we could cut from a budget in deficit. After eight hours, the pad was bare. They had answers for why everything had to be in that budget. *Had* to. Cutting was not an option, only levies.

I also soon learned to verify everything told to me because *everyone* lied to me at one time or another. When I went to outside sources to determine if what I had been told was true and learned it wasn't, I always went back to that person and told them. For example, "You have to stop saying we will be in receivership if the levy doesn't pass. I have talked to the state, and it's not true."

My first year on the board, I wanted to attend the OSBA annual convention, but there was no money in the budget for the trip. I paid my own way, which was quite a sacrifice for a family with the financial resources we had at the time. But that was why I had run, to get to go through doors that regular citizens can't. When the district's law firm found out I would attend, they sent me a very fancy invitation to dine with them; I'm talking steak and lobster. I wrote back saying thank you, and I would not dream of accepting such an invitation. In fact, during the entirety of my time in elected service, I did not allow anyone to pay for so much as a meal for me. Avoid the appearance of evil.

One of the hardest people to deal with as a school board member at that time was the treasurer. He was not very qualified, having been a middle school science teacher and a school board member before becoming the CFO of a $20 million business. He actually told us in a training meeting that he wasn't very good at math! He was at the heart of some of the worst gossip in the district, and he had aligned himself firmly with one cohort of employees, causing the other to resent and mistrust him. He was also closely allied with the lone remaining holdover from the old board.

One of the things that had to change was the practice begun by the prior board of allowing him to function as both the treasurer and the business manager. When we removed business manager duties from him, we allowed "his" people to meet with us to air their objections. They couldn't understand why the guy with the purse should not also be the guy who decides what to spend. Then I held up for them pages from Ohio state law that *specifically forbids* this practice for obvious reasons. It was literally against the law. Their response? "But it works so well!"

We had told him on multiple occasions that we did not want him to present new information to us during a meeting. We wanted to be able to review everything ahead of time, yet he continued to hand us new material at meetings. Once he gave us a "report" that he had handwritten on a legal pad and photocopied. It contained a large mathematical error. When I noted the error during a meeting, I'm pretty sure how I felt showed on my face. At his next opportunity, he told me that the audience was able to read our faces, and I should be much more careful about my facial expressions. I remember thinking as he lectured me, "You *do* know I am 20 percent of your boss, right?"

One night, a day or two before a meeting, I received a phone call from the man who was then the board president. He told me he was thinking of making a motion of nonrenewal of the treasurer's contract, which had about eighteen months left on it. He had consulted OSBA about proper wording. He felt it would be good to give the treasurer plenty of time to find another job. I immediately said I would support him but advised him not to make the motion unless he was sure it would pass.

The following night at the end of a long meeting and in front of an audience of about fifty people, the board president offered the motion. Jack was there that night and heard the union president lean to the lady next to her and say, "Did they just do what I think they just did?" I was sitting next to the treasurer, and when he heard the motion, he made a little grunting sound. Our practice was that the treasurer would call the roll for all votes, but he declined to do it. The superintendent called the roll. The vote was three in favor, one abstention and one no—that vote belonging to the holdover from the old board. The motion passed.

The no voter who was the treasurer's ally began to express her strong disagreement with this action. Actually, she yelled at us, including a bit of colorful language and name-calling. Then she jumped up and threw her satchel full of papers onto the table so that it spilled across and onto the floor. Then she shouted, "And furthermore, I resign!" and stalked out of the meeting room. There was a stunned silence.

One of my fellow board members calmly turned to the superintendent and said, "Don't we have to vote to accept her resignation?"

My only thought in that moment had been, *When you do the right thing, God rewards you*, because this board member had not been easy to work with. To her credit, she really meant it and never showed up at any event I attended.

One of the real challenges during the first couple years of my public service was for Jack to figure out his place in the whole thing.

At first, he came to all the meetings, critiqued everything I did, and blurted things out in meetings that were confidential. Now I talked to him all the time about the work because I did need his input on some things, but when I was taken aside by the board president and cautioned about his behavior, we really had to talk. Once he stepped back and let me do my job, of course, things were smoother, but I think he always felt he had to guide and direct my thinking on everything.

In particular, he once required me to write a letter to the editor about an issue in Judie's school district, something I felt was not my place. He was *very* insistent that I was like Esther, in my position for just such a time, who knew things that the public needed to know, and I was the one to tell it. I did write the letter and got a call of protest from the president of the neighboring board. It was not a comfortable position to be in.

I used to say if he thought he should be in charge of the job, he should run for it. He always said that he did not have the personal qualities that it took to run for office, and I did. Yet he often left me feeling that I wasn't really meeting his expectations in this area. Still, I forged on and still believe I did a credible job.

One of the things we did that was not the norm was to meet with the guiding committee of the teachers' union at their union hall. This had never been done before. I was board president at the time and had been in a meeting with the union president during which, in a side bar, she said to me in a challenging way that, of course, I would never think of meeting with their committee. Our board met with anyone who wanted to meet with us. So I said, of course, I would meet with the committee. She seemed surprised but set it up. One of my fellow board members learned of my plan to meet with them and insisted on going with me. I'm glad he did because I really had had no idea the group was comprised of upwards of thirty people. These meetings were done quarterly for some time and mostly consisted of them telling us about things that bothered them while we tried to fix what we could or explained why we couldn't. I remember one in which one of the squeakier wheel guys was kind enough to say, "You know, we know that realistically, there's probably not much you can do about these things, but it means a lot that you came here and listened." It wasn't long after that that the union declined to have us back.

One initiative of which I am justly proud was mine. We began to ask the administration to develop a semester course in consumer economics. We wanted kids to come out of school knowing what a checking account is and how to balance it, what's the difference between buying and leasing a car, what kinds of insurance there are and why we need it, how credit cards and debit cards work. We wanted them ready to be independent adults. We got a lot of resistance from the administrators on this, but eventually, we pretty much ordered them, and they did it. And we wanted all students to *have* to take it in order to graduate. It is my understanding that school districts around the state are now requiring similar courses.

While I was board president, I once sat in on a negotiating session with representatives from our bus drivers' union. They were not happy with the health insurance, and as the union rep laid out their objections, it became clear she had not understood what had been presented. At the end of her presentation, she concluded by saying, "We're done here!" The assistant superintendent in attendance acted like he was prepared to wrap up, and I literally jabbed him in the ribs and whispered, "She just doesn't understand. Explain it to her!" He sighed and just about rolled his eyes, but he got up and explained it again. This time, they got it, and we were able to conclude the contract. Why would you have to be told to do that? That night, the president of that union called my home to thank me. "If you hadn't been there, we would not have gotten this done."

One day, a voter called me and said she had been told by a teacher that he had not had a raise in eight years. She wanted to know if that was true. I went to the treasurer and asked for a list of that teacher's salary for the past eight years. I got the information and wrote it down to give to the voter. His salary had gone from about $36K to about $53K during the eight years in question.

Public employee salaries are a public record and available to anyone who wants to know. It did not seem right to me to have given the information to a member of the public without informing the teacher in question. As this teacher always attended board meetings, I decided to give him a copy of what I had given to the voter. On it, I wrote, "You told a citizen you had not had a raise in eight years. I was asked if this was true. This is the information I gave her." He went nuts.

When the union president arrived at the meeting, he dragged her outside the room's glass doors, and I saw a lot of yelling and arm waving. After the meeting, she came up to me so angry she was almost spitting.

"You have violated state law! You have violated the contract! You have…" You get the gist.

I stepped back and said, "I don't think I've done any of those things, and I am going to walk away now because I'm not going to have you talk to me in this way." I walked away. Later, I told the superintendent what I had done, and he almost snorted with laughter.

"You haven't done anything wrong," he assured me.

I already knew that, but it was nice to hear.

One time I think I made a difference was in a conversation the board had one night with administrators regarding an employee who was retiring due to health issues. The superintendent wanted to give him a lump sum payout that he did not qualify for under the contract. He told us that the man would probably die as soon as that summer. As we went around the room, I could see the other members of the board were leaning toward being compassionate and giving him the bucket of money. When they came to me, I said, "You know, if this was my money, I would be happy to give it to him. But it's not. It's the taxpayers' money, and he does not qualify to receive it. I think that doing this will set a precedent that is very unwise." As a result of my words, the board chose not to proceed.

Here's how they got around it. They went to the board member who seemed softest on this and worked with him to create a super specific policy (I came to call it the John Smith [not his real name] policy) in order to make the gift. The policy passed 3/2, and the payout was made. The man, as far as I know, is still alive today. That is not the way to make policy.

I spent eight years on the school board. In those eight years, our board took a $1 to $2 million dollar deficit and turned it into a $5 million dollar carryover without raising general fund taxes. One of the main ways we did it was through the cooperation of all the union employees in accepting a couple of years of salary freezes. We repaired buildings, set up a bus buying rotation plan, got the pit in the high school parking lot paved, and brought together disparate volunteer groups to cooperate on building a field house for the district. We hired a firm to help us formulate a plan to keep all the buildings in good repair for the next twenty years. And we actually read it and challenged a number of the conclusions; something you could tell this firm found surprising. We restored faith in the board and administration.

At the end of my second term, I decided to run for township trustee instead of another school board term. Part of the reason was because I feel that in eight years, you have done about what you can, and you begin to lose your edge. In addition, I liked the work, but the school board pay was less than $2,000 per year while a trustee earned more than $10,000. Still not stellar pay but not bad for a part-time job. Once again, I was looking to be part of fixing a not-great situation.

In my township, there was a lot of unrest and lack of trust among citizens toward the leadership at that time. There was a group called Leroy Citizens for Quality Government that made life for the township kind of challenging. They videotaped the meetings, published their take on trustee decisions, followed township employees around, and questioned their work. It did not help that there was an obvious issue with nepotism, and that the four key elected positions had been in the same people's hands for a long time. The longest serving trustee had finally decided to step down so that there was an open seat. Since the incumbent would almost certainly retain his seat (in fact, he is still there today), that meant that six people were effectively vying for the one seat that was open.

As before, I immediately began attending trustee meetings and educating myself about the issues. I had signs and literature printed. And I decided to go door to door to all the registered voters in the township. There are about one thousand homes in Leroy, so it was quite a task. I began in July and kept on until the day before the election. At a candidate forum, I told the audience I was doing these visits. A week later, I knocked on a door, and the lady who answered said, "When you said you were knocking on all our doors, I leaned over to my husband and said she hasn't knocked on our door."

"Well, here I am," I replied. That is such a Leroy moment!

Once again, I was blessed by God to serve as an elected official. I served three terms as a trustee. The day after I was elected, I went over to the township office at the fire station. I asked the lady who was the longtime fiscal officer where the book was.

She said, "What book?"

I said, "The book that tells you how to be a trustee." Because there is always a book that lays out the duties and responsibilities of an elected position.

After I read the book, I went back to her with some questions regarding how we were performing these duties. As it happened, one of the issues was something the Leroy Citizens for Quality Government had been banging on the board about, and she got mad. "I know the president of the Leroy Citizens gave you money for your campaign, so I suppose you have to do what he says," she said.

And that was the one time in my service to Leroy that I got mad at a coworker. "Now you listen to me, no one tells me how to do this job, except God and my husband!"

Nepotism was a real issue in Leroy. There were two employees in the road department. One was the son of the fiscal officer and the other the son of one of the trustees. They were good guys and did their work, but no wonder people were suspicious. It was that way when I got there, and it was still that way when I left. I will say that the fiscal officer called me one day to say they were looking for summer help and asked if I wanted to send my son over! I declined. Avoid the appearance of evil.

The first time it snowed after I was elected, I looked out my front window and saw my driveway had been plowed. I called the road department and asked if they had plowed my driveway, and they had. I thanked them for plowing and said, "Please don't ever do that again." They didn't.

Over time, we were able to come together as a good working unit and get people to see we were doing the best we could with the limited resources available to township government. I was placed in charge of zoning and recreation. In those roles, I spearheaded the first update of the comprehensive plan in some years. I attended every recreation board meeting and every event, every zoning board and zoning appeals board meeting, every comprehensive plan committee meeting. So many meetings...I got the trustee board to start using meeting agendas. We started to have employee evaluations and job descriptions. The zoning inspector quit immediately after his first employment evaluation, not because he got a bad review, but because he was so insulted that we would dare to evaluate him at all. That is so Leroy.

I also wrote a Community Development Block Grant, Leroy's first, and secured $90,000 with which we built a large community meeting room as an addition onto the fire station. It was done as an addition in order to avoid having to build a commercial septic system. It was also built with almost all volunteer labor, for which we had to get special permission from HUD as one of the goals for CDBG grants is to give work to minority and women-owned businesses. Before I left my service with Leroy, I also secured $15,000 of state capitol budget money through a couple phone calls to a state rep and state senator I knew. It was used to help save and refurbish a dilapidated historic building, the South Leroy Meeting House.

Not too long after I took on the zoning department, it came to our attention that a member of the Zoning Board had had an interaction with a citizen in which he gave incorrect information apparently to benefit himself. I asked him to attend the next trustee meeting and to stay after the regular meeting was over. I told him that we knew what he had done, and that he should never do that again. Being a mother of boys, I could tell by his attitude and swagger as he headed toward the door that he had not received this reprimand as intended.

"If anything like this happens again, you will be removed from the board and reported to the prosecutor," I said to his back.

He swung around on one heel and came boiling back up to the trustee table, shouting, "Are you threatening me? Are you threatening me?"

"No," I replied calmly. "I'm just telling you what's going to happen if you do something like this again. Don't do it." I could tell the fiscal officer and the other trustees were a little taken aback by this exchange, but he had to receive the reprimand, or he would have disrespected the office. Apparently, he got the message that time because he called my home later that night to apologize profusely and promised to behave.

An elected office does not ever represent a person; it represents the consent of the governed, the will of the people. It is, in my opinion, paramount that those privileged to hold office remember it's not about them nor respect for them but about requiring respect for the people who put them there to take care of their money and their things.

At one point during my service, we had a female firefighter accuse a male firefighter of sexual harassment. We had to spend $25,000 to investigate the claim while this woman strutted around our fire station, telling anyone who would listen what she was going to do with the money she took from Leroy. The investigation was inconclusive (we were told he passed his lie detector test, and she failed), but that did not prevent her from filing a federal lawsuit.

The lawyer representing OTARMA, our insurance carrier, told us we had to settle. He figured we could be done for $12,000. I was incensed. I said in no uncertain terms that it was wrong to pay her off. But he said it was a cheap price to pay to avoid going to court.

"But it's wrong!"

"This is not a matter of morality," he said smugly. In the most condescending way possible, he informed me that this was how you manage risk.

"No," I replied, "this is how you *create* risk. Every time you pay off a liar, all the other liars line up with their hands out."

"Well, if you don't take this deal, OTARMA will not cover the cost of the suit."

Say what? That's what we have insurance for? To be browbeaten into liar-paying "risk management"? These are the kinds of things that drive good people right out of elected service. That and the soul-crushing begging you have to do to get the resources needed to pay for a credible political campaign. The next time you ask yourself how it is we get such awful people in high office, remind yourself what a person has to do to get there, and you will understand.

I served three terms as a Leroy Township trustee. I should have served two. The last term really started to drag in part because the nepotism made it so we could not practically switch up duties. Also, I chose to run for county commissioner during that last term and got walloped in the Republican primary. I was outspent three dollars to one and beaten by a fairly unworthy opponent. It really soured me on elected service. Walking away the night of the primary, I confided in Jack how relieved I was to have lost. Trying to be and stay a county commissioner would probably have been really hard on our marriage.

In addition, having even a little local political power can be seductive in much the same way that the ring of power was seductive for the characters in the *Lord of the Ring*. Some people cannot bring themselves to lay it down. So it was kind of a relief to effectively put the envelope with the ring on the mantel and walk away. As an aside, I actually went through a kind of grieving process when I realized that season in my life was over. It had become a sizable part of my personal identity, and I had to come to terms with it being gone.

The other thing that caused me to step away from elected service was when I saw how quickly good work gets undone by those who come after. Especially on the school board, when we had been so proactive and innovative, we were no sooner off the board than things slowly but surely slid right back to many of the ways they had been before. If I think about it, I want to cry.

When Abby went to school, I began to look for paid employment after thirty years out of the workplace. I was fortunate to secure a bank job but did not enjoy the sales-driven atmosphere. I had been there for about two years when I began to seriously look around for other work. I ended up applying for a budget officer position in the office of the Geauga County Commissioners.

Now I was barely qualified for that job. But I knew a lot about how government works, and I knew I could learn to do it. As it turned out, I applied for that job twice in ten months and was interviewed five times. Both times, the job went to clearly better qualified candidates, as it should have. However, the second time, the last interview was with the board of commissioners. They decided they wanted to hire me too, so they created a job to offer me called special projects coordinator. What a perfect job for a self-motivated slightly ADD person like me. I got to do such an interesting variety of things in the three years I did it.

In the interview with the commissioners, I told the board I knew I would not be able to do the budget job walking in the door, but that I had a lot of faith in my ability to learn. Those words turned out to be kind of prophetic. In every job I had with Geauga County, I ended up having to teach myself the duties.

One of the best things about the special projects job was that it was totally new. My basic function was to do whatever my boss, the county administrator, came up with that was useful to him. This allowed the job to be shaped in the direction of my skill set and interests. That said, I spent a lot of time teaching myself the things I needed to know to be most helpful in as many ways as possible.

In the special projects role, I initiated the county auction, an online auction of things no longer needed in the county like old vehicles, office furniture, computers, and printers. That was really fun! It took me all around the county, so I got to meet and help out a lot of offices and departments. To the degree I could, I did records management for the ten departments under the commissioners. I assisted with two large capital improvement projects by attending project meetings and reporting to the commissioners. I did a lot of research on things that were being considered and wrote brief and concise reports about what I learned. I managed the mail room, which took a lot more effort than you might think and also involved a lot of crying.

After three years in the commissioners' office, I was promoted to a department director position when the commissioners and the recorder agreed to let the county Records Center come under the purview of the board. The Records Center was about twenty years old when I took over and had been run by the same person that whole time. Though she had done an excellent job of gathering and organizing the records for all the county officials into one facility, she had for several years sort of lost interest in keeping things moving. Government records are generated continuously, and there are rules for what to keep and for how long. If you drop that ball, pretty soon, you will drown in a giant pile of paper. That was what was happening to the Records Center and by extension to the offices and departments of the county. When the former director left, she chose to never respond to any phone call or email I sent her as I delved into what it would take to get the Records Center back on track. Once again, I was stuck having to teach myself how to do a pretty important job.

I did have a lot of fun there because my favorite thing ever is to clean up a mess, and the functioning of the Records Center was kind of a mess. It was truly time for fresh eyes. I know it was hard on some members of the staff when I took over because though I had done records management for the departments under the commissioners, I did not have the credentials that some of them thought a person in that job should have. I'm pretty sure they thought I didn't know what I was doing. But you know, no one is born knowing this work, and records management is not rocket science. It does take organization and tact which, funnily enough, in this setting, I was able to muster.

In my first year, I disposed of two thousand boxes, so you can see how constipated the process had become. By the time I left the role six years later, the county's alimentary system was flowing smoothly. I started a scanning program to convert paper records to electronically available digital records. I got a new copier that could also scan to email so we could respond to records requests very quickly and conveniently. I initiated the effort that led to getting the courts' digital records to film for permanent retention. I reduced a bloated staff while greatly improving customer service.

The Bible says the one who would lead must be the servant of all. I truly tried to emulate that point of view as a boss and as a resource to the elected officials. In addition, after spearheading the update of the state records management manual for all counties, something that had not been done in twenty years, I was elected chairman of the state association of records managers. So I think I was reasonably successful at the Records Center.

When the Human Resources person in the commissioners' office was preparing to retire, there was a lot of going back and forth about what would happen to that function. Eventually, I was promoted to a position called director of administrative services that encompassed HR and risk management while leaving me in charge of the Records Center, making me de facto office manager of the commissioners' office and allowing me to still dabble in special projects. I was also the backup for the county administrator.

The person who was leaving had had a different plan for her job, and maybe that was why she gave me almost no help at all in transitioning into that role. During the thirty days between when the commissioners promoted me and her last day, she allowed me to sit with her twice for one hour each time. She said no when I asked to shadow her. And she withheld the book into which she had organized the descriptions of her duties until her last day of work. At her retirement party, when so many people I'd be working with came to say goodbye, she did not introduce me as her replacement to any of them.

If you have read the description of my duties above, you will have at least an inkling of the size and importance of the job. And once again, I had to teach myself how to do it. I freely admit it was terrifying. I worked very hard at absorbing what I needed to know. My guiding principles were to not mess up and get the county into trouble and to try to be good to the employees. (And as petty as it is, to *never* have to call on my predecessor for any reason…ever. At which I was successful.)

Around the time I went back to the commissioners' office, politics everywhere began to be disrupted by Tea Party Republicans. Now in the main, these were well-intentioned and good-hearted people who wanted to make government more responsible and less expensive. Who doesn't want that? But the guy who was elected to the board of commissioners during that time was very challenging to work for.

The main challenge was that he was clearly afflicted with some iteration of attention deficit issues. He would demand reams of information, the gathering of which was very time-consuming, and then forget to do anything with it. Making actual decisions also seemed hard for him. In addition, he *refused* to recognize that there were areas of county government that were not within the purview of the board of commissioners. He had formed the view that if the board paid for it, he was in charge of it. Unfortunately for him, under Ohio law, each county officer is elected separately and has authority for separate functions. Commissioners do not get to tell other elected officials how to do their jobs. They only get to tell them how much money they get to do them.

One time fairly early on, a car dealer guy came to the commissioners' office to drop off the title for a vehicle the board had purchased. This requires a commissioner's signature, and the only one in the office at the time was the gentleman I am describing. He hemmed and hawed and loudly complained that he was not going to sign this because how did he know proper procedures had been followed, and he had not approved this purchase, etc., all in front of a business owner from the community. He was literally saying he did not trust his staff to do their jobs correctly. After he eventually signed the title and the car guy left, I stepped quietly to his desk and said, "Commissioner, with respect, you approved the purchase of that vehicle."

"No, I didn't!"

"Yes, you did. When you approved the financials at your meeting, the purchase of that vehicle was a part of the things you approved."

"Oh…well, I didn't know."

Yikes!

In his time on the board, he hosed up hiring, wrecked the county's relationship with the area highway planning agency, shook up county development planning, muddled up drug addiction services, and obliterated the regional solid waste district. He was like a wrecking ball. The sad thing is, he often had very good ideas and was right about problems with all of these agencies. He just could not figure out how to bring his ideas to bear in a useful way much less garner support for real change.

I found this gentleman very likable and interesting on a personal level. But he was *very* hard to work for. After about the fifth time I did a mountain of work for him for nothing, I went to my boss, the county administrator, and told him I was not doing that anymore. I would only do it if *two* commissioners asked for whatever it was this one commissioner wanted. "They are paying me too much money for me to waste my time like this."

Throughout my nearly four years in that job, I vacillated about when to retire. I always held onto the hope that there might be one more step up for me since I had been pretty severely underpaid since becoming a department head. I was always trying to catch up in building my retirement. After a while, it became clear that that was very likely not going to happen, so I set my sights on retiring as soon as I reached the age to qualify for Medicare. I think Jack and I always thought we might do a few things like trips after retirement, but by the time I was old enough, he was never going to go anywhere due to the requirements of his condition.

At the very end, one of the commissioners was kind enough to ask what they could offer me to get me to stay. There was nothing by then. I really wanted my time. Interestingly, he was also the only one of the commissioners who attended my retirement party, which was a tad hurtful. Made it pretty easy to walk out without a backward glance.

After all my years of elected service, I have come up with a list of suggestions to give to people considering service on an elected board. Sadly, a lot of people run for office without really knowing what they are getting into or how to function effectively in their role when they get there. Below are my thoughts on that score for anyone who might have an interest.

* * * * *

Boardmanship is the art of board members functioning together cooperatively and professionally to accomplish the work of the board. It encompasses the collective traits contributing to a board's interpersonal interactions in the performance of their assigned responsibilities. There is often a real adjustment for a new board member to what it means to function effectively as part of a board. Listed below are some suggestions on how to ease that transition.

1.   Decisions Belong to the Board

One of the first and most important things to grasp about being a member of a board is that *the board* is the entity that makes the decisions. The members are its collective parts, the arms and legs and eyes and ears if you will. But it is *the board as a whole*, separate and distinct, that decides. That board existed before you were a member and will continue to exist after you are gone.

2.   Show Up

Once the office is acquired, there is actual work to be done. Obviously, anyone honored by fellow citizens with the privilege of leadership has an obligation to do the work.

3.   Be Prepared

One of the most disappointing things I have observed over the years is the board member who arrives at the board table just in time to open the board packet. This disrespects the staff, the electors, and the work.

4.   No Surprises

The last thing the staff and your fellow board members need during a meeting is for someone to lob a hand grenade into an orderly process. It also means that questions that will be asked at the table should be asked privately first, so whomever is responsible for answers has time to prepare. This is professional courtesy.

5.   Grudges

One of the big adjustments to board membership is learning to walk away after a loss. As in everything, on the board, you win some, and you lose some. If a loss is going to cause you endless hurt feelings or anger, board membership is not for you.

6. Try Not to Micromanage Too Much

This is tough because one person's micromanagement is another person's constituent service. In general, administration belongs to administrators. The board paints the broad strokes and administration carries out the will of the board. If you are writing job descriptions or selecting bus stops, you are micromanaging.

7. Not All at Once

Some people, upon election to a board, want to fix it all *right now. That's why they were elected!* That approach will cause chaos. While you get your bearings, it may be a good idea to focus on issues that are low-hanging or ethically, legally, or morally questionable.

8. Some People Should Not Be on a Board

As I have shared, I knew a lady who, when she became overwhelmed during board meetings, would jump up and run out of the room, crying. This is a person who should not be on a board. If you find the rigors of board membership that upsetting, it's okay to walk away.

9. Know When to Quit

It is my personal opinion that you will get done most of what you came to do in two terms. It is also my opinion that after eight years, you may start to lose the objectivity that is necessary to keep the whole thing honest. And the truth is, no one has all the answers and a little bit of churn keeps the board as a whole fresh and forward-looking. You are a great board member. And the person who comes after you will be a great board member too. When the time is right, give someone else the privilege of service.

On Laughter

The Bible says laughter is like a medicine, and I believe it. Think about those times when you have a good, hard belly laugh. When you laugh so hard, you fall on the floor, and tears run down your face. Think how *good* you feel after. I recently watched a recording of one of our Christmases, and Jack must have said something that struck me funny. Just watching myself laugh that hard made me happy all over again.

Laughter has always been important to me. I was probably in about the third grade when I realized I like to make people laugh. I began throwing out the occasional wisecrack to get my classmates laughing. It felt good. Jack was also a bit of a wise guy from an early age. It's a good thing to have in common.

I love to kid, and I kid a lot, maybe sometimes too much. I do think joking and laughing is a particularly American trait. A quick mosey through Facebook or YouTube gives ample proof of how much we as a people like to laugh.

When we went on our mission trip to Bolivia, it was quickly striking to me that the people there seemed taken aback by the American habit of joking and laughing. Though we went to build classrooms at a church and we worked hard and built them, none of us thought it amiss to enjoy the experience and mix in plenty of kidding around. Often our hosts seemed just, I don't know, puzzled by our propensity for humor. It could be that the safety and security and reasonable expectation of honest business and government in America make it possible for us to look for the fun in our circumstances. That kind of security is quite lacking in the third world.

I personally feel that laughter can often be a saving grace in a relationship. I would never want to be with someone who is humorless. And I know they would never want to be with me. Jack and I laughed together *daily* for all our years together. And my son Michael can make me laugh so hard I start to cough. Sometimes I wish he still lived around here so I could laugh more and better.

Our family has always been into humor, usually the sarcastic kind. Throw in a little black humor as well. For example, when we discussed what kind of memorial Jack wanted, there was consideration given to black T-shirts that said, "My dad died, and all I got was this lousy T-shirt."

Sometimes the sarcasm can be pretty cutting, and I wish we could back it off a little.

Quite often, Jack would show me things that struck him funny on the Internet, and we would chortle together. I was able to coax a snort out of him right up until the final few days of his life. By then, he was deep inside himself, mostly unreachable. I so really miss having someone to show funny names in the obituaries to. (I'm looking at you, Myrtle Daisy Cornbloom).

Anyway, I recommend laughter. It's good for what ails you.

On Letting Go

There are many dementia stories out there. Almost everyone I know has a relative or friend dealing with this challenge. Our dementia story actually began a few years before we realized what was coming. I had bought my mom a simple little DVD player that operated with nothing but a lid and an on and off button. I remember being puzzled at the time because she could not learn how to operate the machine.

Mom's condition became clearer when she started losing weight. Then she stopped sleeping in her bed. She started having trouble waking up enough to get to the bathroom at night. When she told me my niece now worked at the jail and that she had visited Emily's apartment there, I knew it was time to gather my siblings.

Two of my brothers thought Mom was fine. As we talked with Mom that night about the need for appointing powers of attorney for her financial and medical care, there was some sighing and eye-rolling. One brother decided to experiment by asking Mom to show him where her pills were. She led him to the door of her little kitchen where she paused for quite a while. The pills were kept in a cupboard she could have opened from where she stood. Then she turned around and began to shuffle toward the laundry room with my brother right behind her.

He looked at me and said, "She's taking me to the basement." Mom's condo had no basement.

That night, Mom appointed her oldest son as her financial power of attorney. She appointed the oldest daughter, me, for her medical needs. Our first challenge was to try to be sure she was eating properly and taking her pills. As a diabetic, Mom's diet and medicine were crucial. We set a schedule where family members would visit each day to be sure she was eating and taking her pills. Unfortunately, that approach only worked for a few months.

After cataract surgeries, we brought her to our house for a few months. Every day, she packed her clothes. I would get home from work and put them away, and the next day, they were back in the suitcase. When I brought some family photos for her from her condo, she interpreted their removal from her home as my having stolen them even though they were in her room. She was so happy and grateful to be cared for by us face-to-face, but when she was alone in her room, I could hear her muttering about how those SOBs were taking all her money.

Eventually, we found an assisted living situation that fairly quickly progressed to a bed in a locked memory care unit. She gradually lost her memories of all of us. Eventually, I was her neighbor, Sarah.

One late summer morning, my work phone rang. It was the assisted living home calling to tell me my mother had fallen from the toilet and had a cut on her leg, so she was being taken to the emergency room. As I drove to the hospital, I wondered how a fall from the toilet would result in a cut.

When I arrived, I couldn't find her. As it turned out, she was in X-ray. Because both legs and both ankles were broken. In fact, both legs were shattered from the knees down. One ankle was dislocated. The cut on her leg was from where the bone had come through. It was a horrendous injury. And it most assuredly did not happen in a fall from the toilet!

The ER doctor immediately began to pressure me to send my mother to surgery. In order to do that, her DNR would have to be lifted, something I didn't want to do. She said surgery must be performed immediately, or my mother would "die in agony." She said no surgeon would touch a patient who has a DNR. I said, Can't we agree beforehand that if my mother were to die during the surgery, that it was okay to let her go? That was apparently not an option.

About the time I was finally worn down enough to consider lifting the DNR, the surgeon arrived. He examined my mother very briefly. She had had to be given so much medicine to control her pain that she was asleep with a blood pressure of sixty over forty. He declined to perform surgery and walked out.

At that point, the ER doctor told me that she wanted to send my mother to a trauma hospital forty miles away because that was the best place to treat injuries of the magnitude my mother had sustained. This was something I didn't want to do. I talked to my husband, my daughter, who is a nurse, and my brother. My mother was already under hospice care, and two ladies from the hospice were with me as well. All of them said in the end, it was my decision on what to do.

It was agonizing. To hold a decision like that over the life of someone else is a tremendous weight. What would she do if she were capable of deciding? What would I want if it were me? If I sent her to the trauma hospital for surgery, what would be the consequences? Her legs were shattered. I wasn't sure they could even be fixed. What if I didn't send her for surgery and instead sent her to hospice? What if she didn't die and I left her with two bags of broken bones at the ends of her legs? What would my five siblings think should be done? What would they say if they thought I chose wrongly? What if some thought one thing and some another?

I sat beside her all day as I was pulled back and forth by the broad range of hard choices and impossible consequences. Ultimately, I had to accept that the decision really was mine and mine alone. That's why she had entrusted it to me. I decided to send her to hospice. They had an approach they called "terminal sedation." That means that aggressive repair is finished. All the machines are removed. Everything is done to keep the patient completely comfortable until life ends.

That's right. I decided to allow my mother a calm, peaceful, dignified end. Part of what drove the decision was my father's death. He had pursued aggressive treatment for a bad heart valve, and the procedure killed him. He died alone far from home. I wanted a better death for my mother. Part of my reasoning was to ask myself if my mom enjoyed being how she was. I believed then and still believe that if she had been aware of herself enough to answer that question, the answer would have been no. So I decided to let her go.

That evening, as my mother was settled into a room, I was talking with my daughter and sharing the agony of what I had chosen to do. The nurse quietly working with my mom could hear the conversation and, when she was done and about to leave, stopped at the door.

Looking at me with great compassion, she said, "For what it's worth, if this were my mother, this is what I would do." It helped.

Twelve days later, in a lovely quiet hospice room with a beautiful garden full of summer flowers just steps away, with the music she had always loved playing softly, she waited to be alone and passed. She was a Christian believer, and she and we know her passing was not her end.

To their credit, my siblings never once criticized my decision. In all honesty, none of them has ever talked with me about it one way or another. I hope they don't think it was done quickly, easily, or lightly.

In the years since her death, I have circled back to this decision many times. I have asked myself again and again what else I could or should have done. In my husband's words, there *were* no good choices. To have chosen to let my mother die is a hard, hard thing. Every time I go through the events of that day, I come back to the same conclusion. In those circumstances, for my mom, I believe it was the right thing to do.

In our current culture, with the multitude of medical interventions available to us, it is harder and harder to choose to let go. There is an undercurrent, always, of pressure to "do something." Even among Christians, there is strong pressure to "choose life." It takes a strong effort of will to resist that kind of pressure. It is probably because of it that I so often go back and reexamine my decision. One day, I, too, will be swept away, down the maelstrom to afterward. When I reach the afterlife, I expect I'll have the chance to see my mother again. I hope she will look right at me and say, "Linda, thank you for letting me go."

On Reading

I am a readaholic. I admit it freely. I read off and on all day every day. I absolutely read every night before sleep for at least half an hour. Sometimes a lot more. I read mostly fiction, but history and biography and memoir show up on my nightstand regularly. I have had as many as six books going at once, and when I tire of one, I go to another.

Since my mother did not drive, when she ran out of cigarettes, she was kind of stuck. I remember on many occasions watching her ransack the house, looking for a cigarette. That's how I am when I don't have a worthwhile read handy.

When I was a homeschooling mom, reading was my way of resting my mind from my labors. Jack and I very seldom went out alone, and our family as a whole took only one family vacation in all those years to Chincoteague Island. That I learned about from a book. Back then, reading probably saved, if not my sanity, at least my ability to soldier on.

I read aloud to our children regularly. We read the entire *Little House* series together, I think, three times. I read all the Elizabeth Enright to them that I could find. I read, obviously, the Tolkien books as well as the *Chronicles of Narnia*, and C. S. Lewis's space trilogy. The Betsy-Tacy books through a couple of times. Francis Hodgson Burnett—you know *Little Princess* and *Secret Garden*. I love reading aloud, and if I could find kids to read aloud to today, I would do it in a heartbeat.

Jack was also a reader, but he read much less fiction. He read serious books and bought a lot of them over the years. He really liked Francis Schaefer, the Christian philosopher. I tried to read Schaefer, I really did. But he is just too dense for me. Jack also had very fond

memories of reading, I think literally, the set of kid-level encyclopedias that his parents had bought their boys. So as an adult, he wanted
to have encyclopedias.

I read through the settlement portion of his divorce record and
note that he got his and Mary's set of *Britannica*. I don't know what
happened to them because when I met him, there were no encyclopedias until somehow the *Britannica* salesman found his way to our
house just months into our marriage. And there, right in front of me,
I saw Jack's eyes start to spin, and he signed up to buy $1,000 worth
of encyclopedias! That was a lot of money back then, and it took a
year to pay off. In the end, I was glad to have them because I can lose
myself in an encyclopedia as fast as Jack could.

That said, that was when I learned my husband had generally
very little sales resistance. I made myself the sales gatekeeper after
that because I have enough for both of us. He was especially vulnerable to knowledge peddlers. In retirement, he liked to purchase stuff
from Great Courses. I mostly stayed out of it as long as he didn't buy
too much. He was entitled to it.

He also brought a whole mahogany bookshelf full of Great Books,
beautifully bound classics to the marriage. Over the years, I read a lot
of them. I don't have the books anymore, but I still have the bookcase.

I have never been one to buy books. I go to the library…a lot.
This is another reason the pandemic has been hard on me. Besides
losing my husband, I have lost my library. They have been closed for
months. Other area libraries are open. Not mine. So in my desper-
ation, I have had to resort to buying books. I read them, and then I
donate them. I do not need to be storing a bunch of books. That's
what libraries are for.

Over the years and even until today, the library is where I go
when I want to learn how to do something. When I wanted to quilt,
when I wanted to garden, when I wanted to raise animals, when I
wanted to learn how to make very small things, the library supplied
me with detailed and varied information to help me move ahead.

One thing all this reading has done for me is to give me a pretty
good vocabulary. I used it when I talked to our children from the day
the first one was born. Jack questioned me about it once.

"Why do you talk to them like that?" he protested. "They don't understand you."

"They will," I said. And they did.

Jack and I shared a deep love for language, and our reading fed it. He especially loved reading and memorizing poetry. As for me, I wrote quite a bit of poetry back in the day. We were fortunate, I think, to share something so esoteric.

On The Trip to Bountiful

One evening, probably sometime in the eighties, I watched the movie, *The Trip to Bountiful*. For some reason, it really resonated with me, how that grandma so longed to see her childhood home one more time. I swear, when she finally got there, I could almost smell it. The following morning, I woke up with the beginnings of a poem in my mind, and below is what I wrote.

Though I find it a little pedestrian, Jack always really loved it and, in fact, asked me to read it at his memorial, which, due to covid, may never happen.

I totally believe the basket of flowers will be on my arm when I get to heaven.

Grandmother's Garden

Come listen to Grandma, I want you to hear
The tales of this house that's so gray and so drear.
Back then, it was white, full of laughter and cheer.
Oh, you'd never imagine, I know it my dears—
T''is the home of my youth, little ones.

Well, I had me a garden, the 'hocks grew so tall
From the vi'lets in spring, to the mums in the fall.
Some did wonderful well, some did nothin' a' tall.
Their faces come back, I can clearly recall.
It's as though they were friends of my youth.

The mem'ries I hold of my life in those days
Are as clear and as sweet as the petals and sprays

Of the blooms in my garden, and even today
I can touch them and smell them; they are a bouquet
Of the days and the times of my youth.

I tell you, my children, I thought I would weep
As we walked up the old path, the grass is so deep.
The air smells the same, why, it makes my heart leap!
I thought Pop and Mom through the window would peek,
To welcome me back to my youth.

Let the scent of the rose draw us backward in time
To those warm, quiet summers when weather was prime.
Oh, the air was so pure I could drink it sometimes,
And the darkness would hum with the old skeeters' whine,
In the soft summer nights of my youth.

Then the sun would rise up, and we'd work it back down
Taking cows up to graze, little brother would clown
Walking pasture fence backward, he'd laugh at my frown.
He was killed in the Big War; we never knew how,
But he still walks the paths of my youth.

Now I want you to think of the goldenrod's hue
Chill mornings and crickets and grass drenched in dew.
When summer sky turns to the eye-achin' blue
Of the days of September, guess you love it too.
Oh, the smoke-misted autumns of youth!

You could come out and sit in the porch swing at night
And you'd barely see stars, that ol' moon was so bright.
We would swing and sing hymns by its sharp-shadowed light
And the skunks danced their dances, perfuming the night
On those leaf-rustlin' fall nights of youth.

No, they didn't have school buses. Mercy me, no!
We just walked to the school with the dust on our toes

A WIDOW'S TALE

Where the desks were all lined up in wood-shinin' rows
And the boys always pullin' a little girl's bows
Oh, the crunch-apple taste of my youth!

Well, the flowers would fade and the fall colors brown,
Till the hills with the redbirds, and holly were crowned.
November winds tumbled Thanksgiving Eve 'round
And with it came Grandma and Grandpa from town
To give thanks in the days of my youth.

Though we couldn't know then, Grandma stood on the brink
Of her heavenly rest. I was thirteen, I think,
When she gave me her locket, right here by the sink.
Oh, it slid from her hand with a soft, golden clink.
I have worn it from days of my youth.

Don't know what I loved best of our Christmases then—
The smell of the tree or the laughter of friends
The babe in the manger, the carols' sweet blend,
Candlelight on dear faces, bright secrets, and then
Christmas mornings in days of my youth.

The skies of midwinter were milky and pale.
The northeast would darken, bring snow, ice, and hail,
As we waited for spring, the seed-catalog mail.
Stuck inside by the stove; the house seemed like a jail.
Sometimes winters were long in my youth.

Then one day, I would putter on out to the pump,
While drawing the water, I'd mutter and grump,
When my eyes would be drawn to the foot of that stump,
And a vision of snowdrops, a small frosted clump,
Was the advent of spring in my youth.

Easter came with the mem'ry of God's sacrifice.
The scent of the lilies, the solemn church rites

Seemed to spark the renewal of life and the flights
Of the Canada geese through the dripping March nights
Sang a song of the freedom of youth.

Into April, it seemed Spring came on with such speed
As though for abundance of flowers Spring's greed
Couldn't spill out the blossoms, from Winter's grip freed
Fast enough to suit Spring (and I must confess, me!)
Oh, I reveled in springs of my youth!

And now I must tell you a secret, my dears,
Something I've never shared down through all the long years.
Though I've loved the sweet summer, fall brought me to tears
There's a certain kind month that's my favorite I fear,
May's the month that I've favored from youth.

Well, it seems to me now that the Mays of that time
Struck a kind of soft balance between April's grime
And the rush of the earth-bursting full summertime.
The year's kindly pause at the foot of the climb
To the harvest in days of my youth.

Well, my sweet little ones, we have talked the year round.
And we've named off the flowers, the gifts of the ground.
Though I know the earth yields us our food, I'll be bound
That a bloom's only duty is beauty. Surround
Your young selves with the blossoms of youth!

Somehow it just seems we remember the best
For the years take the sadness and lay it to rest.
And only the sweet things worth keepin' are left.
Like a basket of flowers all dewy and fresh
Are the kind, painless mem'ries of youth.

Well, I know that the Good Book says bodies must die,
And the day of my passing from earth's drawing nigh.

I believe when I enter those portals on high
I'll have with me this basket of flowers of mine—
All the brightest and best of my life.

Come along, little ones, guess it's time we should go.
Shut the door, brush the dust off. We'll turn away slow.
Bring the flowers you've gathered, wind's starting to blow—
Oh, the sound's just the same as it was long ago!
Say goodnight to your grandmother's garden.

On Forgiveness

One of the great gifts I got from my life with Jack was being in close proximity to his propensity for forgiveness. He was just not a person to hold a grudge. Now it may seem strange for me to say this in the context of his lifelong wounds from his divorce. But I think he truly believed the divorce was his fault.

The lessons I learned from him about forgiveness really came to the fore when we left New Testament Fellowship. This was a small nondenominational church we attended for five years. The leaders were all young, and as often happens, they had wandered into some pretty tall weeds on a few issues. There was a great shaking, and many people were bitterly hurt by some of the things that were said and done, including some close friends of ours.

Now Jack had seen what was happening and had tried to address what he saw as problems with actions of the men in leadership only to be rebuffed. He knew we were probably going to leave. But he was not angry, and he would not allow me to be either. Our friends were not able to make as clean a break, and I would not be surprised if, even now, a discussion of the incidents of those days would drag it all up for them. Jack was never like that. Being with him helped me to know enough to at least try not to be like that either.

On Owning a Cellphone

I held out for a long time against owning a cellphone. I had formed a prejudice against them because I found conversations with the tops of people's heads at the very least insulting.

Attending the meetings of department heads who spent the whole time playing with their phones and taking calls while the person who was talking to them in that moment had to stop and wait was beyond rude. I once invited my grandchildren over to watch a movie with me. This was when I learned that that generation doesn't seem to watch movies or listen to dialogue or get the jokes, much less the subtleties of movies I love and wanted to share. They just want to play with their phones. I only did that once.

I eventually gave in and acquired a cellphone when I had to acknowledge that my children would no longer accept my calls or listen to my voicemails or respond to my emails. The dinosaur had to learn to text, so I did. I will admit I can perceive the convenience of texting, and I do it a lot now.

To my credit, in my opinion, I have not purchased a phone. The phones I have used so far have been the outdated relics of my children's cellphone lives. This is, I admit, a point of pride for me. While I was employed, I never told my employer I had a cellphone, nor did I give the number to coworkers. They knew where I was and how to reach me during work hours, and there was always someone at home if they needed me after hours, which they never really did.

Even now, I do not carry the cellphone around with me, not even at home and certainly not when I go out, unless I am traveling, or there is a specific reason I might need it wherever I'm going. I do not ever go online with my phone and expect I never will. I am determined never to be a slave to a device. My phone, as with my computers, is a decent servant but will never be my master.

On Getting Organized

One of the things that came in the package of me is a propensity for order. I think I was an ordinarily messy little kid, but around the time I turned twelve, something clicked in me, and I started to want to have the space around me neat and tidy.

From her birth until I was a senior in high school, my space was shared with my much younger sister, Susan, someone who was not at all ready for the level of tidy I wanted. You should have seen what was under her bed. But under the bed was out of sight, so… To her credit, she did not seem to mind that I rearranged our room about once a month that whole time. Really.

I started wanting to make a home in the small ways a twelve-year-old can. I got my dad to give me some leftover paint, and I did the best I could to paint our room. I made a garden in our backyard and grew flowers. Every spring for the last three years we lived in the Headlands, I cut and rooted a sprig of pussy willow and planted it back by the woods. I don't know what was in me that made me want to do these things, but I have been garden and farmer and homemaker-hearted for my whole life. I facilitate that with order.

When I got my first job at a bank, every time they put me into a new teller window, the first thing I did was put it in order. Clean out the drawers. Resupply all the needed forms. Fill up the coin dispenser.

While I was raising a large family in small houses, I picked up. Constantly. Because so much of what a mother does is undone *so quickly*. I remember after having Michael by cesarean, my friend Maggie commenting on how still I was. For once. Well, I did have a six-inch zipper up the front of my belly.

When I worked for Geauga County, it was the first time in my life I had an office. I hung pictures and brought in houseplants. I had curtains on the window. More than one person who visited my office commented, sometimes almost uncomfortably, on the fact that my desk either was clean or about to be. That's just how I like it. What clutter there was, was in labeled folders in the drawer. Alphabetical. Clutter makes me crazy.

I enjoyed my job as the records manager for Geauga County because records management is all about order. There is a process. It is easy to follow. Theoretically, you should be able to put your hand on whatever is requested pretty fast. In our case, we often turned around a records request in five minutes. Bam!

My way of organizing at home is logic-based. If you base your system on logic, when you can't remember where you put something, there's a better than even chance you can logic your way to what you did with it. Things we use a lot should be handy. Things we don't should be far away and out of sight. Similar things should be together. Bigger to smaller. Little bins in the drawers to corral the clutter. Clothes we don't wear should be got rid of. When I retired, I simply donated my professional wardrobe.

Jack's way of organizing was that he wanted everything where he could see it. Yikes! His work areas were enough to make me itch. His desk was covered in little slips and snippets of paper in stacks everywhere. And he did in fact know where everything was. Right there, where he could see it. And if I even dusted, he knew and chewed me out for messing up his system. He bought twelve…twelve sets of plastic shelves to store his tools and his stash.

I mean, I have stashes too. Craft supplies and fabric and sewing notions. But they are organized in bins mostly in the basement or in closets. His stash was spread across the plastic shelves in single layers so he could *see* it. *Total* waste of vertical space. After he died and I got rid of all the multiples of things (seriously, who needs *five* coping saws?), I was able to reduce the sets of shelves to four. Those I need because I actually use a lot of our tools.

As time went on, I think my neatness began to grate on him as much as his disorder grated on me. I did get to a place where I made myself turn a blind eye to his office and tool bench. He could not seem to relax and just let me tidy the rest.

It's interesting because he wasn't like that when I first met him. I know this because I spent a good bit of time with him where he lived before we were married. Maybe because he was renting a room in an old lady's house he felt an obligation to keep it orderly. All he had that tipped his hand was a chair in the corner of his room where he piled his clothes. We always had a chair in the corner of every bedroom we ever had because that is where clothes go. Except for the large set of open shelves where he could pile his clothes in stacks. Where he could see them.

In any case, I like to organize, and I am pretty good at it. I am trying to make the spaces I live in now as ready as I can for when I die. I have asked my children to tell me if there are things they want, as my mother did time after time with us. The truth is, most kids don't really want their parents' stuff. Though my kids surprised me by what they wanted of their dad's.

All Beth wanted was the Chock Full O'Nuts coffee can that had been in our garage her whole life. Jeff wanted Jack's little barbell that was always in the living room. When he did a couple curls and we heard the ka-chuck, ka-chuck sound it always made, "That's the sound of my youth," he said. Becca wanted a flannel shirt or two, and she wasn't the only one. But then, I think she still has my dad's flannel shirt.

It has been harder than I expected to pare down some things after Jack's death. There is a finality to dropping that bag of clothes at the Salvation Army that must be endured. I am writing these memories on his computer, which I refused to even touch during his life because he said I would get cooties on it (and as we know, all kidding is half-truth). Also, I knew if I touched it and subsequently something went wonky as happens with all computers at some point, it would be my fault, and who needs that?

I am enjoying being able to keep the whole place as tidy as I want. Though I will confess to slacking sometimes. I will look at yet another set of mucky little puppy prints on the floor, and I will ask myself, "Does anybody care but me?" And if the answer is no, I ask myself how much I care, and whether I care enough to do anything about it. Sometimes I do, and sometimes I just decide to let it go for now. Jack would be so proud.

On Houses

I have shared elsewhere that my parents were real estate hobbyists. I remember even as a kid noting how often they would buy a house, put a lot of money into it, and then sell it for less than what they had spent. Even to a kid, this seemed weird.

Nevertheless, I was able to understand that homeownership seemed like a good idea. By the time we had been married for about a year, I was pregnant and about to be a stay-at-home mom. One Sunday, I decided to look at the classifieds and found an ad for a three-bedroom, one-bath colonial on Wood Street in the Browning School district in Willoughby for about twenty-one thousand dollars. It was 1974, the midst of the fuel crisis that came with the Carter years. Though the times were challenging, I knew home ownership was possible because of Jack's military service, so I showed him the ad. We ended up going to see the house one day in the middle of January.

It was a tiny house, well less than a thousand square feet. It stood on a tiny lot, only fifty by sixty. The back of the house was twelve feet from the side of the house behind. It had been owned by a developmentally disabled family who had moved out after the choking death of one of the children. It was really dirty. But I noticed the coved ceilings, the china cupboard in the dining room, the solid wood doors with crystal knobs, and the colonial moldings. It even had a single garage attached. It was in a very good location on an old tree-lined street walkable to town. It was the only house we looked at.

Because we bought it using the GI Bill, the sale took a long time, months. There were some basic items that came up in the inspection that, by law, were the responsibility of the seller to fix before we moved in. Gutters, plumbing, etc. They were fixed; I saw the certificate signed by the follow-up inspector, saying the repairs were done, except they weren't.

When we finally got the keys, it was spring, and Jack was working and going to school, and I had full-time care of a pretty cranky baby. When we got in to really look, we noted the gutter with the big hole that spilled rainwater down the front of the house was still there. The toilet still shot a geyser from the broken bowl whenever it flushed. The kitchen sink leaked across the floor from the hole in the drainpipe underneath. The level of dirtiness was stunning. There were black handprints around the kitchen cupboard handles and every doorknob. Dried food from old spills stuck to the walls of the breakfast nook. Where the baseboards had been painted, the paint was full of dog hair because no one thought to dust beforehand. In one bedroom, you knew where the furniture had been because they had painted around it. Around it… During our first walk through after our purchase, we asked ourselves why on earth we had bought this awful, awful little house. Then we rolled up our sleeves.

We started by tearing out all the carpet in the whole house. Underneath were decent wood floors. I cleaned and cleaned. I had a baby; it had to be clean. We painted most of the interior before we even moved in. Jack had to remove some of the baseboards to be able to sand off the hair. As the house was only eighteen feet deep, there was no room inside more than nine feet wide. We had to be careful to buy furniture scaled to the size of the rooms and to arrange it in ways that worked.

One of the interesting things we encountered was a design choice where someone took a sponge, dipped it in yellow paint, and carefully used it to make brick prints up the green wall of the stairwell. That's what you call DIY design. We took down the brown plaid tub surround to find big holes in the walls. So we fixed them and put up a nice neutral surround and fresh paint. Small but crisp and clean. We decided to put up paneling in the basement so we could have one room that wasn't unbearably narrow. I made curtains for most of the windows.

While Jack worked and went to school, I plugged away at the rest of the painting when Becca would let me. I painted all the interior doors on both sides, which, let me tell you, gets old. In order to paint the kitchen cupboards, I removed the handles and soaked them in a jar full of paint remover. (We didn't have slow cookers to soften paint back then.) They turned out to be copper and pretty and shone nicely against the clean white cupboard paint. I painted the kitchen yellow. A year later, I painted it pale blue, much better.

We insulated the attic, put up new gutters, and repaired and replaced all the malfunctioning plumbing. Then we started on painting the peeling exterior. This was when I learned that the fluorescent lighting inside a paint store would fool you on color. I thought the paint I chose was light green. When it got painted on the house, it came out yellow. In the end, it was okay. We added black shutters, trimmed the overgrown bushes, and planted petunias. I know for a fact the neighbors appreciated our efforts.

We lived in our first home for two years. It was the first time Jack had ever lived in a normal single family home, having grown up in an apartment at his family's motel. We put fifteen hundred dollars and tons of sweat equity into that little house. By that time, I was pregnant with our second child. Though we could have stayed there—after all, it was no worse than an apartment—the opportunity came to buy a bigger house with a nice yard right around the corner. We decided to sell by owner.

Now I know there are a lot of people who advise not to sell by owner. But it worked out for us. We lived in a desirable area, and we were not unreasonable about the price we set. I wrote and placed the ad in the paper (no zillow then) and started fielding calls. At least half were from real estate agents who wanted to list the house. I always declined politely, told them how much we needed to get and said they were welcome to sell the house for enough to get their own commission provided I got what I needed. In the end, we sold it ourselves in just a few weeks.

One day, a lady called about the house. She said she was newly divorced, had four children, and desperately wanted to be in our neighborhood. I was very honest with her and advised that our house was really small with no yard and probably not suited to a family of that size. She said she wanted to come see it. She did, decided she could make it work, and made an offer. We had hired a real estate attorney to write us a purchase agreement (no free legal documents on the Internet back then), and we all signed. The house we had bought two years before for $21,000 sold for $32,000. And *that* was when I learned about buying the worst house in the best neighborhood. It didn't hurt that inflation then was around 14 percent.

A few weeks later, in June 1977, we moved two blocks to our new house on South Street. The house on South Street was on a corner, and it was like living on an open-air stage because our whole life was exposed to the world. We were like the hub of the wheel of the neighborhood, and lots of kids came to play over the years. Jack let the neighbor boys shoot hoops in the driveway as long as they minded their language, and they mostly did.

I had a lot of fun with that yard over the ten years we lived there. I had vegetable gardens and flower gardens. I planted fruit trees and rhododendrons. Jack raked the leaves into a compost pile in the back corner every fall, and I did actually get some compost out of it eventually. The soil there was heavy clay, which was often my fate. The yard had a hedge along the sidewalk where someone thought it was good to make it out of trimmed down pine trees. Well, they were pricky, so maybe that discouraged people from wading through them.

There were plenty of kids and stay-at-home moms all around us. That was sometimes good and sometimes not so good. Negotiating these types of relationships can be tricky. One friendship I made was with an old lady who lived across from our backyard. Her husband had been the French teacher at South High for many years and was in his eighties. Mrs. Lake was in her seventies. She was a master gardener, and her modest backyard was just beautiful, filled with fruits and flowers rioting together in the shade of a huge old apple tree.

Mrs. Lake was born in France and met her husband during the First World War when she was fifteen. They fell in love, and when the war ended, her parents refused to let her marry her American beau, and eventually he had to go home without her. He managed to get a job with the Red Cross and go back to France. Her parents required her to wait until she was twenty-one to get married. By the time I met them, Mr. Lake was really not with it mentally anymore, and she was caring for him. I used to visit her regularly and listen to her stories and admire her gardens. We would drink tea in her little bitty kitchen.

Eventually, Mr. Lake became a danger to himself and his wife and had to go into a nursing home. He immediately got sick, and then so did she. She was at home with pneumonia when he died. She was very hard on herself for not being with him at his death. Now I am a widow, I understand better what she felt. Jack chose to go when I was just steps away but not with him, and it bothers me a little. Like I failed him in some way.

On a day not long after he died, Mrs. Lake took me down in her basement and showed me a rocking chair she had. It had been in the house when she and Mr. Lake moved in in the 1920s. It was a bentwood style rocker, and the caning was gone before she ever had it, but she had always wanted to redo it. I told her I would be happy to refinish it for her. I was doing a lot of refinishing of furniture during the seventies and eighties, as so many of us did. When it was ready, she had it re-caned at an antique shop in Willoughby.

As I look back, it seems to me that it wasn't that long after Mr. Lake died that Mrs. Lake started to decline. It was like she had had to keep it together for him, but once he was gone, so was her purpose. She became more and more confused. Eventually, she, too, had to go into a safer place. Her son very kindly gave me the rocker I had refinished for her, and it sits in the corner of my bedroom today. I am so glad to have it in Mrs. Lake's memory.

The South Street house was like a tool for me, useful but not something to be in love with. It was oddly configured in that the third bedroom was reached by going through the middle one. The kitchen was a small galley next to a big dining room. Eventually, Jack and I thought we might try to add more living space, so to get ready for that, we rewired that whole house. The basement electric panel had fuses, and many of the wires were knob and tube, so it was time. We learned a lot on that project and eventually did quite a bit of wiring together over the years. I became pretty good at fixing the resulting holes in the walls.

We never were able to do any big projects at that house. The constraints of the lot configuration combined with where we were in life—you know, knee-deep in little kids—kept our focus more on family than house back then.

Eventually, there were enough unpleasant and even wicked incidents in that neighborhood that we had to restrict our kids to our own yard to try to keep them safe. By the time we were expecting our fifth child, we started to look into a move to the country. The search took two years, and by then, I was homeschooling. It was interesting how many of the neighbor kids asked me to homeschool them. Did they think homeschool meant no school?

Because we were raising and homeschooling a large family on a modest income, the house we bought on Callow Road in Leroy was also modest. We went to see it on a day in early March. I remember standing at the backdoor and listening to a quiet that seemed like food to my soul. Quiet and calling crows.

Once again, we sold by owner. We had received the offer of a market analysis from a local realtor. We accepted, got the value, subtracted the 6 percent commission, and set our price. The house sold in five days. The young couple who wanted it brought her dad to look with them. He was in real estate and aggressively challenged me on the price. When I told him how we set it, all he could say was, "Oh." And anyway, as it turned out, Jack accepted a disappointing offer without even asking me. That extra few thousand dollars would have been nice to use on the new house, which had been a rental for some years.

It was a thousand-square foot ranch with three bedrooms and one bath. What it had that made it doable was a full, deep, dry basement. We eventually built two more bedrooms down there. We also converted the pantry closet in the kitchen—I am totally not kidding—into a toilet closet. We *had* to have at least a second toilet, and that's where it stayed until our son bought the house from us and redid much of the interior, including dismantling that closet. We had a great well that never failed to provide enough good water the whole of the twenty-seven years we lived there.

I remember the first day after we moved in. It was in May and I woke up with the sun. I walked to the end of the driveway in complete quiet, checked out the cornfield across the way, looked up and down the street, and said to myself, "I live on a country road."

We had one and a half acres of land with the house, our little piece of the country. We had a patch of woods and a patch of wet ground we called the swamp and an area we did not mow we called the meadow. I got to try a lot of plantings over the years. The fruit trees never prospered. Same with berry canes. Blueberries did well, and once I learned to cover them with net in fruit, I got to harvest a lot of berries. Strawberries came and went because the grass that grew amongst them made them more trouble than it was worth. The grapevine that was already there never gave us any fruit. Every time the grapes were about ripe, some critter came and ate them. Insult added to injury were the empty skins littering the ground. We kept chickens for a while, long before it became the popular trend it is now. We also raised rabbits for 4-H and for food. I didn't mind eating rabbit as far as the meat goes, but it ultimately felt too much like eating a pet, so we didn't do that for long. We definitely ate the eggs and eventually the chickens. The kids did get to show rabbits at the fair a few times, and it was a way for them to create friendships in a place where there were not a lot of kids around. While that was probably hard on them, it was exactly what I was hoping for as a means of protecting them.

At that time, Jack's job required him to work on rotating shifts. There was no way he would be able to sleep inside such a small house where all those kids were doing school. So he partitioned off a corner of the detached two-car garage into an unheated sleeping room. He had a little ceramic heater about half the size of a shoebox to try to keep himself warm, and that's where he slept on third shift. Yes, really.

I loved being a woods runner as a little kid and had always wanted that for my kids. Becca was twelve when we moved to Leroy and never really got into wandering the woods, but the rest of them got to have and enjoy that kind of freedom. We had creeks and cliffs, waterfalls and ponds all around us. Beth eventually made a garden from wild things she brought home. We briefly had both trillium and bluebells back there. I brought in mayapples and jack in the pulpit, which are almost certainly still there today. I spent a lot of money and time trying to start ginseng to no avail.

Over the years, we were able to maintain and even upgrade aspects of that house. We replaced the roof and the septic system—two pricey affairs that were paid for by refinancing the house. We replaced the electric panel and a lot of the old wiring. We connected the garage to the house with a family room. That job grew to include replacing some windows, rewiring, insulating and drywalling the garage, and pouring a patio out back. We renovated the old 1950s kitchen. The last big project was a screened porch built over the patio. I had always wanted one, and we finally did it.

Jack and I often spent time discussing how we wanted to manage our retirement. We eventually agreed that the house on Callow might be pretty hard on two old people, so we started to think about a better house in which to age in place. Ultimately, we bought a lovely old house in the Bank Street, Historic District in Painesville. It was quite solid but a little dated. Not all the choices made for it were quite in keeping with a historic home, but the people who had lived there for fifty years before us had kept it in good repair, so we felt the cosmetic things would be fun but not horribly taxing. In addition, as part of the sale, we got the contents of the house, which included some really nice antiques, a bonus since we had neither the means nor the inclination to acquire such furniture but were glad to have things that were right for such a lovely home. In retrospect, I feel pretty badly about that move because that was around the time Jack's health began to fail.

I remember the day we got the keys. On the way over, I asked him the three main reasons he had decided we could buy this house. He said the yard, the location, and that it made me happy. It did. We agreed we could live there because there were a first-floor full bath and a first-floor laundry. The parlor could easily be used as a bedroom if it ever came to that. We moved there believing it would be our last home.

The first thing Jack did was get to work on the garage. One corner was rotted, and he completely rebuilt it. There was inadequate light and not enough outlets, so he rewired the whole building. He also built a nice little workbench. Then he painted the exterior. It was the first garage we'd had since moving to Leroy that I was allowed to park in, so I really enjoyed it.

We also paid a lot of money to address the large trees in that yard. It was like a jungle, completely unusable for a gardener. We had three big ones removed, and the rest trimmed. We had the tree out front cabled due to the crack between the two main stems. That tree was a linden, and it had a pretty shape and lovely shade, but let me tell you, you will seldom find a messier tree. Every time the wind blew, I was out there picking up the little twigs it shed like it was its job.

I really loved that yard. It had the best soil I will ever get, black and loose and fertile. The cosmos I planted by the garage grew taller than the roof. One day, I picked up a pot that had been sitting in the side garden, and on the underside were nasty little white critters, termites. They liked the soil too. There was old termite damage in the house, and we had it professionally inspected twice while we were there. Had we stayed, I almost certainly would have invested in termite protection.

I spent a lot of time removing 1990s wallpaper in the Bank Street house. So much wallpaper. We painted much of the woodwork, some of the ceilings and almost all the walls. Jack chose many of the paint colors, which were often not what I would have picked. A winner was the mid-tone green he picked for the entrance hall. A loser was the minty green he picked for the kitchen. The stairway had supposedly come from the demolished Parmly Hotel. I was never able to substantiate that claim. Either way, it was lovely but painted completely white. I decided to strip the paint from the handrails, and they turned out to be oak. What a job, but in my opinion, so worth it.

I started to strip the beautiful double front doors, but the wood when revealed was not pretty enough to be worth the effort. I did strip the paint off the hardware in situ. I was afraid if I removed anything, it would never go back together right. Those doors were the glory of that house with their lacy wrought iron window inserts. They were not very weather tight, but with an old house, there are some things you put up with.

We replaced all the leftover knob and tube wiring we could reach. We added outlets and sconces to the front parlor that we used as a dining room. When he opened the wall, Jack discovered the entire house was sheathed in two by eights. You know, actual two-inch thick solid old growth timber. No wonder it was so quiet even though we lived on such a busy street. I had bought an antique light fixture for in there, but we eventually decided the ceiling plaster was too fragile to disturb. Selfish as I am, there was only so much I was willing to put Jack through by then. When we took up the carpeting in that room, we found that a two-foot strip of flooring was missing, replaced with plywood. I had to send to Seattle to get white oak of the right width to repair it. Then the whole thing was professionally finished so it would all match. It was the only room I put wallpaper into. It took me seventeen hours to hang, and that was with the repainted wainscot. So worth it though. I also took a stained glass class and made a window that we mounted into the top of the big picture window. That room was beautiful when it was finished.

Another big effort to restore historical integrity was the front porch. Part of the railing had been replaced with horizontal planks at some point. Though we could not find spindles to match what was there, and they weren't up to code anyway, what we did ended up being very pretty and much closer to right. We replaced the front steps with something that would require no maintenance, and we redid all the lattice skirting. I remember Jack being particularly cranky and hard to work with on that project. It must have been so hard on him to be bent over like that for so long, but he would never just stand back and let me do it for him. I also painted the porch ceiling pale blue, not just for tradition but to try to discourage the spiders. I honestly feel that it helped. Plus, it was pretty.

Everything we did on Bank Street was with the expectation that the house was where we would stay, so we did not go cheap. Instead of repairing the roof, we replaced it. Instead of average light fixtures, we got historical reproduction brass light fixtures. After two years, the house and yard were pretty much done, and I had enjoyed every minute. So I began to talk to Jack about doing a flip, also for fun. Despite his fluctuating health, he was game. When we actually found a house that seemed a good candidate, he suddenly said he didn't want to do all that work for a house that we weren't going to live in. So we moved again.

The house on Willowood Court was a completely different kettle of fish. It was a modern colonial in a subdivision that had been horribly neglected and mistreated. Once again, in the belief that it was our final home, we repaired and replaced as if it was the forever house. All new flooring, heat and air-conditioning, appliances, every single interior surface painted, new roof with tear-off, new shed, new energy efficient toilets. We fixed all the holes and dings in the siding, redid landscaping, we even had various sunken concrete structures raised to level again.

It was super rewarding just to clean that dirty, dirty house. Animal hair and dust and mildew literally clinging to the walls. Subfloors so soaked with pet urine we tried to remove them, couldn't, so sealed them with a rubber coating. Walls full of dings and holes from the apparently wild children who had lived there. The kitchen was so bad; I hired cleaning help. It took a professional cleaner a full eight-hour day just to make it clean enough to use. I had to use a paint scraper to get the gunk off the bathroom floors. In the end, it was fresh and clean and a very pleasant place to live. The backyard looked out over a twenty-acre fallow nursery field. It was very quiet and alive with birds. And eighteen months in, Jack suddenly said he really just wanted to get back to the country. Huh?

So we started to look. As usual, we considered some wrecks. I finally told him I had redone two houses in four years, and I was tired. I had had enough of that kind of fun. One Saturday, we spent two hours combing over a sad little ranch on eleven acres at the back end of nowhere in Leroy, and when we got home, I told him no. The house had too little to work with and was too hard to get to and was just more than I wanted to take on at sixty-six years old. So I opened up the laptop and took another look at what was out there in late March.

And found a house for sale on Girdled Road almost in sight of our Callow Road home. If the woods were cut down, I could see it from my living room window. I knew the house well, having driven past it a million times when we lived in Leroy. I did not care for it, but as I began to scroll through the pictures, I realized this house had been gutted and redone. By *not me*. But by someone whose taste was very similar to mine. In addition, it was situated across the street from a preserved farm, so the view will likely not change in my lifetime. (Everyone who visits this house is breathless at the gorgeous views. It is a feast for my soul just to look out my bedroom window.) I carried the laptop in to Jack at his desk and said, "Look."

And here's the thing. I'm sure people who know us wondered what was going on with us. Why did we keep moving after so many years of stability? I think it was so Jack could let me have a little fun. I think he enjoyed it too. And because the houses let us stair step up to a home value much greater than what we could have realized from the Callow house. It put us in a position to buy the house on Girdled with its five acres and pond and everything new.

I am so sad that Jack got to enjoy this home for less than a year. But the one summer he had was fun for him. He bought and used some tools he enjoyed like a chain saw and a weed whacker. He got to take his machete to the brush out back. There was plenty of mowing to do. He really enjoyed the fish in the pond. He got food for them and would go out and toss it to them every day, usually much more than they needed. The very last time he ventured outside, it was to feed his fish. We spent so many soft relaxing hours side by side out by the pond, just watching the wind blow the riffles across.

As far as I know, this really is my last house. I am trying to plan for whatever I can think of to keep things easy for the kids and to stay here even if getting around gets hard. I have a first-floor bath and laundry but no bedroom. Worst case, I can do as we did for Jack and put a bed in the living room. I have already made it clear to them that I do not want to linger if there is no hope of usefulness. I have had my life, and it has been a good one. I am ready whenever God wants me back. I look forward to seeing Jack again. I hope he is the one who comes for me.

On the England Trip

In 2002, my cousin Don Merriman's wife, Opal, passed away. They had left me 1 percent of their estate. In the end, it came to about $25,000. What a windfall for a low-budget operation like ours! Jack told me immediately that I should use it to take the trip to England I had always wanted. He said he would go with me but then withdrew. So Becca went with me.

The following is a transcription of the journal I kept during our trip. All told, for everything for both of us the cost of the trip came to around $4,000. *So* glad I went, as travel has become physically challenging for me due to my sensitivity to motion.

England Trip

5/02/02

Had my first type-A dream of our trip last night. We found the BandB and the room, but I was in the bathroom when the maid walked in with towels. And for some reason, we were traveling with animals, in particular a hamster. Could not comprehend the Yorkshire accents. Oh well, put new undies into the wash. Unwrapped and tried out new umbrella and "waist security pouch."

5/07/02, 1:59 p.m.

Preparations are winding down, and I'm actually starting to pack. Though I have toyed in my mind with the reality of this trip, I have not really dwelt on it yet.

5/08/02, 10:52 a.m.

On the limo to the airport. The morning ended up passing pretty quickly. We repacked Becky's stuff. Showered and bathed. She colored her hair. Several farewell calls. At the end, Jeff P. was late coming to take us to Quail, but we made the limo anyway. Forgot to recheck the flight. Hope that isn't a problem later...

1:00 p.m.

Waiting at the airport. Had outrageously expensive Pizza Hut for lunch. (Oh well, must get used to that.) The flight appears to be on time so far. Here's a new one. Looks like there may be a seeing eye dog on our flight.

2:20 p.m.

Aboard the plane. Oh yeah, the seats are *so* close together. Light rain from a gray sky. And someone turned the heat on! So glad this is a short flight. Lucky me...I have a worsening sore throat. Find myself wondering if it might be from the scopolamine skin patch, or am I coming down with a cold? Yuck! Lord, please put your big hands around this plane.

2:50 p.m.

Up in the sunlight above the clouds. I love this part. Scopolamine doesn't seem to work all that well for me. Bumping ride today.

4:20 p.m.

Waiting at Charlotte, North Carolina. It's eighty-five degrees! We were obviously *not* prepared for the heat and humidity (I wore jeans and a turtleneck and socks and tennis shoes and jacket). Thank heaven for air-conditioning. Throat continues to hurt. Becky says it could be drying from the patch. Lots of weary children here. Hard to know what to do now. Sleepy but not wanting to sleep yet.

6:20 p.m.

Feel a little better after a walk up the concourse. We stopped at Starbucks for hot choc and Danish. Then called home. Nice to hear

Jacky one more time. Should start boarding soon. Stir sticks from Starbucks would be perfect to finish the attic floor in my dollhouse, maybe on the way back.

6:50 a.m.

Lucky me again, have been chosen twice for random extra checks, have had the little paddle run up and down twice. Yes, I wear a watch, and yes, my pants have rivets.

5/09, 7:15 a.m. (2:15 a.m. home time)

Well, it seems it is morning now. Less than an hour until we arrive. We're in the last seats against the restroom bulkhead, so all night, we heard the rush and swish of flushing. Not at all rested despite the sips of wine with dinner. Mostly dozed all night wishing for earplugs. Will not use the rest of the scopolamine because its drying effect makes my throat so sore. Hope that's all it is anyway.

8:45 a.m.

Safely arrived in London. All the luggage made it. Got cash with the debit card. Seems like it will be pretty easy to find our way from here. After a cleanup, we'll go buy train tickets to Victoria Station. So far so good!

10:00 a.m.

Figured out the train. Sat with a couple guys who were very friendly and helpful. Now riding the tube. Sure hope the hostel will be open when we get there. Time to kick in the travel mantra: "I'm so tired."

10:45 a.m.

Only got lost once on the tube so far. Sitting in Hyde Park trying to imagine it in another time, without the sounds of cars and many diesel engines. Throat still mad sore. Took off the patch and hope it gets better. Checked into the hostel, located in a very pretty street. And an attractive building, but inside is all broken up and painted weird colors. As we went to stow luggage, some guy walked by wearing only a towel around his waist. Hope we have *some* privacy. Over yonder are some chestnut trees (in bloom, white or pink). The park is surrounded by a tall boxwood hedge. Fairly unkempt grass not cut; maybe it's a wildflower garden? Long tree-lined avenues lining asphalt sidewalks. We both feel pretty ragged from lack of sleep. At eleven, we can get into the room, nap?

12:00 p.m.

Lunch at Burger King—duh. London is the most culturally diverse place I've ever been, all kinds of nationalities with their own languages.

12:40 p.m.

Red open-top bus tour and Thames River cruise.

1:00 p.m.

On the tour bus, all the major sites.

1:35 p.m.

Well, this worked out nicely. The bus included a boat ride, and the pier is right under the London Eye. Will try to get on early after the boat ride. If not, there is a Dali exhibit right near the London Aquarium. Whatever we do, we plan to quit early and go to bed. We both fell asleep during the first part of the bus tour. Am still intimidated by trying to find our way through the tube. Everywhere we go, we hear many different languages. Interesting observation, almost all the Germans we've seen appear to be gay. Lots of English women and girls are using bright, Raggedy Ann—red hair dye, whole head or streaks. Saw a condom dispenser in the lady's room at a Burger King. Tour begins with cheesy march music. *Ick.*

3:00 p.m.

On the London Eye, they let us on early. Have to admit I don't enjoy heights much. (I had pre-purchased tickets for the London Eye online and they were scheduled for 5 p.m.)

3:15 p.m.

From up here, we can look down on a kid attraction consisting of trampolines combined with bungee ropes. Two posts stand either side of trampolines with bungees to each and connected by a harness. Kids get strapped in and bounce really high. Becky said she thought Abby would really like that; I think it's scary.

3:40 p.m.

Back on the tour bus. Almost all the buildings touch, and many have window boxes with trailing vines and greens, etc. Lots of pansies (no pun!). Many iron "balconies" full of flowers.

6:40 p.m.

We decided to do the London Dungeon Tour. It was quite grisly. Now we're having Chinese for dinner. After this, we're going back to the hostel and *sleep*. Another interesting observation. Public restrooms are called "toilet." They use the little bins for toilet paper. London is really just another big city, although the old architecture is pretty. The area around Buckingham Palace is like a park, noble statuary and huge old trees, many sycamores (which turned out to be plane trees). Becky and I neither one enjoy the crowds. Having to find our way around really adds to the stress.

8:40 p.m.

Here's a weird European thing. We're sharing our room with a guy. Maybe he'll leave tomorrow. Forgot to mention that part of the dungeon thing was making us walk across a walkway inside a spinning barrel kind of thing where the boards were far apart enough that "flame" showed through. It was a completely disorienting thing. Almost threw up from it. Even now, between planes, trains, and boats, I keep getting these little spasms of dizziness stuff. We're all washed and ready for bed. Our room is in a five-story townhouse filled with faded glory painted over in bizarre colors—purple, salmon, etc.

The room itself is institutional green with some holes punched in the walls. There's a sink in the corner, which is handy and one ill-placed electric socket, which is not (handy, that is) one fluorescent light. Real college dorm ambience going here. Our room has three sets of iron bunks painted bright red. Haven't met our roomie yet.

Later; they are a young French couple.

Friday, 5/10, 9:45 a.m.

Well, we slept. It is so strange sharing a room with complete mixed-gender strangers. Probably would not do that again. Last night, as we got ready for bed, the smoke alarm went off. What a helpless feeling. The ceiling is too high to reach the alarm, and it's so loud. Finally, it just stopped. That was weird. This morning, I went to curl my hair, and the curling iron burned a hunk of my hair off! (Plastic tip also melted off the iron. Clearly, the adapter did not adapt well.) That's one of those "nothing I can do about it" things.

12:00 p.m.

Still wandering the streets looking for the British Museum. Hope we make it to tea okay. As I write, we are sitting on a park bench in Russell Square. It is maybe three to four times the size of the square in Painesville. The ten-meter wide sidewalk is graveled with tiny brown/tan gravel. There is a fountain at the center of the square, and there are sycamores all around. Black wrought iron fence six feet high and gardens lining it. All the grassy areas are temporarily fenced with something similar to our snow fencing, except the wood is natural and not straight, as though chunks were hacked from branches. The fence is to protect newly planted grass. Food here is not "to go" but "takeaway", which is cheaper than the same thing eaten in. Hair still stinks of being burned. Statue in Russell Square. Francis Duke of Bedford erected MDCCCIX twenty feet high on white marble plinth

2:00 p.m.

Well, that was the British Museum. Many very cool things. Did a little shopping. Hope I don't have to jettison too much to make the souvies fit. Throat much better since I took off the patch. Having occasional vertigo, which is weird. We have an hour to find our way to the Charing Cross Hotel.

2:10 p.m.

On the way back to Holborn Station, we ran across Bloomsbury Square. Also surrounded by wrought iron fencing. More secluded as the perimeter plants are very mature. Many sweet-smelling flowering trees. One looked like bright-yellow wisteria. One purple one smelled just like viburnum. (Throughout the trip, we saw a shrub with a blossom like mini lilac that was a dark almost-blue color. Never found anyone who could ID it for us.) There is a slate pavement in the center with benches. Rounded grassy islands with granite curbstones. Pigeons. Off to the tube.

3:20 p.m.

We made it to tea. Scones and clotted cream. Smoked salmon.

5:30 p.m.

Tea was lovely as was our visit with Sheila. (Sheila was a lady I had met at a writers' conference the year before. We had kept in touch and she happened to be in London at the same we were, so we met for tea.) After tea, we began walking down the Mall. Right now, we're sitting on a wooden bench in Saint James Park right across from a large, open, graveled place with bleachers all around. We think that might be for the changing of the guard. Have bought a few souvenirs and was sorely tempted at a store where linens were 70 percent off. Decided to wait on that. Am getting ready to mail out some postcards, which may be a challenge as there are no letter boxes, to avoid bombs. There is a plain black bird that sings very sweetly. ("Four and twenty blackbirds baked in a pie.") The ducks and pigeons are quite unafraid.

6:00 p.m.

Sitting on a park bench on the other side of Saint James Park. Thought a tree dropped seeds on my head and reached up to remove it, it was a bee! And it didn't sting me. Someone is blowing a trumpet across the street. We're about to see Buckingham Palace and walk back to the hostel across Hyde Park. Figured out what mailboxes look like—small, red, tiny slot. (Took a while to find street signs on the sides of buildings too!) Have seen a new kind of one-person car, five to six feet long (actually seven feet, I paced one out). Really tiny. There are weeds in the grass of the park, which I think is quite cool, no chemlawn here. Have observed many ladies draped in shawls and scarves. Way pashmina.

7:30 p.m.

We walked the length of Hyde Park. Now in a restaurant over-looking the park, about to try bangers and mash before going back to the hostel. All over London, they paint on the pavement, which way to look for oncoming traffic before crossing. Pavements often have reddish color. Sidewalks are made of individual rectangles, maybe one and a half by two and a half feet. Lots of cyclists ride in traffic with the cars, mostly the old English racer rather than mountain bikes. Down through the parks, which have big sections unmown and unweeded, people do not leash their dogs to walk them, and the dogs are generally obedient unlike the children. Have seen several examples of a small, stocky pit bullish-looking type, maybe Willy's size. (At that time, the family dog was a Springer Spaniel/beagle mutt of about twenty-five pounds named Willy.) Ordered a lemonade for dinner, and what I got is a glass of white pop with a slice of lemon. Still quite dry from the scopolamine. Drank the whole pot of earl gray at tea. We had cucumber sandwiches and raisin scones with clotted cream. The cream was pale yellow and thick enough to hold its shape. It was not at all sweet, but you put jam on the cream. Black current and strawberry. Chopped tomato sandwich. Then a thick brownie kind of thing. If Sheila had not been there, I would probably have tasted everything, just to see how it tastes. So cool to walk through Hyde Park and think. Regency people saw these hills and even some of the trees. Many chestnuts in bloom and sycamores with knobby trunks. All the walking is finally making me tired.

8:10 p.m.

Unimpressed with bangers and mash, but at least it's filling, and the gravy was good. About to try bread pudding for dessert. Have had tea a couple of times now, and here's the interesting thing, it's been *good*. I hate strong tea and really expected not to like the tea here. But even though it was earl gray with the bag in the pot, it was not too strong. Maybe because it had cream and two lumps.

9:00 p.m.

Dessert was great, then we walked the rest of the way. Found my bed occupied, and learned beds are assigned. Oh well. Means I'm in a top bunk, which also means I have had to climb up using Becky's suitcase. Otherwise, there's no way. Now what do I do about going to the bathroom at night?

5/11, 8:30 a.m.

Well, that was quite a night. I laid awake for hours, not sure if it was the noise, both in and outside the house, or the caffeine from all the tea I drank or normal insomnia, hard to tell. At some point, there was a huge, yelling, swearing fight outside. "Kill me now!" "I'll bite your f——ing face off!" What is that!? I don't feel as badly as I ought considering how little sleep I got. Had to move into the top bunk as the last empty bed here was filled by an Aussie physical therapist. We're thinking of trying to find a hotel for the night if we can find one near enough to get back to here by seven to catch the bus tomorrow. Took some pain med this morning as either the climb or the bad bed has done in my lower back. Hope to walk that off through the day. Want to email and send some postcards this morning.

1:30 p.m.

Back in the room, which is wonderfully quiet after the chaos of the night. Have just set the alarm for tomorrow morning when, hopefully, the bus will show up, and we can get out of here. Just back from the doll's house show, some lovely, wildly expensive things. Bought almost all I wanted except for porcelain and glass, which I am leery of trying to get home without breaking. Met Diane from Avon. We had a nice chat, and they will let me buy from their trade pricelist, which should at least pay for shipping. (I had started a little business making and selling handcrafted dollhouse miniatures and was making connections with possible suppliers at the London

Dollshouse Festival.) My reaction to this trip so far is, I don't realize how much Jack's protection over me means until I get out from under it. It does let me see the world as it is, that's for sure. And how ugly and meaningless. You go to England and *not one* business service person is actually English. You're never sure if they can even understand what you say! Both luggage locks and keys are still missing. Will try again on postcards as I had addresses, stamps and pen but no cards while we were out. Three of four roommates are gone, and I have high hopes number four is leaving as well. Have discovered I can live in so-so conditions, but the utter lack of privacy here is dreadful. Dang! Looks like he's staying, oh well. Can't wait to leave!

7:38 p.m.

Back in the room. We walked around in Hyde Park for a couple hours. Saw Kensington and a beautifully peaceful water garden. Park full of people, mostly not Brits. Saw the Albert memorial. Grotesque! The flower walk was lovely. Love those blackbirds that sing so sweetly. Had Italian for dinner. Got my postcards done. Hope they'll mail them from the desk for me. Hope I have the little travel clock set right. We need to be down at the door at 6:50 a.m. to catch the bus. Lovely to see the sun today. It's clouding up again. Jack emailed there's been a train wreck (here). We heard nothing, but we're so out of the loop here. Feel conspicuously out of place.

Sunday, May 12, 6:20 a.m.

Pam's forty-ninth birthday. She's been gone ten years almost. We got up early to be sure not to miss the bus. My back is hurting pretty good this morning. Oh well, won't it be ironic if, after all the gyrations to do the horseback, I can't even ride!

8:45 a.m.

On the road from London. (We took a seven-day backpacker bus tour all over England that began that morning.) Stopped in Windsor and saw the *huge* castle (but not Queen Mary's famous dollshouse). The countryside could be home until you see a house. And of course, there's the driving on the left thing too.

9:00 a.m.

Played rock, paper, scissors, and I was the bus champ, even though I don't know how to play! Instead of "yield", they have "give way." Roads are incredibly confusing. Wonder if IOM is doable… (I planned to drive around the Isle of Man later in the trip and wondered if I could do it.) Most of the people on the bus are young Aussies or Kiwis. Two American Mormon girls and a retired Chinese guy. I begin to feel extended travel is not worth the hassle if you're not doing something worthwhile. Once again, Jack is right… Just passed a wood carpeted in bluebells. The fields here are hedged, not fenced.

10:15 a.m.

Well, so that was Stonehenge. Very low-key setting in the middle of rolling pastures and mustard (rapeseed) field. Cows, etc. Took a pic of some barrows for Abby. People wander the fields with their unleashed dogs. Decided not to pay for the privilege of walking around that particular pile of rocks. Our guide, Graham, reminds me of Tim in looks and manner. Same hairstyle too. Smells good here and always the birds. I keep trying to get myself accustomed to the left-side driving. London roads so bizarre. Who could tell? Enjoying the countryside. Still having occasional dizziness. The more I get around, the better I like the way Brits do parks, etc. Very low-key and natural. Another cool gray day. Still no rain. Thank you, Lord! Bet Jack is up by now. Miss church today. Some people from the bus were playing catch with a football. Theirs is tan and shaped like ours only with rounded ends and much bigger.

10:45 a.m.

Already making hay here. Crop circle area. They do military maneuvers here because there's enough open space.

12:00 p.m.

Avebury, perfect English village.

1:00 p.m.

Laycock authentic old village, could have spent several days. Did visit a church and cemetery. The day has turned gorgeous. Sunny and warm. Moss on the walls, flint gravel on the sidewalk. Ivy all over. Lilac in bloom. Church felt so old and dead, smelled old, door old and worn. Moss on the slate and thatch roofs. Cornish pasty, wiggly line on top, one-half meat, one-half dessert, and cider. West Country food.

1:10 p.m.

In Box is the longest railway tunnel in Europe. Buying cider, which is fermented, for later. Thought I knew a bit about Brit history and culture, but there's so much I never heard of.

4:00 p.m.

All around Bath. Pasties for lunch. Cider for later. Saw the Assembly Rooms, columned entrance. Four fireplaces in each, huge crystal chandeliers. Hilly town. White gowns, very delicate. White on white embroidery. Narrow alleys. Often, we have seen glass blocks set into sidewalks. Is there something beneath? Roman Baths excav., 1880s though some artifacts were found earlier 1700s. Still sunny and warm. "Beef and stilton", hamburg and cheese and potato cubes with pepper in thick pastry crust.

5:35 p.m.

Cider at Tintern Abbey. In Wales. Cider is *awful*-tasting, sour with an icky taste. Going through the Wye valley. Welsh flag, a red dragon on a green and white ground. In England, all the houses touch. In Wales, they stand alone. Yellow fields in England and Wales are rapeseed. "Sycamores" are actually plane trees.

6:30 p.m.

In Wales. Much nicer hostel in a six-*girl* room. Yah!

11:00 p.m.

Like Wales a lot. Sat up in the pub till ten or so, eating pizza and the others drinking a lot. Becky completely sloshed! Talked for a while with two Mormon girls but couldn't seem to find the differences to talk about. By the way, Welsh pizza was like a crust spread with tomato soup covered in powdered parmesan cheese. Not very pizza-like.

5/13, 8:30 a.m.

At the Black Sheep Hostel in Wales. Wonderful to sleep somewhere quiet! Our group is made up mostly of Aussies and Kiwis between whom there is a brotherly sort of rancor and lots of sheep jokes. We have one retired Chinese man who pretty much keeps to himself. Raining this morning, a pretty, soft, steady rain. Trying to decide how many layers to wear, how to stay dry, etc. Debating what clothes I can jettison to make room for souvenirs.

9:30 a.m.

Took a little walk this morning. All the houses are made of stone or brick or knobby stucco, slate roofs, and slate doorstep. Everyone names their house. Lots of flowers in bloom. (Had *lots* of trouble getting the combination on the lock to actually *open* the front door.) Some wind today, all kind of subdued. None of the drinkers seem worse for wear. Here's a good lesson: fellowship of the cup is fleeting. Group dynamics, also interesting as coalitions form and reform. This hostel is *old*, the floors with some give, walls papered with thick-textured paper painted garishly purple, orange, etc. Room clean with comfy, good bed, good pillow. We're off! Hostel across from the train station. Amtrak? Low clouds scudding along the mountaintops. All signs in Wales in English first, then Welsh. Had a little communication thing this morning. One of the Mormon girls was going to find out about breakfast, which was part of the deal. As she was leaving the room, I said, "Let me know what's up with breakfast," and a Kiwi woman turned on me, almost angry. "What's wrong with the food?"

I said, "That's not what I meant. I just meant what's going on with the food. How do we get breakfast?" So even if you *do* speak the same language… Wales is a lot like Pennsylvania or Kentucky, switchbacks, etc. Forgot to mention, Avebury is a sheep field! No kidding, we had to watch our step. Sore throat again. Been using Becky's motion relief. Wonder if that's the problem. Back still tender, at least with this weather, I won't be tempted to try to ride. Thank you, Lord. Email this morning. *Love* daily contact with home. Makes it more bearable. Oh, the road we're on! Snaking up a mountain with almost no guardrails, wet road. Gorgeous, gorgeous scenery. Going down a coal mine today. Woo-hoo! Rocky, sheepy hillside. Up in the clouds now.

11:30 a.m.

The coal mine was interesting. They hate Thatcher here for closing the mines, even though they admit new mining methods are more cost effective. Waterproof coat—not! It's just pouring today, and the mountaintops are covered in clouds. Got coal stains on my coat. *What* a miserable job—coal mining. Black damp, heavy gas, fire damp, methane, lighter than air. Twll Mawr, Big Pit. The guide says, "It's all good," quite a lot. Still reminding me of Tim. Aussies and Kiwis often say, "Yeah, yeah, yeah," really fast. Vegetation much different from home—grass, lots of gray rocks. (Yesterday, soil around Stonehenge was full of gravel.) Low, evergreeny things and long rust-colored stalks of something weedy. Mine was damp, smelled old, pipes full of rushing water. Low ceilings held up by bricks or planks but mostly by pine tree trunks, maybe five or six inches thick. Red phone boxes are everywhere; sheep have their tails. Lots of wild mulberry in bloom—blossoms stink. Hedges and walls. Vines trained above doors. Lilac up here still in bloom, down in the valley, they're done. There is a vine, often trained up a house front, with a pink, trumpety stephanotis-looking flower with no scent. Wisteria all over.

In Crickhowell with its castle which is one tiny round tower. Gas sold by the liter, usually in the high seventies per liter. Lace curtains at the windows always and everywhere. Rain easing up.

2:00 p.m.

Stopped at Elan to view dams and picnic, ate on the bus in the rain. Cod and chips for lunch. Big fillet (which was very good every time I had it) and fries like American steak fries, very greasy. Served with vinegar and salt. Red Lion most common pub name. Watching the driving a lot and believe I'm becoming a little acclimated. Lots of it is common sense and courtesy. But getting from point A to point B will still be tough. Lunch came wrapped in three pieces of newspaper (unprinted). Didn't do much with the DH show, feeling so dizzy and sick. Wish now I'd bought more muslin and lawn. Otherwise satisfied.

2:45 p.m.

Welsh mountains covered in pine forest. BTW, no one in Australia drinks Fosters. Little sunrooms with glass ceiling very common.

5:15 p.m.

Back from a hike in Snowdonia National Park. Rain quit just in time. Great walk—but scary—"Braveheart", "Princess Bride" looking country. Huge old trees with ferns growing from the moss. Bluebell glens, miles of drystone walls, sheep all over. Lichen on the rocks. Gorse is that evergreen I was seeing—very nasty, prickly, orange/yellow flowers (which were a pretty, orchid-looking thing). So nice to feel fresh air and quiet.

5:35 p.m.

This whole area has the feel of West Virginia, though pretty well-kept. Place names so cool. Our bus is royal blue with multicolored "go!" all over. Sort of an "ice cream truck on steroids" look. *Really* ugly upholstery. But it runs so far.

9:00 p.m.

At the hostel in Caernarvon. We are actually staying *inside* the old city walls. Pretty nice hostel though the bathroom stuff is weird again. Gents up here, "Oh, go ahead and use the gents," Yeah right!

(Bathroom fixtures often very tiny to retrofit into such old buildings.) Had cottage pie for dinner, ground beef and brown gravy covered with baked mash potatoes served with fries and peas! Still getting periodic head spins which I attribute to bus motion. Free breakfast and one and a half hours to tour the castle with a local lady. Hope to have time to shop a little. Leah's telling a bunch of bad jokes. A man walked into a bar and said ouch. (That one made me hysterical. Must have been *really* tired.)

5/14, 11:10 a.m.

Spent the night within town walls of Caernarvon Castle. Stayed in a Georgian house (two hundred years old), where six years ago, the owner found the opening to a medieval tunnel in the basement. Slate and coal are what Wales is all about. They use slate for mulch! Visited a supermarket. Very like ours, but of course, the products are all different. "Plain digestive biscuits?" I asked a Welshman re: digestive. I said in America that would mean medicine, and he turned away to laugh. Boob windows. Walked up on the town walls and picked up a stone up there. Hoping to post cards somewhere today. Amazing how fast the tide sweeps up the quayside ("key side"). Only took an hour! (I went for a walk alone early in the morning around the streets and along the quay. Cold!) Very narrow little streets. King's Gate had six portcullises! We saw grooves in the sandstone rocks where swords and arrowheads were sharpened. Weather today, cool, gray, with blue streaks. Windy! Saw yellow wallflowers on castle walls. Very weird to see old-style brick or stone houses being built because they look old as they're being built. Saw palm trees growing *in* Hyde Park. The colors for houses, in and out, are pretty different. Lots of pastel house fronts, purple door, lace curtains, *never* see wooden buildings, just stone, brick, or stucco. Will even have cement fascia. "Essex girl" means tramp, same with "Welsh girl." Caernarvon, 80 percent Welsh-speaking. Have seen lots of buttercups, not a lot of dandelions. Will paint window surrounds to match door. In Bangor, beautiful wooden front doors, not painted. For sale signs affixed to building fronts. The amount of casual swearing in the British culture is shocking, popular music is full of the stuff (and explicit sexual vulgarity), way beyond home. Every sign in Wales nearly has both Welsh and English, usually Welsh first. Crossed bridge over Menae Strait so narrow the bus barely went through, built in 1815–1830. Trees in full leaf here. Finished our butter crumble cookies (like pitzelles).

12:10 p.m.

On the way to Liverpool. Sun has come out.

1:10 p.m.

Seriously not interested in going to Liverpool. Weather still sunny.

1:30 p.m.

Everyone in Liverpool wears a tracksuit and white trainers (tennis shoes).

3:50 p.m.

Had lunch in a mall in the Albert Dock in Liverpool. Give the Brits credit for preserving many elements of historic buildings, pillars, doors, and windows, stone floors, etc. Had a "ploughman's lunch," two *huge* slabs of cheddar, two French bread rolls with butter, pickle, which was a sweet brown chutney, "salad" which was chopped tomato and cuke and cole slaw. Had carrot cake and clotted cream for dessert. Walked over to the Maritime Museum and Tate Gallery. Don't know why walking around displays is giving me vertigo. Seems a bit odd. People on the tour, Tony and Jane, Aussie teachers, very quiet. She is small but always hungry and eating sprouts and muesli, has three sons, seven to thirteen, though the parents are my age almost. China man and us, the rest are young Aussies and Kiwis, footloose and into drinking and partying pretty much. I've been sitting up front and watching the roads, etc. Stones for these buildings are more often white than brown or gold. There was a tub of something called nut nougat at breakfast, which I wanted to try but chickened out. Also, some Vegemite, which was in a plastic tub like with sour cream and brown and smelled *vile*. Becky tasted it and pronounced it vile. Aussies said that was 'cause she ate it alone instead of on toast. Plan to try some Scots food when we get up there. Just passed a business in an old church. Even new houses have slate roofs. Union Jack is Brit flag, not English.

5:15 p.m.

Skipped bus bowling and riddles. Riding the bus *really* puts me to sleep. Weather has gone gray. Land is rolling, trees in full leaf. Sheep *everywhere*. In Lancaster, rain.

Beautiful green and rolling country. Back into sunshine and stone walls after endless neatly-trimmed hedges. Hills up ahead much more barren than what we've seen so far. Interesting note, battlemented castle tower at Caernarvon meant to be roofed with conical lead and wooden roofs.

9:00 p.m.

We have a room to ourselves, very quiet in Ambleside. Mountain views, the town almost has an Alpine sort of feel, also resorty. We ate in, cooked spaghetti and ate in with Tony and Jane from Australia and Jill and Evan from Canada. Emailed home and ready to shower and maybe sleep…we'll see. The hostel is an 1871 farmhouse. Huge lounge with piano, huge dining room with fireplace, kitchen you can function in. The rhododendron outside has a trunk at least ten inches thick. Learning to function without napkins—there's a trick! Have about decided the dizzy turns are from constantly being in motion on the bus. Don't know why it hits so badly in museums…maybe because there's not much going on then, so it's more noticeable. The shower here is wonderful, especially because of the luxury of privacy. Fifty-six million people on this island, not much of that! Eccles cake/pastry crust full of mincemeat sort of raisony filling. Ew! Jack was right. Fun is not a good enough reason to make a trip like this. Fun is so empty.

5/15, 7:00 a.m.

Gray and heavy clouds lying on the hilltops. Back is slowly healing. Seems a bit better each day. Felt a bit better when one Aussie boy said his back hurt from a bed too. (Took another walk that morning in the cool rain. Lovely quiet time.)

8:45 a.m.

Nice breakfast. Starting to get the hang of these places. Picked up a brochure for a backpacker place in Oxford. May stay there Friday, instead of going back to London. Still gray and rainy. More Aussies getting on. Cars are so small here because if they weren't, no one could get anywhere. Up on the mountains, the ferns grow on stalks. Here, ferns pop out of cracks in the wall. Picked up a dropped rhododendron blossom, smelled pink, that covered my hand. Seems like *all* Ambleside is either hotel or BandB. Love that every little house has a name. This area seems pretty Victorian.

9:35 a.m.

Took a little hike up the hill in the mist. *Huge* black snails on the trail. Country is lovely, but no more so to me than other places we've been. The lakes are nice with treed islands. Once again, sheep everywhere. Don't know why this bus makes me so sleepy (might have been the motion pills!). I love that sheep graze on the soccer field in the middle of a little village. Never see goats. Not a lot of cows, no beef cattle, no chickens running loose. Always sheep. As we go further north, the hills get steeper, all pine trees, streams rushing down the hillsides over rocks. Saw a WWII cement bunker in the middle of a sheep field. They were built all over England in case of invasion. "Matterdale-Unsuitable for motors."

10:30 a.m.

Bus ill, stopping in Carlisle to get it fixed. One big challenge in this country is to find street signs. If they exist, they are on the buildings.

4:00 p.m.

Had an adventure. Stuck in Carlisle for four and a half hours because the bus broke. Saw a beautiful cathedral begun in 1100. Also, saw the castle where Mary Queen of Scots was imprisoned. Kind of creepy inside. Had a moment alone in a large empty room, so big it had two fireplaces. I thought I could actually feel the presence of the soldiers who had been quartered there. Smells old. All the town was built of red rock. Saw the sharpening grooves and portcullis grooves, murder holes filled in. Church full of memorials. Now stuck in rush hour out of Carlisle. The churchyard had places where grass, etc. were allowed to grow uncut. Three wells inside the church. Unbelievable carving inside. This detour makes us too late to do much of anything in Edinburgh. It's gotten sunny and fairly warm but still very windy. Finally decided to go to Hadrian's Wall after all. English cemeteries are hard to enjoy because the stones are so old, they can't be read. Interesting fact about street names in Caernarvon. Pool Street (main shopping street) is named for a millpond that's gone. Many street names are the same. Had a chicken curry jacket potato for lunch. (Icky!)

5:05 p.m.

Just visited Birdoswald on Hadrian's Wall. Built on a ridge crest. Walked along it to a mile fort. You can really tell Roman stonework from local. Have identified the prevalent Brit smell. Sheep!

5:25 p.m.

WC break in Brampton.

5:35 p.m.

Heading on into Scotland. Only about 10 percent of Brit farming we've seen is cultivation. Vast majority is animals, mostly sheep. Amazing that miles of hedges appear to have been trimmed square. (Turns out, there are people who travel around with a machine that prunes the hedges so neatly.) At Hadrian's Wall, we saw two guys doing maintenance. He said private landowners will maintain their portion. They had power washed two times and were weeding! Hadrian's Wall, the northernmost reach of Roman Empire. Churches, homes, even barns fortified against Scots!

5:50 p.m.

Crossed into Scotland. The earth is rust red here.

6:30 p.m.

Pines cover the hills. Daffodils and tulips still in bloom in Scotland. Much more cultivation here. Churches all derelict. Seeing our first "housing development," maybe two acres.

7:00 p.m.

Many tree plantations in Scotland. Daffodil bank under stonewall.

7:40 p.m.

Been driving round and round Edinburgh as the driver keeps missing his turn.

11:30 p.m.

Just back from "Haunted Tour." Ghost stories told in the dark in vaults under Edinburgh and in a graveyard. A little creepy but beats the heck out of pubbing. Have our arrangements made for Friday night in London. Pretty sure we won't have any trouble making the train. Really hate these big city hostels. We are in with sixteen girls from as many countries. Some are really long termers here. What a way to live! Every place we've stayed has deep windows with paneled surrounds. This is the saddest, emptiest place yet. Haven't seen a live church yet. They remind me of futuristic movies. Only it's now. Very sad.

5/16, 7:35 a.m.

Lovely sunny morning. The light lasted until nearly ten last night, and the birds must have started singing at four. Busy room, not a restful night. Have found part of my perception of a place lies in whether or not I like the hostel. Don't like this one, nowhere near enough privacy (men and ladies shared same shower room. Stalls were private but shared a common mixed-gender outer room). At least the dorm was all girls, but so many of them and so noisy! Will probably put in some breakfast and computer time.

Will try to ring Helen sometime today when I see how the time is going. (Helen was a miniaturist I met on a weblog who lived in

York and whom I hoped to meet with there.) Yesterday, Graham said there is some feeling mad cow disease, and foot and mouth were spread on purpose to force Britain further into the EU. Britain has been agricultural, but EU wants it to fill a manufacturing role, so there's the belief that it was all done to shift Britain's focus away from farming. Seems to have put many farmers out of work.

8:30 a.m.

Time to leave Edinburgh. Might have liked it better with more time and different accommodations.

9:05 a.m.

Saw an actual kilt-wearing guy in Edinburgh. People really do not wear jeans much here. At crosswalks, if you look, they will have painted "look right, look left" in the pavement. Saw "Lady Road" painted on the road.

9:20 a.m.

Just passed a hillside covered with white, three-armed, huge windmills. Road is excellent. Long views in every direction. More new construction here than in England or Wales. It seems that a standalone house will have a name but not a row house. Have crossed the Esh, the Clyde, and the Tweed. None more than about sixty feet wide. Saw three fishermen knee-deep in the Tweed under a very high, many-arched bridge.

10:00 a.m.

Here's a weird thing, just took a pic of borderland because it reminded me of central Pennsylvania, and then we passed a trailer park. First time we've seen a vacation park. Weird. Lilliesleaf, town name.

11:00 a.m.

Jedburgh Abbey, eleventh century on the Jed River (which would be a creek at home). Nice little town. Here's a little bit of Scottish stuff—nineteenth-century grave markers rather wordy.

Tasted haggis and black pudding at the breakfast café. Ew! Actually, the pudding was bad, but the haggis, not too bad, except it looked like raccoon droppings. For breakfast, we had a fried egg, fried bread (bitter aftertaste), potato scone, beans (Campbell's, I swear!), toast and marmalade, the usual hammy bacon and no-meat sausage. Tea was good (it always was!). Just passed a steep, tree-shaded pasture with three to four hairy coos (ancient, hairy cattle) red, brown, and black.

11:30 a.m.

Bus driver has revealed an unexpected patriotic side, playing "God Save the Queen", as we crossed from Scotland into England.

11:45 a.m.

Northumbria, pine forests giving way to hardwood. Still rolling, dry stonewalls, sheep.

12:15pm

Durham, didn't expect to see this town/cathedral. Glad to get here, cathedral, beautiful and very old (1093). Saint Cuthbert and the head of Saint Oswald, a king who died in battle. Indoor Market. Woolworth on steroids!

2:45 p.m.

Driver used a marker to divide the left half of the windshield into squares. Twenty pence, buys a square, most dead bugs by the end of the day wins. (Poor Graham was really bored.)

3:05 p.m.

Saw the "Angel of the North" recent sculpture made of metal maybe twenty-five-feet tall, now a rusty brown. *Ugly!* In Newcastle.

3:20 p.m.

Bus bingo, now charades. Figured out why my hair is so soft; the water here is soft compared to ours. (In fact, I have never been any place where the water is as hard as ours!) Much more cultivation here rather than all livestock. Brits do not say "bloody" much, but they do say "bollocks" when ticked. Aussies don't really say "crikey", but they do say "bloke."

3:45 p.m.

Headed into York. Saw an "Elderly People" street sign. Approaches to York much flatter than expected, flattest I've seen in England/Britain. Beautiful agricultural area. Capt. Condom Variety Pack at ladies room in Durham.

7:55 p.m.

Like York. Too late to meet Helen. Had time to see the cathedral and hear part of a service with wonderful singing, a men and boys choir. Walked the castle (town) wall in the long twilight. York has a race meet on, and the town is *full*, but we paid extra for our own room and are at the top of a full out, honest to goodness Georgian townhouse. Across from a churchyard in a business kind of area. This seems to have been one of the nicest houses in the Saint Micklegate Road, the main drag in the walled town. Very heavy wrought iron fencing in front and round the very elegant, inset entrance. Interestingly, the floor is stone, not marble. Very heavy plasterwork on the ceiling, and moldings. Grand staircase (where someone decided tangerine would be a good wall color!) Room to the left off the hall is used as the dining room. Great wide embellished archways from the hall. We are obviously in a maid's room. There is a window ten feet up in the roof operated by dubious-looking string apparatus. At least we're alone, and it's quiet despite the house and town circumstances. Had an English roast beef dinner. Becky wanted to take me for my birthday. You went up to a buffet where the chef sliced some beef (or pork or chicken), you served yourself dressing, overboiled vegetables, potatoes, etc. used horseradish sauce and a lovely green sauce that seemed to be a mix of mint and dill. Really liked that! Had English sherry trifle for dessert, which seemed to be sponge cake and pears in Jell-O with not very sweet cream. Brits do beef and dairy very well. Lucked into a lace shop just as the lady was closing and got some lovely stuff. They have a website where I may be able to order a nightgown. Becky wants to get me a birthday gift. We're leaving here at 7:30 a.m. Can see the jump on, jump off thing is the way to go with this tour. Otherwise, there just isn't time to see anything but what passes the bus windows. Might like York because the weather is so golden. No, I just like the feel of it.

9:00 p.m.

Showered and in our room for the night. Tried streamlining to lighten the loads. Just doesn't seem much better. Oh well, we tried.

5/17, 7:30 a.m.

One of our worst sleeping places yet. For some reason, the room just creeped me out. Lack of ventilation? Don't know. Two beds, a table, a chair, a nonworking lamp, and a wardrobe. Like York though. So sad to visit churches that are no more than museums. Very impressed with the granite road bricks—that took work. And what is the purpose of a chimney pot anyway? The windows here generally have larger squares than American colonial-type windows (Georgian?). The really sad churches are the black ones, all stained from coal smoke and never cleaned. Did not appreciate the urine smell on the landing between stairs five and six on the way up, dragging the two-ton bag. The morning started sunny but is clouding up again. Can't grasp the number of Chinese restaurants in this country. Just noticed the guide is still wearing the same pants. Don't think he's shaved either. English license plates are narrow, about two feet long, yellow on the front of the car and white on the back. And chicken curry is a gimme. At every restaurant, must be that whole imperial, owning/India thing. Pulled out lighter clothes today as yesterday was so hot. Hope that wasn't a mistake. Countryside here remains flat. "Little Chief" is their fast-food franchise. I guess the trees I thought were poplars, were.

8:20 a.m.

Guess we won't be seeing the Yorkshire dales. Just passed a nuke plant with *eight* cooling towers. Can already see another a couple miles to the east. Dodgy. Fifty power lines march all over the flat land. Agriculture here is all cultivation. Haven't seen a sheep in hours. Do see horses occasionally.

8:40 a.m.

Houses here brick instead of stone. Pine tree plantations. Sherwood Forest is white birch! What oaks we saw were universally very short and very stout.

9:25 a.m.

So weird to hear Asian girls speaking in Aussie accents. Guide claimed (with a straight face) the Robin Hood tree had his hair on it.

10:00 a.m.

In Edwinstowe, where Robin and Marian supposedly married. Had breakfast at a BandB. Something called Cobb—huge soft bun with salty bacon, egg, and tomato or bean inside. Left most of the bread behind. Walked up the street a bit. Got a couple muffins for later.

10:10 a.m.

For as much ham and bacon as these people eat, I can't believe I just saw my first pig farm. Did not know the Union Jack is a combination of the English and Scottish flags.

10:35 a.m.

Generally speaking, the British are not an especially handsome people. How those lovely pink and white, apple-cheeked children grow into such unattractive adults is beyond me. In Nottingham now.

11:50 a.m.

Healy-in-Arden pretty little village. Land has become rolling again, treed and well-watered.

2:00 p.m.

Well, that was Stratford (on Avon). Very commercial, pretty tasteful, and expensive, had a real Chagrin Falls feel. Had tea and an éclair. Once again, we see Brits do cream. Had a "salad sandwich." Heard a coo-coo at Hadrian's Wall. Our room was high enough in the roofs last night that we heard doves but did not see them until Sherwood Forest. Very pretty mauves and blues and nearly as big as a chicken. Don't see chickens much and certainly not loose like at home. The weather is nice today, partly cloudy, breezy, probably high sixties. We bought some china here, to be shipped home. I got one piece of cranberry glass, also being shipped in Becky's box. Most building here is brick, some half-timbering. All over, the curtains are very often lace "net" (even in the ritzy palaces). Some fields have eroded until the base of the hedge is two feet higher than the fields on either side. Fields and pastures are universally larger than at home. In the Cotswolds, beginning to see more livestock but not all sheep. "Kennels and Cattery." Village of golden Cotswold stone, wisteria trained up the front. Mossy slate or thatch roof. Thatch held down with chicken wire. Opposites "black and white", "chalk and cheese."

2:50 p.m.

The 1700s Blenheim Palace, Duke of Marlborough, Churchill. Roses in bloom now, red and peace. Yellow wisteria. The Eagle and Child pub where A.A. Milne got blitzed.

4:15 p.m.

Oxford is a college town done old. Either end of the main drag has a church and graveyard. Every once in a while, you'll see a couple acres all broken up into gardens with a real shantytown look. Believe they must be some kind of community gardens. Doesn't do much good to ask the guide much because besides the schpiel he's learned, he doesn't seem to know much. In York, we had passionless prayer. So sad.

6:40 p.m.

Graham seemed genuinely pleased and surprised by the tip we gave him, which genuinely pleases and surprises me. We are at Leinster Hotel in Bayswater. *Heaps* better than Hyde Park. Actually, have our own bath! One guy roommate. An English-educated

Swede who helped us figure out how to confirm our flight. Radar at Heathrow apparently failed today, but the airline said to come at the same time anyway, so it's on the tube by 5:30 a.m. (Ow!) Off to find dinner soon, which is *such* a chore! Want to scope out the length of the walk to the tube station as well. Need to calculate how horridly early we need to get up. (Tube travel was interesting in that there are so many tourists in London at any given time that riding the tube or even dragging noisy luggage along the sidewalk is commonplace.) Can't measure the joy of the bath here—sweet, sweet privacy. So missing Jack and home and familiarity. This place seems pretty quiet and clean. The desk clerk was so pleasant and friendly; we really felt welcomed. May hit the bar downstairs for a quick drink tonight (or not). Think I'll figure out how to set the alarm clock.

8:50 p.m.

Lovely spot, sitting on the windowsill, listening to a nice, soft rain. Pretty quiet here for the middle of London. Back still bothers at the wrong angle. Hope I can still ride. Really nasty shower here. Press the button for water. No control over temp or direction. It comes out unevenly and temperature fluctuates. Ended up with soap in my mouth and my eyes, and then right in the middle, the water flow stops, and you have to press the button again! Trying to let my hair dry here in the window, so I can get to bed. By the way, the cathedrals have what looks like tin roofs! The neighborhood we're in is perfectly lovely gone to seed. Georgian? Edwardian? Row upon row of elegant townhouses and then the beautiful locked squares, just like Notting Hill.

5/18, 5:55 a.m.

On the tube to Heathrow. House was really noisy last night. Friday seems to be London's night to howl. Hope we aren't too late checking in, but there's only so much we can do.

7:35 a.m.

Up into the sunlight. Just lost my pen between the seats. Hope to recover it later. Can smell breakfast. Smells pukey. When we reached the BMI (our airline) area of the terminal, due to the technical failures of the day before, there were queues everywhere, so we joined one. The man in front of us said he'd been in a ticket holder check-in line and been sent to that one to purchase tickets. Waited a few minutes but had only half an hour till takeoff. Saw a BMI guy in an office, told him of our plight, and he hooked us up with a BMI girl (in a very bad hat) who got us to our flight.

7:55 a.m.

Quick breakfast. Tea with tube sugar, egg, tomato, potato patty, and yet another icky sausage. Can't they put *meat* in them? On with the story, which made short is, we just made the flight, and it was only fifteen minutes late taking off. About to visit the loo (a little put off by the turbulence).

9:45 a.m.

Landed in Belfast and picked up by our BandB host. Arrived at Drumgooland House. What relief. In the country, beautiful pond view from our room. Bacony smelling. A monkey-puzzle tree, my first, and a palm tree in view from the window. So tired!

6:40 p.m.

Oh, there are no words for how much I hurt all over. Fully unprepared for four hours on horseback. Roger was a bastard of a horse anyway. Never had to work so hard on a horse in my life! Eventually the guide gave me a heavy stick, and I just had to hit him. Scenery was gorgeous. Mist drifting through pines, bluebell and fern and shamrocks growing wild. Doves cooing and water running and the cuppy sound of the hooves on the mucky ground. Sun has come out, but it's still pretty cold. Glad to have my boiled wool jacket here.

Sunday, 5/19, 7:45 a.m.

Today I really miss home. Maybe it's that I've been away long enough, or that we've slowed down enough, or that it's the Lord's day, and I'd like to be in church. Running out of clean clothes though the undies will last, and that's the important thing. Think I could ride today if my sitting places weren't so bruised and sore. It's very quiet here, yet the front door is locked at all times. (Surprising to someone who lives in an equally rural area.) Can see horses from our window. It was a sunny evening, but the gray is back this morning and still a breeze. Plan to do some walking anyway. My lower back is really talking to me today. Had duck for dinner. Tougher than beef roast and just as dark.

Baked potatoes, carrots with minced mint, and broccoli (over-done by American standards), rhubarb crumble (crumble good, rhubarb sour. Why do people *eat* that stuff?) with vanilla ice cream, altogether a very nice combination. So far, I like England the best of what we've seen. Ireland is very like home, fewer sheep, houses much more like ours, and more likely to be single dwellings. (Mostly without names.) Still have the row housing and pubs and roundabouts. Need to think about what makes it feel different. (Tip to a BandB host, ask after the guests rather than focusing the conversation on oneself). Had a yelling bad dream last night, which I guess scared Becky. Had taken one of her pills to assure sleep and was slow to waken. Have discovered if I keep moving, I don't hurt as badly, but if I stop for any length of time everything stiffens up. Ow…

10:30 a.m.

Got my tickets, managed to get off an email home. Email is wonderful! (ISP was incredibly slow there.) Looking forward to a quiet indoor day. Had porridge for breakfast, oatmeal but extra gooey and good. The bus with the other three riders just left. (We were the only two yesterday.) It is colder, windier, and much wetter today. So glad *not* to be on that bus. The ones who went to the pub last night were out until one.

So glad we stayed in. Still hope to walk a bit if the rain stops pattering on the windows. They have crows here. Same size as ours, but the bodies are gray. And the huge doves.

People here really do say, "So it is", or "so I will" at the end of a sentence. They also say "youse" all the time. Weird to look in the mirror and see myself looking fairly normal. There is a hair dryer here and, with Becky's round brush, was able to at last shape my hair a little. Rain seems to have backed off to that misty drizzle again. May walk a bit…or not!

1:45 p.m.

Had a nice nap and an odd meal. French bread, buttered, with grated cheese and chopped chives. Cheese and onion potato chips, orange squash (like tang) to drink. Still windy and rainy, super day to rest up, but I do wonder about the ferry tomorrow if the weather doesn't clear. Looking forward to a leisurely afternoon to shop and find a pub to try. Need to call the car rental tomorrow morning. Pain seems to be easing up a little, which is good.

4:05 p.m.

Had a nice tramp up the hill and down and back up. Smelled the appleblossoms and met an Irish bee. Queen Anne's lace in bloom, but not like ours. No queen and the flower clusters more discreet. Sweet peas in bloom, smaller and all purple and violet. Clouds have blown away, and though there is still a cool breeze, the sun is shining again. Bluebells and buttercups also. Lovely to watch the wind stroke the long grass up the hillside. Herd of bullocks in a field at the bottom of the drive, very uneasy about me standing by their gate. Never seen a boy cow with its parts intact. Small lake farther down the hill all ruffled with wind, random ducks, and a pair of swans. Horses up the hill across from the house and sheep at the bottom the other way. Horses graze with their back to the wind. By the way, Marmite (Brit vegemite) is a lot like a beef bouillon-flavored spread for toast.

10: 45 p.m.

Actually sat at dinner till now. Finally rested enough.

Monday, 5/20, 7:18 a.m.

T'is another fine fair day in Ireland. Gray and rainy and windy once more. Becky says I woke her up twice, yelling in my sleep last night. I remember doing it once, don't remember the second. Maybe *she* dreamed that. Am trying to mentally prepare myself for driving this evening. The clutch, brake, and accelerator are arranged the same here as at home, but the shifter is on the left. Rules of the road fairly similar except in a roundabout, the car to the right has the right of way, and once you're in it, you do.

1:45 p.m.

Well! We got to Belfast around eleven. The ferry was canceled due to the windy weather. The ferry guy was conspicuously unhelpful. No place to check luggage. Handed us a Belfast street map. We went to the Tourist Welcome Center where we booked a flight at one fifty-five. So now we're sitting in a bitty thirty-seat lear-type jet. Twenty-minute flight! Called Jack, which was nice except he wanted to talk.

4:00 p.m. on Isle of Man

Well, we made it, and a harrowing trip it was, one wrong turn (no, two) two times asking directions (one man was drunk), one wheel over a curb, which takes some doing when all you're driving is a Ford Fiesta about the size of a suitcase. The room is small but nice; the beds are very soft, our own bath, an inviting square across the way. Douglas is a pretty little town. Will take pics.

6:30 p.m.

Just watched an episode of *The Simpsons* while eating Chinese food in our jammies. Talk about cognitive dissonance! And I can see the sea out the window next to me.

7:22 p.m.

Best bed yet, and we're in them! Parking dicey here. You put a disc in the window set to the time you parked the car. You have two hours and then must reset or move the car. We set ours at eight for tomorrow morning, which gives us until ten to leave town. At Drumgooland, we met a Brit woman, maybe Becky's age, physiotherapist, one of those brisk, quick-spoken, down-to-earth sort of women. Part German/Brazilian, she told us lots about foods. Cream puffs made of "shoe pastry." "There's good sausage, and there's very, very bad sausage." (We never did encounter the good kind!) "Of course, British cuisine is much better than American." (Yeah right, pretty sure, it's all in what you're used to.) "And in America, the portion sizes are simply obscene!" (She had me there.) Ate Marmite on her breakfast toast! Did some good shopping in Belfast, though very hurried. Did not have time to mail postcards from Ireland as I'd hoped to. Oh well, hope to do some final shopping tomorrow. Need something for Jeff and Kim and Dyann. Still hoping for a nice nighty for me, as well as some woolens. Now here's an interesting thing: IOM folk are, as a group, a much more physically attractive people than any others in UK. As nice and helpful as he was, poor Dermot in Belfast was a veritable caricature of an ugly man, pasty skin, bad, bad teeth, all in all, so he was. You know, I could live here a week and start talking with an accent, so I could. Stupidly forgot to pack scissors in the suitcase. Oh yeah, I wasn't flying and had them confiscated from my purse at the Belfast City Airport. Can't believe we've managed ourselves so well so far, especially the drive from the airport into Douglas. Sure hope we can get back out again!

5/21, 6:16 a.m.

Full light and birds singing by 4:30 a.m. Sun is out this morning, at least for the moment.

7:04 a.m.

Good shower, once I figured out how to make it work. White tile with blue grout. Never could get the shower at Drumgooland to work. Had two showers, one lukewarm and one lukecool, in a cold house on successive rainy days. This house is a nice one, in a square that is being renovated. The beds are soft, the bath is clean (smells clean though unventilated) plenty of towels and hot water. Had the window to the sea open all night.

Sun still shining. Going to the museum today, then out into the countryside. Hope Becky stops gasping. I don't feel that I'm hugging the roadside, but she acts as if I am. Shortly after we reached the ferry port yesterday, a group of motorcyclists on crotch rockets and dressed in black leathers pulled in. They came inside, three young men, one old man, and a gray-haired little old woman. I interpreted them to be Manx or Scottish. Either way, the accent was so thick I could *barely* understand them. (Scottish-Manx was intelligible!) They were as stranded as we and pulled out their cell phones and started making calls.

Don't know if the accent is that thick here. Seems not to be. Motorcycles are big here, many riders all the time.

7:40 a.m.

Still a lovely sunny day but cool enough for a jacket. Can't believe how much the sunshine lifts my spirits/colors my perception of a place. There's a huge crane by the seaside that is working. Hear occasional horns like from ships. Last night, we walked back in a downpour with lots of strong wind. Ended up eating Chinese, quite literally all there was. Restaurants stop serving meals at four forty-five and close at five thirty. Caught some whiffs of the sea as we searched for food. Once again, a stressful experience.

2:30 p.m.

Drove to Peel and walked around. Had pub lunch and did Mannanan Museum. It was reenactments with robot things, full sensory experience with smells and sounds as well. Romans never got here, Celts and Vikings did. Pretty little town and generally friendly people. Crab salad. Ew! Cake messy but good. Sitting in a picnic area overlooking the sea on the road to Ballaugh. Just starting to rain.

2:45 p.m.

Arrived in Ballaugh, forgot to mention disproportionate number of elderly people here. Visited a church of Saint Mary, no "Crellins" (in the graveyard, but then they were Methodist, not Church of England). Ballaugh the town from which Jack's family emigrated.

4:06 p.m.

Can't believe it! We made it back without hurting ourselves or anyone else! Took mountain route right across the island. Absolutely spectacular! Sulby Glen was enough to make anyone believe in fairies. It's a little hard to grasp the smallness of the island. Lots of antique and secondhand shops in Peel.

6:50 p.m.

Another frustrating forage for food. Actually had to go and drive around. Finally found a seriously Italian restaurant. Bought an extra duffel so we could repack to make room for souvies. Forgot to pick up a stone in Ballaugh. There was a kid who seemed to follow us into the graveyard and who left right after us and was sort of talking to himself. Made me so wary I forgot to get Jack a stone. Feel bad about that. Tomorrow morning, we fly to London. As soon as we're settled at the hostel, we'll consider looking for some theatre tickets. Would prefer a matinee, as I don't want to try to negotiate London at night. It has gone windy and rainy again, and the waves are a little rowdy. Buildings here, the older ones at Peel, including the castle, which was Viking and on a little island, made of red sandstone. The church at Ballaugh had large chunks of slaty stone interspersed among bunches of slate slices all held together with stony mortar. Ballaugh a kind of backwatery sort of place.

5/22, 6:47 a.m.

Constant swishing sound of the sea. It is gray but not raining, still windy and brisk. Slept very badly, oh well. six thirty, half six.

7:49 a.m.

Thoughts really turning toward home.

10:45 a.m.

Aboard another bitty little plane. We walked out and boarded. At least, this one has baggage storage overhead. Actually has the most leg space yet. We were interviewed on the way out of IOM by a very well-dressed but somewhat humorless older woman about why we came and how much we spent. Told her the lack of dinnertime restaurants a real problem. Took bonnine. Sure hope it works!

9:00 p.m.

Finally were able to do some email. The Mike thing has completely hit the fan at home. (Jack and Mike were butting heads.) Not sure how to react. Guess I'll wait till at home to decide. Ended up seeing *Attack of the Clones* at a huge Leister Square movie theater. The square was pretty, right round the corner from Saint Martin's and the National Gallery. But so, so crowded. Tonight, after the movie, there was a middle-aged lady all dressed up who appeared to be "preaching" out in the square. No one seemed to know what to make of that. The theatre was huge, and there were two enormous sculptures of gamboling naked people, mostly young women, of course, up on the theater wall. So ready for home despite the havoc there.

5/24, 6:40 a.m.

Well, another restful night of London sleep—*not!* We are across the hall from a room of toilets, and every time someone goes through (unless the person makes an effort not to), the door bangs and bangs and… This hostel seems to be in a former office building on the top three floors, which is weird. More stairs to climb with ever-heavier luggage.

There are more older people here than we've seen in the other hostels. In fact, the majority of inmates are my age. Beds are new, all WC and sinks are clean, but the stalls are the absolute smallest imaginable. Becky said the shower was good and roomy. I didn't shower, just washed my hair in the sink, which is a real trick when it is small, shallow, and has separate H and C faucets! This country has the smallest, oddest sinks, which makes sense when you consider what they're often trying to retrofit! We're supposed to have breakfast in the hostel this morning. I asked about it at the desk last night, and the girl seemed to say we could pick it up from them boxed. Hard to tell, had a real sense she did not speak English especially well. Still have not met an English service person in London. Pizza Hut was Muslim, Middle Easterners.

8:20 a.m.

Took a taxi from the hostel to Victoria Station. (Becky really got into taxis by the end. After once lifting her luggage, I could see why!) Boy, is that luggage getting heavy! Breakfast was cereal without milk, a bizarre dinner roll type thing with hard chocolate inside. Really tasted gross. Yogurt and nutrigrain bar, which were edible, orange juice. See how all that sets as we go. Now sitting in the train, Gatwick Express, waiting to go off to the airport. At least, we know to look for a luggage trolley now. Becky plans to do some duty-free shopping at the airport. We're hoping they can instruct us at the shop as to what has to be declared and when. It is a sunny day, and the temp is probably in the sixties. Best weather yet, of course… So glad we're getting to the airport early, just want to be sure to be on time for the flight. So ready for home. Though worried about what I'll find when I get there. Bad choice. Picked rear-facing seats. Hope the bonnine holds. I stopped having those little vertigo things when I stopped riding the bus. Brit trainmen are required to wear the *worst* imaginable suits. Basically royal blue, the jacket overlaid with a fairly large red grid, salmony-pink shirt and red-and-blue tie. Eww! Color choices here are generally much stronger, reds, blues, greens, primaries in bright shades. Nothing like we would do. This includes wall paint colors.

10:00 a.m. Fourteen Hours to Home

Waiting at Gatwick. Becky hit the duty-free shop and got scotch and whiskey. We're about to eat fish and chips one last time. It's early, but breakfast was pretty scanty, and I've been up since five fifteen. Just saw something icky. One of the meals at the shop is sausage and chips, and the sausage looks batter fried! (More of that great brit cuisine.) Talk about heart attack food. Finally figured out the baggage is probably keeping my back sore. By the way, you can tell a lot about a person's nationality by looking at their shoes. Some, you just say to yourself, "An American wouldn't wear that." Peckish! Hungry.

11:45 a.m.

Finally aboard the plane for home. Maybe I'll sleep some. Did not get picked on for special checks, which is nice for a change.

7:15 (2:15) p.m.

Apparently about to land. Had one little in flight thing where they asked for people with medical experience for help for someone who was sick. Apparently, there were some doctors, so Becky didn't have to respond. Hope I filled the customs thing out right.

5:10

After all our efforts to keep home apprised of our progress, they just announced our plane is late, so we're leaving late. Rats! (Going through customs in Philly interesting. *Very* long line snaked through stanchions. Then we had to have our feet washed with bleach because we'd been around animals. Then Becky had special stuff because she spent enough to have to declare things and pay some duty.)

6:40 p.m.

Before we finally took off, waited half an hour on the runway. They said the flight should take one hour, so hopefully, we'll get to Cleveland before eight. Really getting tired. (By then, it was nearing 1:00 a.m., our time.) Weather here, lovely, clear, and warm. Guess it's been really cold with some snow last week. Cool to watch the land pass by below.

On Bolivia Trip

In 2000, while attending Leroy Community Chapel, Jack and I, along with our son Michael, went on a mission trip to Bolivia. Now if you had asked me in order of preference what foreign country I would want to visit, I'm not sure Bolivia would even be on the list. That said, I'm very glad I got to go since seeing the Southern Cross was on my life list. Our mission was to help rebuild the church's classrooms destroyed in a recent earthquake. We stayed all together in the home of Eric and Shirley Bender. They had two teenaged children and had just adopted twin Quechua girl babies.

It was a big group of mostly teens and singles. I kind of assigned myself the mom role of carrying the first aid kit, hand sanitizer, and the video camera. I tried to keep a regular video record of the trip. I also carried a spiral notebook into which I jotted constant commentary. I have learned that if I don't write things down, I don't remember to the degree I want to. What follows is a verbatim transcription of what was in the notebook. A copy was provided to the church. Pretty sure no one ever even gave it a glance, but I was faithful to record it. Copies of the video were provided to all team members.

Bolivia Trip
(Or Linda Burhenne's Stream of Consciousness Impressions as Recorded in a Little Spiral Notebook)

Sunday, June 25

We were introduced in church, and the mission committee asked for "elven for eleven" people to pray for each of us during the trip. Then in each service, the whole congregation came forward and laid hands on us and prayed for us and the trip. It was an awesome experience. I felt like a cup that had been emptied by creeping fear, filled afresh with new faith through the prayers of my brothers and sisters. We spent the afternoon learning skits and songs. Jack will play God. I *think* I'm ready to become a fool for Christ. We're going to a place where people actually worship false gods. My prayer is to have the faith to allow God to show himself *mighty* through us. He is the great King above all gods. May our faith be sufficient to dare much in his name! The pile of goods in our room for the trip is growing. I will be the medic/mom, a familiar role. I'm really starting to feel the tide of events carrying me along. I want to be open to letting God deal with selfishness and the competitive spirit that so often motivates me. I hope to learn to die to myself like never before.

Monday, June 26. Very little sleep last night. Before bed, Beth came into our room. She had gotten Jack's prayer card, and he filled her in on how he hoped she'd pray for him. One of his big concerns is his health, and when she came in, she said she believed God wanted her to pray for him then. She anointed him with oil. Then I put the vial of oil in my purse in hopes that God will have a use for it. Jack woke me at four thirty this morning with concerns about our leaders and how they have a cliquish kind of mindset toward the walk of faith. I told him I think that's why God let us be on the team, to show them stuff they haven't seen before. But I told him I thought we had to first gain credibility by acting as servants. Down = Up.

Wednesday, June 28. Spent the day yesterday washing, marking, folding, and packing Mike's and my clothes. Amazing how long it took. Managed to compress most meds into a bag borrowed from Beth. What's *really* interesting is that ten pounds of stuff really does fit into a five-pound bag! Still can't decide what to do about my hair.

Later that night.

Spent from 7:00 p.m. till after 10:00 p.m. at the Cornerstone packing. *Amazing* how much stuff is going! Chaotic piles reduced to twenty-two parcels with bright-orange tags and duct tape.

Thursday, June 29, the Big Day. This morning at seven, just before waking, I had one of those classic type-A dreams. Running around an airport, wearing a sheet, trying not to miss my plane, miss my plane. *Arghh!* The morning is cool and gray. Once again, I can hear water drip in the downspout and a mourning dove call. The air smells of woodsmoke. A jet passes over, and I think, *Pretty soon, that'll be us!* The weather worries me a little (only because rain will wreck what little style might stay in my hair), but there are bright streaks in the overcast. Maybe it'll clear up.

12:00 p.m.

Skies gray and rumbly all morning. Tornado watch and heavy rain at eleven, but now the sky is almost clear, and the sun shines. Did banking, bought food, and fielded several supportive phone calls. Mike is in the shower. I'm next.

6:00 p.m.

Arrived at airport before five, but check-in took a long time. Two trolleys full of bags, and the airline computers appeared to be down. Before leaving Cornerstone, Becky asked if I was excited. Excitement struck just as we passed under the W130ᵗʰ Street bridge. Right in the stomach. Saw some kids on a ball diamond on the way here, and I thought, *Yeah, it's Thursday night, ballgame time.* Life goes on as usual outside our adventure. We have an hour to wait at gate C11. Windows to the right show a very dark bank of clouds. Windows to the left, sunny. We will eat pizza here in the waiting area.

8:15 p.m.

Finally in the air. Got our itty-bitty snacky thing. The flight attendant tells us about a man who insisted he be allowed to smoke on the plane despite airline policy forbidding smoking. "But I am *French!*"

10:40 p.m. (Home Time)

Waiting in the Houston terminal for the next leg of the journey. We were in the very back of the plane for the first step. What windows we had were blocked by the engines. Motion not too bad and singing helped me get through the landing. We seem to be eating our way to Bolivia. Pizza at the airport, sandwiches on the first plane. The flight attendant said they will give us dinner and probably breakfast before we get to Lima at 5:00 a.m.

6:25 a.m. (Home Time)

In the terminal in Lima, Peru. Not much rest on the plane. Plenty of food though. Used seatbelts most of the way because of mild turbulence. Coming into Lima in the dark, there was a huge grid of lights, some yellow, some more bluish. Grid interrupted here and there by dark conical hills. At the airport, we debarked down stairs onto the tarmac, cool and damp. Air smelled of diesel.

During the flight, every announcement was in English, then in Spanish. Here in the terminal, most everything is in Spanish. There are duty-free shops, and we've been given little laminated passes to let us out of the "holding corral" to circulate to the shops and restrooms. Very tired but not hungry.

7:15 a.m.

Walked around and looked at the shops. Mostly jewelry in Aztec themes and nice woven stuff. Bought a couple postcards so home can get "mail from South America." Passed a large poster for some apparently luridly yellow beverage called "Inca Cola, the drink of Peru." In the ladies' restroom, there was a poster that said, "Ahora! (Now.) This is your last chance. Dump it!" Over a picture of a bag of drugs being dropped into a wastebasket. Had a conversation with a salesgirl when I bought the postcards using rudimentary Spanish. Very cool, being understood. Dave Gehring has lost his boarding pass twice, so far.

8:10 a.m.

On board, nearly empty flight to Santa Cruz. We'll spread out and sleep once we're in the air. For now, the flight attendant wants us in our seats (as always in the rear). Our weight is needed in the tail to balance the cargo. Hope it wasn't a major error not taking another dramamine. Lima dull and gray, *looks* like winter. Strong smell of diesel.

8:25 a.m.

Above the clouds and heading to cross the Andes. Dark-red mountains just above a sea of cloud. No snow! Everything looks so dry. How can people live here? Puddle of green water in the lap of red foothills pierced by round gray rock and traced by tiny worm trails of switchback roads.

Snowcapped peaks here and there. Occasional towns in the creases of the hills. Ears keep popping. Air pillow that was nearly flat in Lima is now nice and fat again. (This is strangely weird for me!) Hope to catch a nap. Time has become disembodied. It just keeps flowing. Out the left window, a huge isolated thunderhead rears into blue sky. Ahead, the mountains are covered in cloud. Odd to be on this side of the cloud, fundamentally unnatural. Breakfast is an adventure, crepes with a little boxed drinky (that's what it says!). Is it apricot? In the fruit salad, I recognize grapefruit and strawberry, but the orange stuff cut into three-inch rectangles defies identification. Taste it. Yuck. (Autumn later said it was mango. I say it was *old* mango.) Crepes served with carrot and zucchini and a little thing of what looks like cream of mushroom soup. Aha! Crepes stuffed with chicken breast. (At least it *looks* like chicken breast.) Is this what Peruvians eat for breakfast? Mountains below now cloaked in forest. We're crossing over a braided river. Blobs of puffy cloud dot the distance. Wildly meandering little rivers cross the jungle below. Now a bigger river with a clearing in one elbow. This enormous expanse below us is only one tiny corner of the Amazon Basin.

9:10 AM

Big clearings in the jungle. We just crossed from Brazil into Bolivia.

10:05 a.m.

Mostly cleared below and now a bunch of good-sized lakes. This plane seems warm. Maybe it's the sunlight. Sky well-dotted with puffs of cloud. Ears popping, must be descending. As we come down, the area around Santa Cruz reminds me of Ohio until I see the palm trees.

11:55 AM

Saw my first Bolivian soldier, dressed in green and armed, strolling through the airport. The airport in Santa Cruz is well maintained with a real sixties ambiance. Comparable in landscaping and upkeep to what you might find in a medium-sized Florida or California airport. Parking lot striped, etc. There's a Subway restaurant about two hundred feet from where I'm sitting. That's a little bizarre! Lydia leaned against a wooden counter, and it almost tipped over. Most of the people are small and dark. I was prepared by National Geographic and Discovery Channel to see small Indian-looking people. But it's funny to see them in dress pants, dress shoes, and regular shirts or nice cardigans. Dan from SAM (sounds like Dr. Seuss but means South America Missions) is taking us into Santa Cruz. We divide up. Some ride with Dan, and the rest of us go in a small bus. The dashboard area, very personalized with a quilted dash cover and Catholic stuff. Cool and rainy. Sensory overload as I try to take in everything. Awful traffic, cars way, way closer than we would ever drive. Inches apart at full speed. Phone booth shaped like a flamingo. Long-legged, muscular chickens. Eighty percent of vehicles are Toyotas. Brown thatch and red-tile roofs. Beautiful square at city center. Tiled walks and huge, exotic trees in bloom. Instead of a squirrel, saw a sloth in a tree. Old cathedral faces the square. All the bricks were handmade. Jack gives money to a blind beggar seated at the door and a little girl who saw gloms on to him and won't stop begging until we drive away. At a city restaurant for lunch, Dan suggests we have ice cream. Is he nuts? Choosing something from a menu you can't understand when you don't know what's safe a real chore. Thirteen of us to eat—chaos. Find myself trying to figure out how much risk to take. This restaurant is all bright colors. Tablecloths and tiny napkins. Spanish music and fresh flowers. A colorful wall painting (eight by twelve?) of fish with water like a waterfall flowing down the front. Food choices include ice cream, bakery goods, meats, fish, and alcoholic beverages. Weird combo for us. Across the street is a storefront McDonald's. As we walked to get here, you could glance down alleys into pretty courtyards at the centers of rundown city blocks. Santa Cruz is arranged in nine concentric circles about one kilometer apart radiating out from the plaza and pierced by boulevards like spokes. Driving here reminds me of DC. Saw a cemetery coming in. Remains are housed in niches in little building-looking structures. The buildings here are all random but close together. *Everything* is close together and all jumbled up. Old and new, rich and poor. So, so poor. During a pause at a traffic circle, a woman dressed native, blue poncho, bowler hat and all, carrying a baby, was begging window to window, car to car. Dan said beggars sometimes borrow babies to make their beg more appealing. Later, we saw a woman with a child slung across her front hold up very primitive-looking bow and arrows to us as we passed. Another, larger bus passed our little one, and I noticed people hang their heads out to watch. I thought it odd until I found myself doing the same thing. Many street vendors. Narrow, uneven sidewalks, usually covered by a colonnade. Even the very center of town is very old and not well maintained. Not that there isn't money here. You see the SUVs and young people very well dressed, usually right next to some woman in a fat skirt and braids. Constant clash of rich and poor, native and foreign. A lady with a pushcart and native dress peels the skin from an orange in one long, narrow strip while standing under a Kodak sign. Dan says Bolivian government is the most corrupt in the world. Driving back to the airport, we pass La Patita Pekin, a Bolivian Chinese Restaurant! (OWW, cognitive dissonance!) The road back to Viru Viru Airport is modern, four lane with a landscaped median strip. And on the side of the road is a rough wooden wagon on old car tires being pulled by a skinny horse. Carrying our bags this whole time is a pain. Mine holds first aid kit, video camera, enough personal stuff to last a couple days if the luggage disappears…heavy.

3:35 p.m.

On yet another airplane for the last leg into Cochabamba. This one is not the puddle/jumper I feared we'd ride in. The trip is only forty-five minutes. Hope my lunch (scrambled Philly beef and cheese) stays put. Customs in Santa Cruz was weird. It took the time needed to walk past a couple guys. No looking in the bags, no searches… weird. First time we'd seen our luggage since Cleveland, got twenty-two of twenty-two. This trip is the final test. Will the tools duct taped into two golf bags make it to Cochabamba? On this plane, *all* the talk is in Spanish. Haven't heard a word of *Ingles* yet. Am *so* tired. When we landed at Santa Cruz, the music on the plane was James Taylor, so incongruous in that palm tree-plain setting. On this plane, Spanish-flavored classical music. No James Taylor for Bolivians.

5:55 PM

In Cochabamba. Ceiling in the airport is ribbed copper (really!). All luggage here. God must have put angels around us, as both trips through customs were embarrassingly brief. Not one box or bag opened. US Customs apparently opened one of the plastic bins on its way *out* of Houston. When we got it in Coch, it was taped shut with red tape, saying US Customs had opened it. Because of daylight savings time, I don't have to adjust my watch. Time is the same as at home. Everything here is walled-brick or wrought iron. Biggest, fattest palm trees I've ever seen. Mimosa. Though it is winter here, things are in bloom. We walked to the New Tribes Mission guest-house along a quiet street (closed for construction), where cement lay in rectangular slabs over the old cobbles. At every turn, am surprised by the sight of mountains rising beyond every vista. Clouds lie along the tops like lumpy gray cotton. Saw the huge Cristo on the hill above the city. It seems way too barren here to support four hundred thousand people. Beautiful flowers, pink and magenta (whose name I could never learn. Nobody, even natives, knows the names of hardly anything around here!) pour over the tops of the walls. Eric was glad we're here. We know because he said so *several* times. Even the dogs here beg! For supper, *empanatas* (dry, slightly cheesy puff) and peanut soup with shredded carrot, potato, and celery. Altitude making me breathless. Hope to feel better after some sleep. Met old-time missionary staying here whose wife is sick. Had a way about him like a New Jersey used-car salesman. He was so regular. So I find missionaries are, after all, just folks. Jeff Allem was already sick. Struck again by the contradictions of this place, in a quiet cobbled street overhung with huge trees and flower-festooned walls, a boy rides a skateboard. Eric told us tonight, his main frustration in his work with the Quechua is their take on the world. *En Ingles*: I'm cold. *En Espanol*: I have coldness. In Quechua: The cold has me! You don't put toilet paper in the toilets here. You put it in a handy bin. Have been given a pitcher of boiled water for drinking, washing, brushing teeth, etc. Saw the Southern Cross. Tomorrow we tour NTM hangar and a radio station. The doors here at the guesthouse are heavy wooden screen doors nicely varnished, but the rooms are bare, no toilet, a curtain on a string for under the sink in the corner and another across the closet opening. Good double bed though. Didn't expect a bed! We're staying near the Iglesia de Cala Cala (in Aymara means "rocky place", in Quechua, "bare naked." Take your pick). The guesthouse annex is right next to a big white colonial-style house in dreadful repair behind the inevitable wall. Five ratty dogs behind the house. Two men with machetes were building the framework for something large from poles. Found out NTM will take uncertified teachers for their MK (missionary kids) school in Tambo. Everything here is like a fortress behind a thick wall or bars. You keep a dog in the courtyard for an alarm. But sometimes a thief will throw in poisoned meat and come over the wall a couple hours later when the dog is dead. (Learned Bolivians say, "It's no wonder there is so much crime in America, no walls!)

4:00 a.m.

It *looks* like air, but it's really not. Noisy all night in the city.

Saturday, July 1, 7:15 a.m.

Very slight headache, not so breathless. Took the book and magazine from my bag. Put water bottle and poncho in. Could have used the poncho in the rain during the ride through Santa Cruz yesterday when we all piled into the truck bed for the trip back to the airport. Stayed up late last night, talking to Eric. Surprised by his son's very American appearance. Bleached spikes in his hair, necklace, etc. When he graduates next year, he plans to go to college in the US and study accounting. Seems an oddly ordinary ambition given his upbringing. Lips cracked this morning. Little nosebleed last night. From dryness and/or pollution. Coch fourth most polluted air in the world. Tranca, tollbooth, checkpoint. After tours, ate at Panchita/sort of outdoors, fried chicken, pieces small, not much meat but tasty. Fries just like at home. Square pitchers of lemonade. After all the leaders drank, I did too. Figured we could all get sick together. Garnish for the meal was half a lime about one and a half inches across and fried banana chunks and little fried sweet potatoes. Neither the banana nor the sweet potato, actually very sweet. Banana had weird texture. (Maybe plantain?)

Hand sanitizer for all. People all over the streets, selling peanuts, oranges, little stands with belts and watches, fake name brand stuff. Outdoor "restaurant" set up in a median near a traffic circle. Cobbled streets, pretty but rough. Sidewalks varied, colored, marked randomly with decorative imprints. Inside of houses cool and almost always some kind of courtyard. Doors at the NTM (New Tribes Mission) hangar beautiful, handmade, shiny varnish, out of place in a steel and cement airplane hangar.

1:20 p.m.

On the flota (bus) waiting to go to Aiquile. (Found out later, Lydia had her watch stolen right off her wrist while we waited to board.) God in his kindness gave me a window seat. It's probably going to be a hot, smelly, three- to five-and-a-half-hour trip, no rest stop. Indian women are so tiny. Wear stiff white wide-brimmed hats with pastel ribbons that stream down the back. Just discovered my seat is wet. Ick! Do not want to speculate what I've been sitting in. Spread my poncho as a seat cover. Don't know how a plastic seat will feel heatwise after a few hours but better than sitting in the unknown. When I pull the poncho from my bag, JP says, "You really *are* a mother!" People still standing in bus aisle, will they stand all the way to Aiquile? Have not seen a speed limit sign or a garbage truck yet in Bolivia. Coch has had traffic lights less than a year. Traffic chaotic, yet it works. Never see an accident. Motorcycles everywhere. Old-timey nuns in habits. Saw one sweeping the street. We pull out of Cochabamba and immediately are on a dirt road. Dust billows continuously. Hand-painted billboards and political signs in hot pink and bright blue. Pink paint still on livestock heads and throats after San Juan celebration last week. Bare, dry Utah-looking country. Often pass scene of women washing clothes beside little streams, the bright-colored fabric hung all around on the bushes. Pass is thirteen thousand feet. Sky up here, very blue. Watched clouds pour over a mountaintop. Road *very bad!* Flota often comes to near stop to negotiate hairpin turns in the rock and dust. Not as hot a ride as I feared. Landscape sort of Italian-looking, Dr. Seuss trees dot all the valleys. Pines and some kind of blue (no, really blue!) broadleaf tree. Pass a greener valley covered with sagebrush sort of bushes. Corn laid out to dry on corrugated tin roof. The roof is held down with rocks so the wind won't blow it away. Whenever the flota pauses, people crowd the windows to sell food and drink. Stopped now in a little village. Guess we're here for a while, waiting for the driver to eat. There are hotels and restaurants. Windy, dry, lots of kids. See my first loaded burro. Tire being changed. Let me tell you about the bathroom here. Sent Todd to scout and, with his description, felt mentally prepared. Unisex bathroom with wooden stalls with doors on a damp cement floor. Open the door, oh, a hole in the floor with a white fiberglass surround molded with raised places for your feet when you squat. Little paper bag for the toilet paper. Had there *been* toilet paper... (Thanks for the heads-up, Todd!) On the way out, a little boy, maybe ten, twiddled his fingers at us. Fifty centavos apiece for the privilege of squatting in the *baño*. I admire his entrepreneurial spirit. On the way again at last. Dust wafts into the window. Cacti everywhere like spiky Ping-Pong paddles and gigantic mother-in-law tongue. Tiny stone shrines along the roadside. Dust in my teeth. Interesting that the men tend to dress like us, but many women remain traditional with very full, knee-length, often pleated and velvet skirts, lacy blouses, and hats. Double braids down the back. Finally roll into Aiquile at eight twenty, one and a half hours late. Poor Eric has been waiting. Dust everywhere.

Sunday, July 7, 7:01 a.m.
    Slept badly. We are in a great bed in a loft open to the living room in the Benders' house. Not much privacy, but right next to the bathroom. Still using the toilet paper bins. Floors downstairs are

very nice ceramic tile, up here, cement. Shower is open corner of bathroom. Water heated by cylindrical showerhead that only works if there's enough water pressure. Today, there isn't. I took a lukewarm shower last night. Didn't care. It cut the dust. Water seems soft. My hair, after being slept on damp, is really something. Dogs barking and roosters crowing, it seemed, all night. The chorus really cranked up this morning and continues now. We're supposed to have gone to the market at seven this morning, but there's no sound of stirring downstairs. Babies up at least three times last night. Mike just came in to get Tums, said he had some stomach cramping last night. I have a little headache; guts seem okay so far. Uncomfortable with the level of sarcasm among the team, especially the young guys. May have to say something. Interesting exchanges among the missionaries we've met so far. They all seem comfortable with something close to contempt for the Pentecostal brothers in Bolivia. When there *is* cooperation, they seem almost apologetic. Starting to develop some real questions about our conduct in some areas. JP told us to get on the flota as early as possible to snag window seats. Did it, but it turned out the seats were assigned. Felt bad at having acted like a pushy gringo. Several people had to stand, sit/squat the whole way while we sat in seats. Did they agree to that, or was it tough luck? Should some of us have shared? Jack suggests sharing our food, and JP says, "How much? Till it's gone? Then what?" Well, then there's no more. We didn't share anything. Is that an example of Jesus? So what if there's none left. Fat gringos have plenty more in their suitcases. Of ten of our people in the seats, five listened to CD players during the trip. We did do some singing in the starlight. The stars are incredible this high up. Actually, saw the Milky Way for hours. Just discovered the clock in our room is one hour fast, and I got up at five forty, not six forty. (After being up until midnight...so tired.) So I guess the trip to the *mercado* this morning will happen at seven after all. Nose-bleeding and sore. Banged knee climbing into the Toyota in the dark last night. Pretty sore this morning. Babies are cute, two months old, lots of thick, very black hair. Appear plump and healthy. Though they are not identical, they still look a lot alike, so the pinky finger-nails of one are marked with nail polish to tell them apart. When we opened the bins from home, the packaging for the baby wipes was all puffed up tight from the change in air pressure due to the altitude. I guess stuff sometimes will burst.

10:00 a.m.

Went to the market this morning with Shirley, Autumn, and Andy. Lots of rebuilding going on. Market stalls about two feet high with a cloth spread over tables of wire mesh. Lots of familiar vegetables and some strange ones. Tomato, lettuce, cukes, carrot (short and fat like the ones I grow!), achocha (something new), and chicha/corn beer. Lots of social interaction in the market between boys and girls. Market divided as to vegetable, fruit, household goods. Pots are aluminum, now I know why Shirley asked for a steel pot. Plastic goods/ some kind of scuffed up and used-looking. After the market, went to buy eggs. Drove down rough alleys and through the dry riverbed full of plastic grocery bags of garbage. Shirley says people throw garbage in the riverbed, expecting it to go away when the rains come. To do otherwise is dirty. Got a huge basket of fresh brown eggs (forty cents per dozen), a ropa (twenty-four pounds) of azucar (sugar). Somewhere else for chickens (*mercado pollo* too skinny). Market days travel from pueblo to pueblo. Sunday happens to be market day in Aiquile. You do it then or not at all. After shopping, Lauren, Shirley, and I took the babies to the goverment clinic for shots. Polio drops, Hep. B. Catholic Hospital beautiful, landscaped, and flowers over the wall. Clinic pretty simple. Babies weighed in a blanket sling hooked to a handheld scale. People stand in the doorway and watch and listen as we get doctored. The doctor is a lady who happened to ride on the flota with us last night. First comment was about the gringos complaining of the smell. Ouch! Ugly Americans. Quinoa, tiny grain that expands with cooking into a C-shape used to thicken soup.

1:30 p.m.

Spent rest of morning chopping veggies, cleaning house, showering, etc. Found and tuned the guitar and practiced a little. Lovely instrument. Chicken soup and pumpkin bread for lunch. Always fruit drinks. Big plastic water container always on the counter and full of filtered and treated water for drinking. Loro-green parrots that roost near the hospital at night and fly out and steal corn all day. Illegal, but many people keep them as pets. Charango, little ten-string guitar.

4:00 p.m.

Practice for the service tonight. Shirley told us her babies came to her because the Quechua think twins come from either infidelity or the devil. They have a way to figure out which is the bad child, and that one is abandoned. The Catholic Hospital where the girls were born called the Benders after three days basically because they thought the abandoned baby was going to die. "You can try to save her if you want." The parents ended up giving both girls to the Americans. Quechua also believe supposedly that they have two brothers in their chests. If you take their picture with a camera, you steal the little brother, and the big brother will grieve to death, and they will die. I have to say in all my picture-taking, I did not encounter evidence of this fear.

10:30 p.m.

Back from the service at the Dios Es Amor Church (Iglesia Christiana Evangelica). What an experience! It was one of those times where you just know God is there. We sang and heard Todd's testimony, then more music, then the drama in whiteface. Finished with the dirty rag object lesson. Interspersed was lots of singing and prayer in Spanish and some Quechua. JP said they had tried to practice the object lesson three times without success, yet it went off without a hitch tonight. Eric said he thought the people saw/heard new things tonight. We were asked to do a second service on Thursday. Plan is to knock off work early Tuesday, so we and the church people can canvas with invitations. We will also go out into the campo (countryside) Wednesday and try to relate to some real campesinos. After tonight's service, the people wanted to shake our hands. You shake once, lightly embrace at the elbows, and then shake again. All evening, since before the service, there has been a huge mass of clouds piled on the mountaintops full of flashing white lights and streaks of lightning. I believe it is a picture of the spiritual battle taking place here and now. God and his angels and the prayers of the saints doing battle in the heavenlies on our behalf. After the service, we handed out candy and balloons and offered face painting to the children. At first, they held back, but once a few came up, they all wanted face paint.

Monday, July 2, 6:15 a.m.
JP sick. Today we begin the physical labor that brought us here. I fully believe the spiritual labor began last night. We broke bread with the people last night. The little elder man who prayed for the bread looked like the mummy of Seti. The bread was soft, and the wine was bright red and tasted like cough medicine. Finding that I seem to be rattling cages all the time. Hope, hope, hope eyes and hearts become more open to the huge possibilities of what God can do. Jack and I had an anointed spiritual warfare prayer time this morning. (Slept pretty well.) I'm finding that I have to learn to be patient with what God is doing. I keep expecting to see instant results, both in our people and the Quechua, but think now that we're planting seeds (hopefully fast-growing seeds). These ideas need time to grow and mature. Hoping to see us be open to faith enough that God can do some miraculous stuff. Roosters crowing all over town. Place filled with hungry dogs of many kinds, though none bigger than a small German shepherd. Always dust and grit in teeth. Will try to remember to pray blessing if people touch me. Will ask about acceptability of calling people *hermano* and *hermana* (brother and sister).

1:45 p.m.
Managed to do two loads of laundry by bailing buckets of water (five each time) from the fifty-five-gallon drums outside the back door. Spent the morning mostly on food prep. Probably spend afternoon on same. Between forty-five minutes of cleaning blueberries by hand and hand-mixing chicken in marinade, my hands are irretrievably black in the cracks and around the nails.

4:40 p.m.

No siesta for me today. Too much to do. Finally got water back when the men went out to clear dead possum from the waterline. Laundry (seventeen people here) moving along. So good to hang clothes out again. Have met killer bees; they are between honey bee and bumble bee in size, mostly black, very aggressive with a high-pitched, cranky buzz. If you kill one, as it dies, it releases a hormone scent, and in minutes, hundreds are swarming. Small brown crickets. Chagas bugs in the girls' dorm the other night. "Not to worry. Only 10 percent carry chagas" (Shirley). (Boy, doesn't that make you feel better?) She calls herself Juana here (middle name is Jean) because Quechua cannot pronounce her name. Saw pictures of the babies' family way out in the campo. Men wear heavily embroidered pants, which they sew themselves. And huge yarn pom-poms arranged on their bodies to demonstrate marital status. Women wear knee-length, often pleated, very full skirts. They are short, squat, strong, often carrying bundles considerably larger than themselves. The farmers weave straw birds and hang them on rope from poles on the hill-tops to catch the constant wind scarecrows. Inca/Quechua, "don't lie, don't cheat, don't be lazy." (Moral foundation and Inca greeting.) Bus and car dashboards are often decorated with quilted cover of gray velvet. Quechua view of life is that they face the past, the known, and the future comes from behind. (We face the future.) Compete opposite approach to life. Actually, their's is the more logical. House has square doorknobs.

9:05 p.m.

No rest all day, pretty whacked. Want to sleep, but our bed is in a loft over the living room where the boys are watching *Mission Impossible*. Hope sleep will be stronger than noise. Borrowed a Louis L'Amour from Eric. Great sleep-inducing brain candy, I hope.

Tuesday, July 4, 7:10 a.m.

Imperado makes 7Bs (boliviano, their money) per square meter, making cobbled streets from round rock. What a rotten job! Went to work all morning on the quartos. Great fun, good camaraderie. After working all morning, they served us a hot lunch. Peanut soup with french fries as a garnish and each bowl with a big chunk of galena (chicken). Coke in bottles with straws. We had fun twisting and popping the straws; Sonya especially seemed to like this trick. Bad night for sleep last night. No siesta yesterday, so I went to bed at nine to nine thirty. Jack came to get dirty clothes to put in the canasta (basket) and missed his footing going down the stairs. Went down cement steps headfirst. Long scrape on right shin and pulled muscles in right arm. He stayed home this morning to work on handouts for the door-to-door tonight. Taco salad for supper tonight. Have seen lots of skinny dogs, no cats so far. Here they come out at night. Guinea pigs well caged, or the cats will eat them.

7:05 p.m.

All afternoon with hands in brick water. Back and legs hurt and will hurt more later. Took ibuprofen with dinner. Another couple, Paul and Dori, with infant arrived today. Oh joy! (Nineteen people in the house, three of them infants!) Tonight, we go back to town to canvas streets with flyers inviting townspeople to our service on Thursday night. We'll go in teams partnered with people from the church. Good-sized group of people showed up for work this afternoon more than the morning. Are we getting a rep? Jack was mad at me for saddling him with flyer prep without asking. Mike queasy tonight. After food and shower, he's better. Overwork? Too much sun? Went to charanga shop tonight. Costs 280 Bs/$47 US for beautiful handmade, carved, inlaid little ten-string guitarras. While I waited in the car, a lady came to the window to tell me about another charanga shop. I understood! We conversed! Turns out Aiquile is Bolivia's center for charanga production because it's the only place to find the best kind of wood. *Narajita*(?), mock orange(?).

Ironically, few people in the town actually play. Thought about getting one, but realized if I had it, I (1) could not play it, (2) could not tune it, and (3) could never replace broken strings. Decided to skip it. Earlier this week, a few of us went with Eric across the street to his neighbor's house. As we stepped over the threshold into the courtyard, Eric casually mentioned we should avoid the ants swarming on the doorstep. "They bite." The wall is white brick with embrasures erupting with gorgeous morning glories that daily rival the deep blue of the sky. The man who lives here is an artist and art professor who works mostly in watercolor and oils. Really like his work and would like to buy as I feel it is very representative of the feel of this place, but $100 US seems a little steep. (Found out later a New York buyer comes once a year to clean him out. No wonder he knows the worth of the work.) My head still feels like I have my hat on. Face feels sun/wind burned. Shower parade begins. We do fifteen in an hour.

9:35 p.m.

Back from walking the nighttime streets of Aiquile. Many people were out and about, hanging out in front of the movie theater where the sound is incredibly loud. Everyone took the flyers, and we easily gave away all 250 long before we finished our routes. We gave suckers to the kids we encountered. Some said they would come. We went two by two with two of us and two of them. Esther speaks no English, all we had was my poor Spanish to communicate with our companions. In a dark place along a deserted street, we had a run in with five drunk young men, one of whom was pretty aggressive and wanted to challenge us, I thought. We came out okay. One guy thought we were selling something and thawed visibly when he found out the flyer was free. The big piece was a pretty placard with John 3:16 in English on one side and Spanish on the other. A Gospel tract and printed invitation to the Thursday service completed the contents of the plastic bag we handed out. In Bolivia, people beep horns a lot while driving to clear a path or let someone know they're coming through. It's first come, first served, though vehicle size and gender of the driver come into play. In town here, a man who sells LP gas from the back of his truck beeps his horns to call customers, starting at 6:30 a.m.! People use short sharp whistles to get each others' attention. There is a poor person's version of the flota; it's a big, stake-bed truck. They just pile in with all their stuff in the open bed. Saw a family debark in Totora and just sit down right there in the middle of the intersection to eat! Mercado stalls and street vendors use square white canvas umbrellas on metal frames. Find the noise level in our group, as well as the constant fooling around wearing. Sometimes I wish people could lay off a bit. Loud card game (Mafia, I went to Bolivia on a mission trip and learned to play a card game about murder?) going on. No devotions planned until ten twenty too late for me. JP said I could go to bed.

Wednesday, July 5, 8:25 a.m.

Feeling better and got some decent sleep. Yesterday, I spent the whole day keeping bricks wet in a big plastic bin and handing them to whoever call, "Ladrillo!" The maestro (master) uses very few tools to build. Plumb Bob. Mari macho/little hand pick used to break bricks, chop out notches in old walls to tie in the new one, and to smooth lumpy adobe on walls we are building up against. Cement is mixed in wooden troughs one part cement to four parts sand and water to the right consistency. Mortar is pretty sloppy, but these walls will be coated inside and out with a plaster kind of finish, so doesn't really matter. At one point, I worked alone for quite a while with Carlos who was up on the scaffold. He let me know he wanted me to shovel dry cement from a wheelbarrow up into the trough, about four feet up. Heavy! Didn't know if I should let him ask this of me, then just did it. The people here keep commenting on all the kidding and laughter as we work/call us "jokesters." At one point, some of the kids were playing Frisbee, and it went up on the roof. What gyrations, getting it down. Finally, Aaron stood in hand-saddles and used a rake to coax it down. One of the jobs here is to shovel the sand through a chicken wire screen to clean it before mixing it with the cement. Another is cutting lengths of ribar and then bending it into squares for use in reinforcing the cement headers we will pour. Mike has gotten pretty banged up with little cuts, etc. JP has had *lots* of intestinal trouble. Jack has a large bruised swelling on his forearm. Went to the worksite anyway. Taking Tylenol for inflammation. We've had a few nosebleeds from heightened blood pressure from altitude, also from dryness of the air. Lydia's lasted twenty minutes and made her dizzy for a while. Autumn had a little one, and Aaron had one in the car. Dryness has made my nose very sore/ am using Chapstick in my nose (ew). Seems to help. Lips also dry. Am a collection of bruises in the knee, head (banged it on the scaffold/twice), or shoulder (bumped it getting into the car.) The scaffold involved posts set into holes and braced with rocks overlaid with wired-on boards.

2:20 p.m.

Spent all of this morning baking industrial-sized batch of chocolate chip cookies for the freezer. And silently enjoying varying levels of older new/mom overkill with these babies. Try not to say too much. These are strong women who *know*. Around forty thirty, we will go up into the campo and have "mote" (boiled corn). Should I eat it? Jack's arm injury is, I think, more serious than first thought. Looks as though a muscle or tendon broke and the ends retracted. Trying to decide if he needs any medical attention before we return to the states. Emailed Becky for advice, though she probably will overreact. Just read a note from Buffy Gehring with a Scripture about how God will be our help in the heavens! "Sacra wayra", dust devil, if one hits you, a demon gets you. Cure is to use green toilet paper! Bitter taste in mouth recurs, from the quinine in the malaria pills?

9:30 p.m.

Back from the campo. The drive up, maybe five miles, takes thirty to forty-five minutes. Took Mike, Autumn, Derek, etc. one and a half hours to *walk* it. Unbelievable road through dry riverbeds, over huge rocks, around foot-deep ruts. Big trucks actually go this way to carry goods to the pueblo *mercados*. *Dust*. Women walking by the side of the road carry mesh bags full of wool. They wind it a few times around their wrist and work at twisting it into yarn and winding it onto a drop spindle as they walk along. At Forto's house, we had a good hike to get up to the house place. A tree outside the compound all stacked with his corn to keep it from the animals. We later watched the chickens one by one go up onto the house roof and walk over to the tree side and flap across to roost in the same tree. Chickens, puppies, baby pigs wander a dry, dusty cornfield lying fallow in the winter season. Up the hill, a number of chest-high rock enclosures topped with thorn bush. One is full of goats and sheep being watched by a couple of little boys. They do not geld any livestock. The compound is an adobe enclosure around a fifteen-by-twenty courtyard. First thing we saw upon entering was a bunch of skinny raw meat hung to dry over a wire strung across the courtyard. There were a few wooden stools (eight inches high) and planks that Forto covered with beautiful, colorful thick woolen blankets for us to sit on. Baby chicks allowed to peck around inside, scrawny puppies kicked out. Dogs in Bolivia tend not to be treated as beloved pets. Often see them hit or kicked. A blanket spread on the corn piled in one corner makes another seat. We were served bowls of "mote." The kernels about the size of corn pop cereal. Cold, absolutely no flavor with gummy to crumbly consistency. Even icky with salt. Bowls of roasted peanuts, such a relief to taste something familiar. Later we have large communal bowls of big chunks of boiled potato garnished with sliced hard-boiled egg. (Egg is usually served almost raw/cooked today for the gringos' benefit.) We ate all with salt we brought, pretty good. Later learned the hostess was surprised we did not eat a lot more. If you empty your dish, Quechua hospitality includes an immediate refill, which you are expected to eat or take with you. Lydia could no longer bear the cramps and nausea she'd been fighting all evening, and Cliff (Cliffy es bueno!) agreed to take her home and come back for us. After dinner, we walked through the starry dusk over to the tiny church. Adobe building maybe twelve-by-twenty, no windows. On the wall are hand-painted the words, "*Aqui oramos por nueb(v)a vida para todos.*" Here we pray for new life for everyone. A small chalkboard hangs behind a round table next to a small gas light on a five-foot metal pole, the only light in the church. A poster with the Twenty-third Psalm in Spanish hangs on the wall.

Wooden pegs are set into the adobe, and a rough plank lays across for a shelf. The seats are worn, hand-planed planks four to five inches thick set on five to six inches high adobe bricks. Almost like sitting right on the dusty, dirt floor. Service consists of our songs and three testimonies from us and two from them. Takes so long to go from English to Spanish to Quechua and back. Eric has brain cramp! Neat that the problems they face, drunkenness, adultery, worldliness, are so familiar and similar. Answer the same for all, God's Truth in his Word. Once again, at the end, the people lined us up to shake hands and say, "*bienvenido*" (welcome). On the ride home, we almost bonked a huge black ox at the side of the road.

Thursday, July 6, 8:00 a.m.
    Going back to the work site.

10:55 a.m.
    And back. *Nothing* to do. Lydia really sick with altitude sickness. Woke up dizzy and in tears. Altitude sickness can make a person feel panicky like drowning. Jeff Allem had a bout early on for two and a half hours in the first night here. Have a wicked headache today, could be lack of sleep, which remains chronic. Hard when sleeping place is *always* open to the world. Just came in from sitting a while behind the house to dry my hair. Nice and warm on the bench against the brick, listening to the corrugated tin roof tick in the afternoon warmth. Very little downtime here. My brain is getting tired. Paul and Dori back again, still messing around with lawyer and judge for their adoption. The other evening, I was sitting in the bathroom and felt warmth coming off the brick wall. (Houses here all built from brick, cement, adobe, rock, tiles, dirt, nothing soft. The kitchen cupboards are set into cement! Wrought iron railings, very little of wood anywhere.) My first thought was, *This must be the south wall.* Duh! Here, *north* is warm. Sure wish I could get a nap. Lydia's in our bed, where she'd been all day. So tired. After a week, we've about used up willpower-type courtesies. Illness, injury (cuts, bruises so far), lack of sleep, close quarters, etc. begin to wear. No gringos willing to go back to the work site and stand around all afternoon as we did all morning. General impatience with a people who won't be efficient! *Llaqwa*, general term for pastes used to flavor food. Can be like fine ground salsa, all pepper (*molla*, from pepper tree), peanut mash with spices. I have hit the wall! Went and had a good cry. Finally realized I had just not allowed for enough brain rest. Will try to ease up. Tonight is our big presentation. Wish I could believe we are really trusting in God.

10:05 p.m.

Back from the service. Nice turnout. Did six songs, three mimes. The chemicals did not work for the Pedro the Sock lesson. Lydia, a little better. Everyone getting stretched a little thin. Have a sense we have never really developed much unity. Dave seems tired of stuff. Seems to me the bumpy; rumbly roads are getting to me. Outside town—awful! In town—not paved mostly but cobbled. Dogs, kids, drunks wander in the streets. Dust always. Leche and fruit frozen in a cup with a stick (no, a *real* stick). Shirley calls it "diarrhea in a cup." Housekeeping here so inconvenient in some ways. No wastebaskets except in the kitchen. Compost for nonburnables, big bin for burnables, which includes foil and used diapers. Burn barrel in the yard used daily or as needed. In the middle of baking cookies yesterday, the stove ran out of LP gas, and we had to haul in a new tank from the garage. Always huge pots of faucet water heating to wash dishes (remember, no hot water here), and there are *always* dishes. Two big plastic pails need to be full of filtered water always for all personal needs, except washing. Baby bottles everywhere. Huge meals disappear in no time. Then there are the 110 gallons of faucet water outside for just in case and washing the floors, which is done with a foot-wide squeegee on a short stick that pushes around a two-foot square rag that you repeatedly rinse. We sweep a lot, but the floor is almost always dirty. Don't bother dusting. Doors often stand open; flies are mostly ignored. Furniture is wooden, not upholstered, pretty but not real comfortable. Jack got cut across three fingers today. Also grew a blister on a pinky that now seems infected. *Argh!* Animal choruses here occasionally really loud. Sometimes start as early as 3:30 a.m. Roosters all around, seems like I'm pretty used to them. (It is 11:15 p.m., and one just started and is being answered. Go figure!) Lately, there's been a turkey too. I can usually handle the poultry, but when the dogs get in on it. Wow! Dogs everywhere, asleep beside walls or against curbs. None look very healthy, and some are dreadful. (I did see the office of a vet in town.) Don't really seem to be pets. I'm told most are not fed and fend for themselves. Benders have two small dogs, Patches and? That patrol the compound here and sometimes go bonkers, often at night and for no apparent reason. That'll wake you up. Lauren seemed really weary today. Think she's tired of all the chaos. We all are, the adults at least. Am trying to discipline myself to let some of the work fall on the others. Weird, depending on the temperature, there are crickets (in winter!). Cool tonight and finally have the window open. The moon seems to have grown slowly this week. Or maybe time is just messed up because of this unreal existence. How did I get so whacked this afternoon?

Hormones? Altitude? Competition? (I'll be the *best* work teamer ever, and they'll all notice?) Upstairs floors are all cement, so feet always dirty. Wore sandals in the campo. Nobody told me we would be walking around in sandy dirt. Mike, Andy, Aaron, and Autumn hiked up! She wore new hiking boots and stepped on a branch of thorns (the kind the locals use for nails), and the thorn went all the way through the boot and into her foot. I was lucky. My sandals are scuffed and feet got dirty but no hurts. We sprayed with *deet* to keep off "church" fleas. Should have sprayed our rears, which were as close to the ground as our feet. Nothing bothered us flea-wise.

Friday, July 7, 6:30 a.m.

Stomach is now trying to decide what kind of day I'll have. Wonder what sort of goody things are swimming around in there. Yesterday and today, we've seen a lot of teenage young men walking around town dressed in camo fatigues. Yesterday, we could hear target practice. High school ROTC. Last night, the plaza was full of them, sweeping with leafy branches. Shirley said they could get time off from required military service by working like that now. Was able to eat some breakfast. Stomach's only a little unsettled. There was no work to do yesterday; some doubt about what could be done today, so I asked if the Benders had anything we could do here. They need a cistern dug, so Shirley and I set out to try to move on that. Jeff and Jeff said to stop, "It's a *really* good idea, but…" Not fair? I totally do not get it. Did we come to work or not? Better we should play Frisbee? Made chitimoya breadfruit blended with milk, for the morning snack drink. On the way back, Shirley showed me the cock-fight corner where the young men meet every afternoon for cock-fighting. Every street is lined with walls, either house walls or fence walls. In town, business signs are painted right on the walls. Many, many political signs everywhere on walls, rocks, cliffsides, etc. Even way out in the campo. Lots of loaded burros in the streets all the time. As we came back from delivering the snack, an unloaded burro skittered across the road, and the door in the wall slammed behind it. "It's going out to eat and breed," said Shirley. They just turn the mares loose to find a stud and hope for the best. Wind rattles the aluminum roof overhead. Achocha for lunch/veggie pod slightly boiled, split, seeded, stuffed with cheese and salsa, batter fried, and served with more salsa.

4:50 p.m.

Quiet day. Forms built and cement being poured at the work site. Stayed to keep the babies so Shirley could sleep. So nice to hang laundry out. Just now was like a late-summer early evening, crickets, low gold sun, little soft warm breeze. Just me and Tumnus, the billy goat. He and I often exchange greetings when I come out with a basket of wet laundry under my arm. Constant tick and ping of the metal roof. Big sheets of egg carton Styrofoam insulation on the inside of the ceiling walls. Shirley went to buy alfalfa for the rabbits to eat. She gets big bundles cut fresh and tied. At home, it has to be cut up and spread out on rugs in the sun to dry, so it will keep. All that just for rabbit feed. The shop where we bought the alfalfa was just a little storefront. When you go to the store, you stand outside and call out. When you get an answer, that's when you step inside. This store had a glass counter full of toothpaste, etc. The owner is a doctor. It was through him that Paul and Dori got their little boy. The wife is a dentist. Such a pair in the states would be rich, but here, they seem to have average income. Milk comes in plastic bags carried over in unrefrigerated flotas so usually sour. When the shower goes on in the Benders' house, the lights dim. Lydia still bothered with nosebleeds daily. Tonight is movie night, *The Princess Bride*…in Bolivia! Just now, the testosterone erupts; the boys are wrestling and laughing wildly. It apparently involves underwear on someone's head. Real scrum, boys against the men.

Saturday, July 8, 8:00 a.m.

Last night, there was a parade, and this morning at five thirty, a band went by in the back of a truck playing merrily. When Autumn came to breakfast this morning, she said very pleasantly, "This is our last day here, and you hired a band!" Cannon firing, guns shooting, shots in groups of threes. Today, the twenty-third anniversary of Aiquile's founding. Big fiesta. All thoughts turning toward home and enduring the journey. Shirley said we could have gotten here much quicker through Miami. Would have cost more but less than half the travel time. Worth considering for a return visit. Pretty sure Jack's thinking about coming back. Have learned some nasty things about myself, how comfortable I am not relying wholly on God, how much I want people to know and appreciate what I know and have done. Yucky! Everything here's metric. People carry heavy loads by balancing them on a bike. Went to the market with Jeff, Jeff, and Todd for some last pictures of the quartos we worked on.

1:15 p.m.

Quiet today, no work, just getting ready to leave. Laundry, pictures, etc. Benders will take the trufi with us as they are going to USA in a week. Hoping adoption of babies will be complete in time to allow them to go along. Right now looking doubtful.

6:00 p.m.

Big water fight this afternoon. Super soakers and water balloons. J. Allem the ringleader. Actually squirted water into the house. Eric and Shirley, not home fortunately. We got it cleaned up pretty well, even where someone heaved a water balloon through the open upstairs' bathroom window. Todd and JP carried Dave down, kicking and fussing and forced him to briefly participate. He did not like that! Then Esteban and Joas came for a music lesson. I drew up some simple info, and Derek translated. Then Esteban asked me to sing a few songs into a tiny tape player he brought. When Esteban asked about the "Frump, Frump" song, we were stumped, so he referred us to Mike. I guess while the boys were cutting ribar together at the church yesterday, they sang "Frump, Frump" to the tune of "you are my all in all", and he wanted the real words. Lydia, Autumn, Jack, and eventually Eric and Lauren and I spent a nice while just singing through the music I had brought. I guess I thought we would have worship times; this was as close as we got, and it was good. Got kind of close to reality during devotions when we tried to "clean slate" with each other. Sent some digital pictures to the church and to CLIF.

9:10 p.m.

The church just left. They came to say goodbye. Brought a three-layered cake with heated (caramelized), sweetened condensed milk between the layers. Gifts were given. Aaron got mini pan pipes, Autumn got a woven work purse with a ten centavo coin inside (she had mentioned wanting money to take home), and I got a pretty beaded hair scrunchy. (The scrunchy hangs today on the mirror of my dressing table.) During a requested prayer time, Jack's arm was substantially healed. Shirley reminded me to record that yesterday, she sent me to the market alone, except for Lydia. We went and bought "*Quatro pesos de tomates*" and didn't even pay for the bag. When we came out of the *mercado*, Shirley was waiting in the car, and as we walked toward her, I held up the bag and called, "*Quatros pesos de tomates!*" proudly. The ladies under the umbrella on the corner laughed at me because I was so proud of myself. So as we drove away past the ladies, I called it out the window again, exaggerated, and they laughed again. *Loco gringos!* Never say *estupido* in Bolivia, very bad word. Got a tape of us singing "Solo Tu Eres Santo" with the church here. Neat that they sang the song we brought. They were lovingly firm tonight that they appreciate what we did in coming here, but that we are in all ways equals and brothers in the Lord. So glad they feel that way! The thing I still find hard, even at this time of life, about brief intense experiences like this trip is the ending. Endings are hard for me. To know I'll probably never see this place or these people again. I wonder how those of us on the team will be after this. Even Aaron will leave after summer, and who knows if we'll ever see him again. I know these things must and will be but something in me just protests it. Downstairs, most everyone is playing a really loud game. It's a sneaky adult trick to keep the boys from their planned free for all tonight. They have to be quiet after ten, and the game will probably last till then. Glass in the windows in town often pressed into beautiful intricate patterns. Went to the work site a couple days ago, and someone was burning garbage with something in it that really made my eyes burn and water like crying. Tonight the house is full of a throat-scratching burn smell almost electrical. The wind must have changed to blow the burn barrel smoke this way (ewww!). Or maybe my throat is just rough from all the singing.

Sunday, July 9, 5:30 a.m.

Another night of so-so sleep. Another light show on the mountaintops. More streetlight in this house at night than at home. Life in a "stone" house is noisy, echoy, doors warp (more of those ever-present, beautiful wooden Bolivian doors). Jack said he and Eric had a good talk sitting out on the curb, waiting for Esteban yesterday. Eric tentatively probed our view on demons, etc. Told Jack there are half a dozen witch doctors in the area. Some work with herbs, etc., some spiritually. Jack told him we believe demons are as active today as in Jesus's time. Can't find Scripture to dispute it. Eric said Shirley has gift of discernment. There was a time she told him a certain man was at the gate, and he was. He says he will pray before a service to tell spirits to stay away, and certain people will just not be there. It's maddening that the church recruits these people and then sends them out completely unprepared to do spiritual battle. They tell them demons are no more, and the gifts no longer operate and then toss them naked and blind into a place where there are witch doctors! Scratchy throat again this morning and pumping out some pretty good snot. Bowels doing their usual morning grumble. Wonder if God might have work for us here. Can't see me here forever, but for a time, maybe. Sabbatical? Early retirement? Jack says he thinks we accomplished all God had for us to do here. He thinks it was the young boys that really helped break down barriers. Autumn, too, in her ministry to the children. He also said he did not think there had ever been a gathering quite like last night. Off in the trufi (small bus) for Coch. Plaza in town, Plaza Zenon Delgadillo. Avenue Bolivar. Orange road signs. Sugarcane seven- to eight-foot stalks stacked against the wall to sell. Ladies all wear fedoras. Still some tent camps left in Aiquile from the sismo (earthquake), Campmento, Mexico. See a lot of *Taquina* (*cervesa, beer*) signs. Sometimes seem to catch a whiff of marijuana. One man and three burros walk up the road as one sow and six piggies walk down. Bolivian standoff? Garbage everywhere just laying around. Big gray clouds over the mountains we're heading into. Brush corrals. Trees full of corn. Turned out the road was cobbled all the way to Coch with concrete curbs. I can't even imagine the amount of labor to build such a road. Going out a different way than we came, flota's too big to make the turns on this route. This way greener, more trees. Phone poles out in the middle of nowhere. Andes mountains have distinctive pointy silhouette. Would never think it's the Rockies. Real Wild West ambiance here. Freedom and lack of care for the environment. Very little wildlife. Rising sun strikes the clouds, turning them bright yellow. Bitter taste in mouth again. Shirley says roads can mess up your kidneys. They're so bad. Railroad built here, brought out by Brazil, and *never* used. Now the sunlight lays on the tops of the green hills to our left. Mauve clouds over mountains ahead. In Coch, there's a kind of Spanish moss thing that grows in softball-size wads on the electric wires. Skirting a pretty green valley patched with onion fields. Passing through a little town and saw two kids just squatting to potty right out in sight. Passed a man on horseback. Big, completely bare dirt soccer field, lighted basketball court, and sand volleyball court. Yard full of drying adobes. In Santa Cruz, saw Jewish moneylender office. Once in a while, a big rock hits the underside of the bus. Hope nothing critical gets wrecked. Kind of cold, did not wear a jacket and wish I had one now. Often pass clusters of little shrines supposed to be for saints but probably for older gods. Some ceilings are of tacked-up cloth. Passed old Toyota van being used as a shed; the roof neatly stacked with firewood. At the bottom of the valley to the right, there is a huge crack in the earth. Can't see to the bottom of the gorge. Half the group walking down to cross antique bridge while we drive over to meet them on the other side. Right in the wall at window level at the worst place in the road, we passed a rock shrine with *lighted* candles. Drivers want to keep the "saints" happy so the trufi doesn't fall off the road. Those who walked down to the old bridge made it safely back up the other side; walk must have looked worse than it was. Long needle pines planted along the road and a kind of fernlike arborvitae. How can a people live their whole life here and not know the names of any of the flowers or trees? Just passed through Kuri, more thatched roofs than tile. Some tin with rocks. Passed six little cement shrines set into the cliff at the right. Derek says a trufi went off the road here, and twenty people died. Begin to see little springs of water beside the road. Unbelievable drop-offs with no guardrails. The driver takes the curves in a way that makes me wonder if he's *trying* to scare the gringos. I just do not look. Dramamine, Tums, seat change have helped motion sickness. Tums a godsend on this trip. Sides of this valley covered in little farms where *not one* square foot is level. Do they level house floors?

11:45 a.m.

Trip taking longer than expected (again!). Boy, do I need the *baño*! Down from the fourteen-thousand-foot passes and into a valley leading to Coch. Good paved road. Mechanic signs painted on old tires. Personal and public vehicles often very personalized inside and out.

12:15 p.m.

Cochabamba at last. Palm trees. Broken bottles set in the cement atop the walls. Still not to Cala Cala and the New Tribes guesthouse. Just saw my very first Bolivian lawn. Air already bad.

3:05 p.m.

Lunch at McDonald's. Everything safe and wonderfully familiar. *Llaqwa* in the catsup dispenser! Met a friend of Derek's from Tambo (missionary kids school). She is Korean, the daughter of Baptist missionaries from Korea to Bolivia. So weird to hear her go easily from English to Spanish to Korean. Another of those Bolivian cognitive dissonances.

5:30 p.m.

Went to the *concha* (market). We all bought stuff, and no one got robbed. Success! Got some nice stuff for only $50 US. Paid too much for all but don't care; these people so poor. Concha was several streets of stalls plus block-long hallways with little stalls on either side or people sitting on the floor beside their piles of stuff. We bought two pieces of weaving from a little Quechua. Got enough that if the other shopping trip doesn't work out, I still have some nice things. Nasty sore throat/bad air doesn't help. Mike also sick. He seemed to have a little altitude sickness after the breathless ride over the pass. I was trying to sleep, kept popping awake gulping for air.

9:30 p.m.

Just back from steak dinner. Filet mignon for fourteen people, $540 Bs, less than $100 US. Tip 20 Bs, tops. We gave the street girl who guarded our car (Cliff's car "lost" a mirror while he was parked outside the church in Aiquile) two Bs and Autumn's leftover chicken. Tomorrow the get-home ordeal begins. Many in the group with misc. illnesses, etc.

Monday, July 10, 6:20 a.m.

Overnight at the NTM guesthouse again. Same room, same towels and pitcher unmoved since we left ten days ago! Actually rained last night. Enough to make the cement outside in the courtyard smell summery. Clouds kept the night from getting too cold. Dinner at the steakhouse was good. Linen tablecloths and napkins. Waiters in plaid vests and matching bowties. Steaks were cooked on open-fire grill right in the dining room. There was a salad bar, but we only ate cooked or peeled things. Not a huge variety. Side dishes were served family-style in little metal dishes about the size of the steaks. (Meals were actually about the right amount of food instead of grossly huge like here.) We had steak fries served with little metal bowls of ketchup. Fried yucca, very much like potato but with an interesting flavor. *Arroz con queso* (rice with cheese) looked like cream of wheat with melted yellowish mozzarella kind of cheese mixed in. Tasty. Drinks were served warm in heavy mugs. Two glass buckets of ice with tongs that were supposedly filled with clean commercial ice. Said I'd rather have one piece of that ice than my whole steak. We dug in. Red straws, the bendy kind, served standing up in a tall, thin glass. After we were done, Aaron had a little piece of meat, and he and the boys started to play with it. They poked it full of toothpicks, and Aaron made it talk. "Mr. Meat would like to go to America." McD straws also red and came wrapped in brittle clear plastic that took a lot of time to get off because it kept shredding into smaller and smaller pieces. Still feel like I have dust in my teeth. Those who ordered diet pop got warm plastic bottled pop and tall skinny glasses. Autumn ordered chicken and got a whole half chicken grilled. This morning at nine, we go to the 777 shop.

7:30 a.m.

Water here must all be soft; soap lathers pretty well. Did I mention how we were told to carry our money in the concha yesterday? I took 150 Bs in my pocket with my hand on it and 150 Bs in my bra! Good to wear tunic top to cover pockets. Saw a drunk trufi driver pay off a policeman right out in the open on the street in front of the concha. Saw an electric pole with about six hundred wires tied to it. Looked like spaghetti.

12:20 p.m.

After an orgy of spending ($200 US was *so* enough), we are at the airport, waiting for the second group to catch up. Used Jack's sea bag for all our goodies. Feeling a little better. Throat still bad. Another of those Bolivian contradictions right before us, two nuns in old-timey habits stand ten feet from a girl dressed in a blouse laced with a six-inch opening all the way up the back over leather short shorts.

1:20 p.m.

Biggest plane yet. Four center seats, two each in two outside rows. Beth's right about flying with a cold. My ears won't pop, and I'm almost deaf. Some pain.

3:30 p.m.

Eating at Subway restaurant at Viru Viru airport. Ears very bad. Forty-five degrees outside here in Santa Cruz. Rain and clouds so heavy the mountains are hidden. Heavy, gray overcast. We'll be thoroughly chilled by the time we get on the next plane this evening. Saw a bike decorated with a Bolivian flag. People do not use dustpans like at home; their's has a long handle so you don't have to bend over. In the restaurant, killing time. Takes forever to get our order. JP has gathered up all the Bs we have left to pay the airport tax. Yes, they charge you $25 US ($275, altogether 1,650 Bs) apiece to *leave* the country. Probably figure we're willing to pay that to be headed home. Could be right! Passed a souvenir shop in the airport and am tempted to compare prices; thought Autumn similarly tempted. Learned if you are shopping in the *mercado* or the *concha* it is very unsporting to argue down and settle on a lower price and then not buy. Arguing equals commitment to purchase. Interestingly, when we went through the x-ray at Coch, the only carry-ons opened and searched were mine and Lydia's (Autumn had a lock on hers). Throat so sore. Will try Tylenol Sinus. Don't want to even *think* about six hours of the kind of pain I had on the flight from Coch. Paper napkins are always tiny, maybe four-inches square. Sometimes, teenage girls hold hands or walk arm in arm. The Latin *bubble* of personal space much smaller than at home. Girls' jeans sometimes are *very* tight. At McD, told Derek and Mike to stop staring at a pair of so-clad chicas. Derek put his open hand over his eyes and said he wasn't staring. All the cigarette smoke and pollution have not done my throat any good at all. On the plane to Lima, one of the flight attendants is a Christian from Kent, which is weird because he talks with a Spanish accent. No trick to unstop ears. Rats!

8:15 p.m.

Ears…okay, bearable. The Lord is with me. Singing through. Lightning outside, some turbulence. Easing back into a world where time matters, phones ring, etc. Good breakfast this morning at the guesthouse. Just the night before, I had been thinking how good oatmeal would be, and lo and behold, we had oatmeal with brown sugar and cold, fresh, rich, safe milk. Have really missed milk. It comes in a plastic, one-liter bag. You set it into a squared plastic jug and snip off the corner to pour it. Can't say I miss baby duty, so glad I'm past that time of life. Hoping for sleep during this flight.

Tuesday, July 11, 5:50 a.m.

Almost home. So good to hear the American voice of the pilot with its little Texas twang. Food still Peruvian. About to do documentation for customs to enter USA. We spent less than $200, so have nothing to declare. In Houston airport, we are carefully and repeatedly checked out by a chocolate lab drug dog. The only one singled out and sent for checking is Jeff Allem and his trolley of four duffel bags. Nose stuffy and raw. Still using meds. Hope my ears can take one more flight. Can't wait to open our bag of goodies at home. Like Christmas!

On the flight to Cleveland

A little while ago, a brown cat went streaking down the airplane aisle. Some lady behind us carrying it in her purse! Well, I didn't see it, but JP did. Or he *claims* he did.

7/11 p.m.

Good to come home to empty house. All mowed and clean and lasagna (again) in the fridge (thanks to all!). Gave us time to clean up, unpack, nap, etc. Arrival at airport, emotional. Families brought signs and applauded. Hard not to cry. Spent evening debriefing with kids. Best meal on any flight ever: Honey Nut Cheerios in 2 percent milk. Really missed milk!

* * * * *

As it turned out, I caught some kind of virus in Bolivia that really kicked my butt. I was sick with a deep and juicy cough for weeks. Of course, we never went back, though we continued to support both the Benders and Cliff Peters until each left the mission field. The Benders visited us two years later while transitioning back to the US.

One of my biggest takeaways from this trip was how rich we are in America. How greedy and piggy and unappreciative we are. I kind of wish everyone could visit the third world so they could know what *real* poverty is.

I am glad I got to go.

In Conclusion

If you are a widow like me, you may have opened this book hoping to find help in your bereavement. I did that a lot at first, looking for wisdom in the experience of others. Truthfully, I didn't find much that was helpful to me. What does help is time. After a while, you stop having those startled moments when you recall your dear one is gone. Eventually, the things you berate yourself for assume perspective and anger cools. In time, forgiveness grows, sadness mellows, and you will stop crying so much. There comes a moment when you contemplate becoming whole instead of half of a whole that is no more. It just takes time. If there is anything I can offer you, it is to counsel patience to let time do its work.

In these essays, I have tried pretty hard to download a really big chunk of my life, as well as to share my grief journey so far as honestly as I can. I have shared the stories of how I came to be the person I am, what I hope I have contributed, and a little of what the significance of that may be. I have tried to share experiences that led to wisdom and things that made me laugh. I hope that these things will inform, illuminate, and maybe even guide others through increasingly dark times. I have tried to honor the memory of my husband as I wait to see him again.

In Jack's last music mix his final song selection was "And So It Goes" by John Denver and the Nitty Gritty Dirt Band. The following are the words to the chorus. As hard as he tried and thought everyone should try to change the trajectory of the church and the country by the force of his effort and will, in the end, he knew that the only thing that lasts is love. Not human love but God's love.

LINDA SWAN BURHENNE

Ashes to ashes, dust into dust
Buildings will crumble, bridges will rust,
Mountains will disappear, rivers will dry on
And so it goes with everything but love,
So it goes, with everything but love

About the Author

Linda Swan Burhenne lives in Leroy, Ohio, the home that her husband, Jack, called "the last best place." Now that he is gone, she has to talk to the cat and the dog, who don't seem to mind.